"It takes real talent to do what Koplewicz has accomplished ..i this book, which is assemble the best science and probe the wisest clinical minds (including his own), and then weave everything together into a highly readable and relatable narrative that's both useful and *fun*. With a unique mix of personal anecdote and professional insight, he breaks with received wisdom, delivers up some eye-opening surprises, and sends the greatly reassuring message to parents that if we take care of ourselves, our kids will be okay."

–Judith Warner, *New York Times* bestselling author of
Perfect Madness* and *And Then They Stopped Talking to Me

"Drawing on decades of clinical expertise and an organization that does some of the most compelling research on kids and mental health in this country, Dr. Koplewicz has written a practical, engrossing, and singularly useful book. Healthy adults don't 'just happen.' They happen because we give them a robust foundation of safety and confidence. Step by step, Dr. Koplewicz illustrates how this foundation is best built."

–Madeline Levine, PhD, *New York Times* bestselling author of
The Price of Privilege* and *Ready or Not

"This book is written with so much understanding and so much sympathy—for both children and their parents. Harold Koplewicz brings science and clinical experience together with his own family experiences to create a book that is always practical and compassionate, and manages to be firm, gentle, and encouraging in all the right ways."

–Perri Klass, MD, professor of journalism and pediatrics,
New York University, and author of *A Good Time to Be Born*

"This compassionate, witty, and street-smart guide to helping kids become independent young adults is a gift to parents everywhere. Harold Koplewicz gives us the tools to build strong, safe support around our children, and then trust that they will launch all the better for it and grow into their own destiny."

–Catherine Steiner-Adair, EdD, author of *The Big Disconnect*

"Scaffolding is about passing the torch of knowledge, self-confidence, and empathy to your child so that she is not fearful of taking chances and grows increasingly confident of making her own decisions. This book is a true gift to parents and their children. As both a neuroscientist and dyslexia advocate, a parent, and now a grandparent, I loved this book."

—Sally Shaywitz, MD, Audrey G. Ratner Professor, codirector, Yale Center for Dyslexia & Creativity, and coauthor of *Overcoming Dyslexia* (2nd Edition, 2020)

"A master synthesizer of attachment science, medical practice, and his own experience as a father, Harold Koplewicz capably and compassionately leads us through the art of scaffolding, from early childhood through the important adolescent period, and then finally to the moment in our own parenting journey when we will let the scaffold down and see our kids move out into the larger world with kindness, strength, and security."

—Daniel J. Siegel, MD, *New York Times* bestselling coauthor of *The Whole-Brain Child* and *No-Drama Discipline*

"In this era of searing fear and uncertainty, and out of the turbulent sea of contradictory parenting advice, emerges, blessedly, Harold Koplewicz's authoritative counsel. A true giant of child psychiatry, Koplewicz has condensed his immense knowledge, wisdom, and experience into a practical and actionable plan. This book is an instant classic—a godsend for us all."

—Edward M. Hallowell, *New York Times* bestselling coauthor of *Driven to Distraction* and *ADHD 2.0*

"Parenting advice tends to swing like a pendulum—from one extreme, trendy position to another—every few years. The steady, deeply sensible, and dependable position is *Scaffold Parenting*. Full of vivid examples of the evergreen effectiveness of scaffolding—the best way to support children as they grow (and grow away from us)—it's a book for the ages."

—Wendy Mogel, *New York Times* bestselling author of *The Blessing of a Skinned Knee*

"Scaffold parenting . . . shares the 'sweet spot' between permissive and controlling parenting . . . (and) reminds caregivers that it is never too late to help your children become the best versions of themselves, which is all any parent can hope for."

—*Booklist*

Also by Harold S. Koplewicz, MD

More Than Moody: Recognizing and Treating Adolescent Depression

It's Nobody's Fault: New Hope and Help for Difficult Children and Their Parents

Scaffold Parenting

Raising Resilient, Self-Reliant, and Secure Kids in an Age of Anxiety

Previously published as The Scaffold Effect

Harold S. Koplewicz, MD

HARMONY BOOKS
New York

Copyright © 2021 by Child Mind Institute, Inc.

All rights reserved.
Published in the United States by Harmony Books,
an imprint of Random House, a division of
Penguin Random House LLC, New York.
harmonybooks.com

Harmony Books is a registered trademark, and the Circle colophon
is a trademark of Penguin Random House LLC.

Originally published in hardcover as *The Scaffold Effect* by
Harold S. Koplewicz, MD, in the United States by Harmony Books,
an imprint of Random House, a division of
Penguin Random House LLC, New York, in 2021.

The Library of Congress has catalogued the hardcover edition as follows:
Names: Koplewicz, Harold S., author.
Title: The Scaffold effect / Harold Koplewicz.
Description: First Edition. | New York : Harmony Books, 2021. |
Includes bibliographical references.
Identifiers: LCCN 2020021226 (print) | LCCN 2020021227 (ebook) |
ISBN 9780593139349 (hardcover) | ISBN 9780593139356 (epub)
Subjects: LCSH: Parenting. | Child rearing. | Self-reliance in children.
Classification: LCC HQ755.8 .K67 2021 (print) | LCC HQ755.8 (ebook) |
DDC 649/.1—dc23
LC record available at https://lccn.loc.gov/2020021226
LC ebook record available at https://lccn.loc.gov/2020021227

ISBN 978-0-593-13936-3
Ebook ISBN 978-0-593-13935-6

Printed in the United States of America

Book design by Ashley Tucker
Cover design by Pete Garceau

10 9 8 7 6 5 4 3 2 1

First Paperback Edition

To Joshua, Adam, and Sam
The greatest joy of my life is being a father.
As much as I've taught my three sons,
they have taught me so much more.

Contents

Introduction

A family came to see me recently because the son, a six-year-old boy named Henry, was kicked out of his first-grade class. He got frustrated during a reading lesson and started throwing pencils and growling like a gorilla at another student. The teacher was so unnerved, the school administrators told the parents he wasn't allowed back until he'd been evaluated by a professional.

Physically, Henry was angelic. His parents were all-American good-looking, tall with firm handshakes. They were obviously upset and embarrassed about their son's outburst and his being kicked out of class. They were worried he might have attention deficit hyperactivity disorder (ADHD), anxiety, or a behavioral problem. Henry's father asked, "Is the school overreacting?"

That was what we had to find out.

After speaking with Henry for a few minutes, it was clear that his verbal skills were terrific. He was shy at first, but when he talked about summer sports, he had a glint in his eye. He eventually revealed the reason he got so upset during that lesson: The kid next to him had made fun of how slowly he was writing his letters and called him "dumb." I took out a book and he tried to read it, but clearly couldn't decode, meaning he couldn't make the connection between a letter and a specific sound. Henry admitted that he was slower than the other kids and that "dumb" remark hit home.

Quickly, we determined that Henry has some kind of dyslexia—like his mother and grandfather—not a behavioral issue. I have no idea why his teachers hadn't figured that out after two years, but suffice it to say, he needed a diagnostic evaluation that would include specialized testing to evaluate his academic strengths and weaknesses with special emphasis on his reading skills, and then remediation to deal with the problem. Dyslexia is treatable. With help, this bright child would learn to read.

At the end of the session, Henry's parents had a plan of action to fix the problem, and Henry felt so much better about himself. The strategies we discussed focused on support—therapeutic and emotional—to teach him not only how to cope with the practical problems of having a learning disability, but his, and his parents', acceptance of it. When he left, Henry hugged me and asked when we'd see each other again.

It's been several months since that first session. Henry is in an intensive reading program that uses a multisensory approach, and the specialized testing determined he qualifies for extra time on tests. Along with learning how to read, he's learning to accept his dyslexia, not as something to be ashamed of but as a part of who he is. It'll always take him longer to read, but he will make the necessary adjustments. Years from today, when he's applying to colleges and taking the SATs, he will be entitled to receive extra time and he'll have a decade's worth of time management training—and the confidence that comes from overcoming challenges—to back him up. In a way, he'll be better prepared for the rigors of the process than his peers who don't have a learning disability.

His parents' role is to guide Henry to accept and own his problem, understand what he needs, and show him how to cope. In effect, they will train him from a very young age to be an adult. With this parental guidance, Henry will be able to turn a deficit or weakness into a strength. I've seen it happen, too many times to count. The whole family will look back at the "dumb" bad day as a blip.

However, if Henry's parents had insisted that nothing was wrong—as many do when they're upset, embarrassed, or defensive— and reacted by switching schools or blaming the teachers, Henry's problems would have only gotten worse, and the trajectory of his life would have been altered. If left untreated, dyslexia is linked with self-harm, suicide, and antisocial behaviors. Seventy percent of kids in the juvenile justice system have dyslexia.

If his parents had overreacted and gone to the other extreme, treating Henry as if he were damaged goods who would never manage on his own, they could have harmed him just as severely. The parents weren't happy about the situation, but they put aside their discomfort, got their son the help he needed, and, in so doing, prevented a host of potentially serious problems for him and the whole family down the road.

Being able to prevent problems and minimize suffering very early on in someone's life is why I decided to specialize in child and adolescent psychiatry. I can treat a kid for six months and significantly improve his functioning and behavior before unhealthy patterns are locked in. Getting early, effective care for children and families who are suffering is also why I founded the Child Mind Institute in 2009. I was convinced we needed an independent nonprofit dedicated to children's mental health to confront a public health crisis. According to the findings of the Child Mind Institute's Children's Mental Health Report, seventeen million kids under the age of eighteen have a diagnosable mental health disorder. That's one in five. More kids are affected by mental illness than asthma, peanut allergies, diabetes, and cancer combined. And yet two-thirds of them will never get help due to misinformation and stigma. This leads to increased risk for school dropout, substance use disorder, suicidal ideation and attempts.

At the Child Mind Institute clinical centers in New York City and the San Francisco Bay Area, our team of clinicians interacts with children in need—and their parents—every day. We've changed the lives of more than ten thousand young people from forty-eight states and forty-four nations. We are also always looking for and innovating ways of helping more children in need. Through our school and community programs, we have reached more than 100,000 children in communities across the country. Our interactive website, childmind.org, brings hope and answers to over two million visitors a month. And our cutting-edge open science research program is pursuing the biomarkers of mental health disorders that will revolutionize diagnosis and treatment. We share our data freely with thousands of scientists around the world, accelerating discovery. The vision of the Child Mind Institute is a future where no child suffers, and to address this crisis, we have built a movement that cuts across the silos of research, medicine, and community programs.

Still, our most important alliance is with parents. Despite the tremendous volume of care we provide and the diversity of our patients, we couldn't help noticing common issues and concerns among the parents. They are all worried they're making mistakes that will hurt their kids. They worry about doing too much for their children, or not doing enough. They wonder if they should be harder on them, or if they're not tough enough. No matter the reason that brings them to the Child Mind Institute, an underlying concern is common to all: Will their kids grow up to be self-reliant? Every day, we all hear new stats and studies about college grads moving back home for good, that parents continue to support their kids financially into their twenties and thirties (and beyond). Many parents have told me that they're afraid for their kids' ability to deal with the challenges of life on their own. "What if something happens to me, and I won't be there to make sure everything is okay?" they ask.

I understand parents' fears, and their frustrations. Before their kids were born, they fantasized about raising a future president, a neurosurgeon, or an artist. It's only natural to go into parenting with a rosy vision of what it's going to be like, the group hugs, proud mama moments in the front row, Instagram-worthy vacations. Joys are anticipated; problems always seem to take parents by surprise.

This is true whether your child has mental health disorders or not. There are so many causes of concern in modern parenting, from social media bullying, dangerous YouTube challenges like eating Tide pods, to the increasing pressure and competition to get into colleges, even among those who have every advantage going in (case in point: Operation Varsity Blues, aka the college admissions scandal that ensnared actresses Felicity Huffman and Lori Loughlin). You hear about helicopter, snowplow, concierge, and Tiger Mom parenting. Which is right? Being authoritative or permissive? Perhaps something in between?

Parents are not always searching in the right places for guidance about how to raise emotionally healthy, brave, independent kids. When they consult Dr. Google, they get a flood of instantaneous information that is not necessarily factual, practical, or up-to-date with the latest research. Child Mind Institute clinicians have to address online noise with parents every day. I don't blame people for googling. They might be desperate for knowledge and are only using the tools at hand. But those tools aren't guaranteed to be verified and approved by trained experts. The conclusions of Mommy Bloggers are not necessarily based on scientific evidence. Kids and parents are in dire need of strength-building strategies that have been validated by research and proved to teach competence and resilience in everyday life *as well as* prevent anxiety and depression in young people.

Since the same concerns and questions about raising kids to be independent adults keep coming up with our patient families, our clinicians and I got together to outline and create parenting guidelines that would work for every family and every kid at every age and developmental stage.

No small task!

But, then again, who better to do it than us? Combined, Child Mind Institute clinicians and I have hundreds of years of experience working with families. I consulted with a select group of my colleagues to formulate the cohesive parenting strategy in this book. These colleagues—listed on the following page—have a remarkable breadth and depth of knowledge both from their unparalleled and varied experiences as clinicians and, most importantly, as parents themselves.

- David Anderson, PhD, senior director of National Programs and Outreach and a specialist in treating children and adolescents with ADHD and behavioral disorders

- Jerry Bubrick, PhD, senior clinical psychologist in the Anxiety Disorders Center and director of the Obsessive-Compulsive Disorder Service

- Rachel Busman, PsyD, senior director of the Anxiety Disorders Center and director of the Selective Mutism Service

- Matthew M. Cruger, PhD, senior director of the Learning and Development Center

- Jill Emanuele, PhD, senior director of the Mood Disorders Center

- Jamie M. Howard, PhD, senior clinical psychologist in the Anxiety Disorders Center and the director of the Center's Trauma and Resilience Service

- Stephanie Lee, PsyD, senior director of the ADHD and Behavioral Disorders Center

- Paul Mitrani, MD, PhD, New York City clinical director and a child and adolescent psychiatrist

- Mark Reinecke, PhD, ABPP, San Francisco Bay Area clinical director and a senior clinical psychologist

The strategies we teach parents are based on scientific research, our firsthand experience as clinicians, and our personal experiences as parents, aimed at encouraging prosocial, proactive behaviors that help kids cope with current problems, prevent future ones, learn to bounce back, and develop a strong independent streak so that they won't be so reliant on their parents to solve their problems for them.

The sooner you teach these strategies, the better off your kids will be.

Our philosophy is that good parenting is *not* about rescuing kids. It's about teaching them how to use coping tools, and then encouraging them to pick and choose the right tool for the right situation so they flourish on their own and take inevitable setbacks in stride. Kids can't always succeed at everything, but they should try, and parents should teach them how. It's also about giving kids the support to fail and grow without hurting themselves. If children aren't guided to make their own decisions, even if they're wrong, they won't learn how to make smarter ones. Permissive or controlling parenting is not the way to go.

So what is?

The sweet spot, philosophically and practically, for raising resilient, self-advocating kids who can cope with stress and learn from their mistakes is what we call "scaffold parenting." Parents are the scaffold that provides structure and support for the child as he or she grows up. They are there to protect and guide, but they don't impede learning and risk-taking.

Building the framework for scaffolding begins as soon as you bring a baby home, in the way you create a supportive environment for them. The coaching aspects of scaffolding begin at age four or five, when children start interacting socially and facing challenges. But scaffolding via support and encouragement continues through childhood, adolescence, and into young adulthood. As you'll see, in each chapter, I've denoted specific guidance for parenting children (ages four to twelve) and teens (ages thirteen to nineteen). Your scaffold will be modified to meet the different demands as your child grows, but the basic philosophy stays the same. Your scaffold exists to provide structure and support, not to control or rescue.

Since we have worked with many thousands of kids in our clinical practice, I have numerous examples to tell about how scaffolding has worked for families like yours. The stories in this book are real, but I have changed names and identifying details to protect the privacy of the families mentioned. Whether your child has a diagnosed disorder or not, I'm sure you'll find common ground with the families on these pages and gain valuable insight through their experiences.

Scaffold parenting strategies are more relevant than ever. Even the healthiest kids with the most stable parents deal with more stress than in previous generations. Moms and dads are working longer hours, having to rely on the Internet as a virtual babysitter. The "village" of multigenerational families and close-knit communities is fast diminishing, if not gone for many. The emergence of faulty parenting styles seems designed to *increase* a child's anxiety, dependence, and incompetence. Overly permissive and authoritarian parenting is not the answer. Scaffold parenting is the single most effective way to encourage kids to climb higher, try new things, and grow from mistakes, while you provide unshakable support. It works for the families who come to the Child Mind Institute, and it will work for yours.

1

The Architecture of Parental Support — Understanding Scaffolding

In 1976, American psychologist Jerome Bruner originally used the word *scaffolding* as a metaphor for the best way to educate a child. His theory was about collaborative learning, that a parent or teacher has to guide the student while he learns a new math skill, for example, and then, once the child has achieved mastery of it, the parent or teacher stops instruction of that task and moves on to the next.

We've taken Dr. Bruner's core scaffolding idea of an authority figure guiding a child toward independence and expanded and redefined it into parental support and guidance not just in an educational context, but in an emotional, social, and behavioral one, too.

The metaphor of the parental scaffold is visual, intuitive, and simple.

Think of it this way: Your child is the "building." You, the parent, are the scaffold that surrounds the building. Your purpose as the scaffold is to provide support and structure, not prohibit your child's growth in any particular direction or style.

Every effective scaffold has vertical posts or pillars as well as horizontal planks—the combination makes the whole structure safe and secure.

The scaffold rises at the same pace as the building.

It is wider at the early "stories," providing that solid foundation that allows for strength and growth. It becomes less important as the building rises ever higher.

If a piece of the building falls off, the scaffolding is there to catch it and make fast repairs.

Eventually, when the building is finished and ready to stand completely on its own, the parental scaffold can come down. It may come down one section at a time, since all parts of the building might not be completed at exactly the same time. And, as needed, parts of the scaffold can go back up.

Scaffolding Pillars

The framework of all your decisions and efforts as parents is the three pillars of your scaffold: **structure, support,** and **encouragement.** By relying on these pillars, you will boost your kids' confidence, self-esteem, and coping skills, so that they develop into adults who support, encourage, and provide structure for themselves. You scaffold a child so that, eventually, he'll be able to scaffold himself.

Structure encompasses routines, communication style, house rules, ways of thinking—all the underlying infrastructure of your scaffold. Crucial to a child's sense of security are predictable routines in the home, like bedtimes and homework hours, family bonding rituals like Sunday brunch or Friday movie night, consistently setting limits and consequences for breaking the rules, and parental availability and attention, regardless of whether a kid seems to want it. By building a structured home environment when your children are young, you will be role modeling stability, a necessary component of being a successful adult, and setting up a secure bond between you and your children that will strengthen and grow as they become adults.

Support with emotional empathy and validation. A child's feelings need to be heard and acknowledged, not judged or dismissed. If parents tell children, "There's nothing to cry about," it invalidates their emotions and makes them doubt themselves on a fundamental level. What they feel is not wrong. It just is. Children who are taught to name their emotions and discuss them openly with their parents learn how to process difficult feelings, which will help them bounce back from rejection and failures. They're less likely to develop psychological issues—anxiety and depression—that might otherwise plague them into adulthood and negatively affect their relationships and careers. Providing support also means intervening when necessary. If your child needs a tutor or a therapist, don't wait until a situation becomes dire before bringing in professionals. Last, giving support means offering instruction. Your child may need help learning a range of skills—from preparing for a test to making a friend. Your role as the scaffold will be to coach and instruct, but never to take over and do the work for your child. Although you can outsource tutoring your child in math, you shouldn't hire someone to give him instructions about life skills and values. The strongest support comes from the parent directly.

Encouragement is gently pushing your child to try new things and take risks. When kids fail, as they inevitably will, encourage their future boldness by talking through the "why" of what happened. Empowered by the knowledge of what went wrong and what they can improve upon, kids will be excited to get back on the bike, stage, or field again. If you don't encourage your children to risk failure, you're teaching them to be afraid and dependent.

Throughout the process, you will need to role model and teach positive behaviors, giving corrective feedback and boosting your child's sense of competence. Role modeling doesn't breed dependency, it encourages independence. In our patient population, we see a lot of pain and suffering that could have been prevented if parents focused on the scaffolding pillars.

Scaffolding Planks

The planks of your parenting scaffold are **patience, warmth, awareness, dispassion,** and **monitoring.** You will stand on these planks to support your kids as they develop into the kind of adults you can be proud of. We use them at home with our own kids and have trained thousands of parents to do the same, with great success.

Patience. Stay steady, even when you have to teach the same lesson, over and over again.

Warmth. Model empathy, affection, and kindness. Show your love and compassion, even when setting limits. It may seem counterintuitive that being warm will foster independence, but the scientific evidence proves it.

Awareness. Tune in to your child's emotional and practical needs and motivations—as well as your own.

Dispassion. Stay calm, no matter how upset you are or how challenging parenting can be.

Monitoring. Keep close tabs on what's going on with your child and make sure your support is benefiting her.

Scaffolding Strategies

As with a literal architectural scaffold, this supportive grid is erected through certain specific construction strategies. In the realm of parenting, there are ten strategies that allow you to best provide structure, support, and encouragement and that use your plank skill set. If you adopt our strategies, you'll raise your kids to be strong, competent adults. The chapters that follow detail the how and why of these strategies, but here is the thumbnail view of each.

Secure Yourself First. Self-care is an essential scaffold parenting skill. If your scaffold isn't secure, it won't be strong enough to catch bits and pieces of the child's "building" when they fall off. It won't be stable enough to guide the building's upward growth. If the scaffold is shaky, one good crisis could topple the whole complex—scaffold and building—to the ground.

Draw a New Blueprint. A blueprint in architecture is a technical drawing, a plan, of a structure's design. Any construction project starts with such a plan. Our brains are the blueprint for our behavior, drawn by millions of years of evolution. Some aspects of the brain blueprint, however, are outdated and don't make a lot of sense for modern life. To build a scaffold that works for parenting now, you have to scrap the old, outdated blueprint, and draw a new one with an open plan that's less claustrophobic, with plenty of space for additions and room for growth.

Lay a Solid Foundation. The parent-child relationship is the foundation, the base, upon which you will build your scaffold. If the foundation is poured from a concrete mixture of emotional availability, positive reinforcement, clear messaging, and consistent rules, your child will rise and grow securely from that solid base. If the foundation is poured from a shoddy mixture of emotional distance, negative reinforcement, ambiguous messaging, and inconsistent rules, your child will struggle to rise and grow from an insecure base.

Hold Steady. Even if you have secured yourself, drawn a beautiful blueprint, and poured a solid foundation, there will be times in life when your scaffold, as well as the child's building, is rocked by circumstances beyond your control. If the scaffold isn't steady during those unfortunate, unforeseeable circumstances, your kids will be vulnerable and exposed to emotions and experiences they aren't developmentally equipped to deal with. But if you tighten all the screws and batten down the scaffold, you can guide kids through tumultuous times, so they emerge confident, safe, and secure, and ready to face the next challenge.

Stay on Their Level. Imagine being on the ground floor of a house and trying to talk to someone on the roof. Not so easy. The person on the roof will have to "talk down" to you, or yell. He might decide it's too much trouble to talk at all. The distance between you makes easy, open communication impossible. Now picture the child's building and your scaffold being on the same level. You can speak directly from a short distance, look each other in the eye, and communicate effectively. To establish and maintain open lines of communication, keep your scaffold on the same level as your child's building. And stay "on the level," too, by being honest and authentic.

Empower Growth. As a child learns new skills, his building will ascend and expand. Since learning means trying and sometimes failing, the child's construction is a process of adding new sections and parts. The scaffold is always there to catch pieces of the building when they fall and help gather materials and choose tools for new additions. Some kids' buildings will expand straight upward, like a skyscraper. Others might expand outward, like a sprawling ranch house. The style of the child's construction is not up to you. The parental scaffold should accommodate the shape the child is growing into. Any effort from you to block or control growth will actually stunt it.

Build Strength. Your child's building is growing, and your scaffold is rising along with it at a close but clear distance. To fortify all that impressive growth, you can help your child to install steel beams like courage, confidence, resilience, and tenacity. With that internal strength, she'll have more than just a building to "live" in. She'll have a fortress that will withstand bad weather and difficult times. You can reinforce her inner steel with guidance and support, and by modeling through your own behavior which tools are most useful when you are tested and need to stay strong.

Set Realistic Limitations. Your scaffolding should never impede growth or block the child's building from taking whatever shape it's going to take. However, the building needs to meet safety standards. Like the head contractor at a construction site, parents need to maintain quality control of their children's development and to make sure that their growth is "up to code." You do that by setting limits and applying consequences for bad behavior. If you let things slide, the building won't be safe and secure to live in.

Support Unconditionally. The architecture of your child's building might not be to your taste. But your personal preferences do not matter. What does matter is that the child's building is stable and strong, and that your scaffold is there to provide structure and to catch pieces that fall off. If you try to change his luxury condo into a whimsical Victorian or fool yourself into believing that his building will one day miraculously transform into *your* dream house, your scaffold won't fit the construction properly or provide the necessary support. Accept his building for what it is, even if it seems strange to you. When it's all done, he'll live in it. You won't.

Repair and Minimize Cracks. As the building goes up, the construction team is always looking for cracks. Not all of them are significant. Some are just cosmetic and take very little to cement over. Some are bigger and require special attention. Along with scanning for cracks in the building, you need to check for damage to the scaffold, too. Keeping the scaffold in a state of good repair is just as important to the construction as maintenance on the building itself.

I know how hard it is to raise kids under the pressures of modern life. I know that you're probably anxious about making a mistake or doing something that might inadvertently harm your child. Just getting your kids through life is stressful and can cause anxiety for you about whether you're doing it right. All this is made harder by a mental health or behavioral disorder.

You can put an end to those worries by using the scaffolding strategies just discussed. They are the solution you are looking for to guide your children through life's obstacles and setbacks, alleviate family tension at home, and put an end to tantrums, slammed doors, and awkward dinner conversations.

If you remember the pillars (structure, support, and encouragement) and nail down those planks (patience, warmth, awareness, dispassion, and monitoring), you will be a better parent, especially when things get rough. If you use these strategies, you'll raise empowered, curious, capable kids who will grow up to be the best version of themselves. You'll also build bonds that survive adolescence and grow stronger into adulthood, which is what we all want for our kids and ourselves.

2

Secure Yourself First

The parental scaffold is the external structure and support around the child's "building." In the early days, the building doesn't yet have a solid framework. Fortunately, the strong parental scaffold that surrounds it keeps the building from falling down.

Now, if the scaffold itself isn't secure, it won't be strong and stable enough to guide the building's upward growth. If the scaffold is too shoddy, one good crisis could topple the whole complex—scaffold and building—to the ground.

It's essential that you secure and fortify your scaffold first to be able to raise your child effectively.

When Lisa, forty, brought in her son, Max, ten, for his weekly session, she asked if she could speak to me alone for a few minutes first. This is not an uncommon request, so Max waited in the reception area while Lisa followed me into my office.

Lisa took a seat, dropped her heavy bag on the floor, and started shaking her head. "I screwed up," she said. "Big-time."

"What happened?"

The saga started over the weekend. "Every kid in fourth grade was supposed to bring a homemade Rube-Goldberg machine—you know those things, when one action triggers another and another—to school on Monday. I didn't hear about the project until Saturday morning. I called another mother to complain about this sudden-death project, and she said that she and her son had been working on theirs for weeks already. I asked Max why he didn't tell me sooner, and he just shrugged."

Lisa works full time at a high-pressure job in finance. Max's father happened to be out of town that weekend, so Lisa was on her own to help her son get the project together. "I'm not mechanically inclined, and neither is Max, which is probably why he avoided working on it," she said. "I found out the Rube-Goldberg machine was a term project and accounted for a quarter of his grade. Some of the parents in his class are engineers, and they texted me photos of their machines with train tracks, pulleys, and hanging baskets. I almost started crying. All we had was a Ping-Pong ball, Scotch tape, and old blocks. I'd had a miserable workweek and hoped to chill out over the weekend. I felt blindsided by this. And when I feel helpless, I get angry."

I thought Lisa was going to tell me she vented her frustration on her son, a slip that every parent makes at one point or another. "If only I yelled at Max!" said Lisa. "I did something far worse. I tracked down the teacher's phone number, called her at home on a Saturday, and screamed at her! In front of Max."

That *was* bad.

"I mean, why did the teacher give little kids such a complicated assignment?" Lisa asked.

"You just know none of the students was doing their own work. The assignment might as well have been given directly to the parents. Some of us have other things to do than rummage in the trash for empty paper towel rolls. I asked the teacher, 'Is the point of this assignment to make everyone feel like idiots?' I just went *off* on her. Meanwhile, Max was begging me to hang up. He was so embarrassed. When I stopped ranting, the teacher said, 'No one has ever spoken to me like that before.'"

All I could say was, "Wow."

"Yeah."

If Lisa had had an easier workweek or her husband were home to help Max with his project, she might have taken the surprise in stride and seen helping Max as a bonding opportunity. She might even have had some fun with her son. Instead, her frustration, insecurity, and annoyance proved to be an overwhelming combination, and she exploded on an innocent bystander.

"Every parent has a story like this," I assured her. "It was just your turn."

I've watched parental pressure increase steadily over the course of my decades-long career. It's never been more intense than it is now. Parents are feeling it from every front—financial, technological, personal, and logistical. It's not your fault that you're exhausted and distracted. But it is your responsibility as parents to do something to neutralize your own stress. If your parental scaffold is so shaky that a strong wind—or in this case, an unexpected weekend science project—sends it crashing to the ground, you won't be able to provide the structure, support, and encouragement a child needs to learn essential coping skills like emotional control and resilience from you.

Self-Care *Is* Childcare

You might be inwardly groaning right now that you have to add self-care to your already endless to-do list.

Not only does self-care need to be added to the list, it should be put at the very top.

Let's be honest: I'm talking to mothers more than fathers here. Fathers today are doing more than their fathers and grandfathers, but they do less than their partners when it comes to childcare. Our country does not have a maternity leave policy like other first-world nations. In Sweden, both parents can take up to eighteen months' leave after the child is born. In Japan, it's a year. But in the United States, mothers have only twelve *weeks* of unpaid leave (fathers, too, are able to take unpaid leave, but they must be eligible by working for a covered employer; and often a couple cannot afford for both parents to take that much time off from work unpaid). The message from the government seems to be that if a mother needs or wants to work outside the home, she's going to have to work doubly hard to manage it. On top of coping with their "second shift," working mothers have the added pressure of believing that they should be able to handle it. Of course, they're tired and stressed! But they feel guilty about the "selfish" pursuit of a satisfying career when they "should" be spending more time with their kids. Guilt only makes parenting more difficult.

"Self-care is an incredibly overlooked and important aspect of childcare because if you don't tend to your own well-being, you can't effectively parent," says Jill Emanuele, our in-house self-care expert at the Child Mind Institute. "It's like the announcement we hear on every airplane flight, to put the oxygen mask on yourself first, and then tend to your children. If you're running around, exhausted, overwhelmed, doing too much, you're not going to be able to pay attention to your kids. Your stress is going to build up over time, and after you explode or implode, you're going to feel really bad about it."

When Lisa's son, Max, came in to talk to me after his mother left the room, he said that he'd been embarrassed by how his mom talked to his teacher. He'd been fearful how he'd face the woman in school on Monday. But even more than that, he was upset *for* his mother. "She was so freaked out," he told me. "You should have seen her face. I didn't want to tell her about the project because I needed help, and she was really tired. I knew it'd just make her feel worse."

In your daily grind, you might not have the time or bandwidth to keep track of your kids' emotional ups and downs. But make no mistake: They are definitely keeping track of yours, especially preteens who are reliant on you for their very survival. They're watching, listening, and absorbing every signal you put out, even the ones you don't realize you're transmitting. Furthermore, when a child spends an entire hour telling her doctor how worried she is about her dad's hectic work schedule, that child is not working through her own issues or progressing in therapy. In a nontherapeutic context, if your child is too afraid to tell you about an important school project or reveal a personal problem because he's afraid to upset you or add to your burden, that child is unsupported and suffering alone with his worries.

To support a child emotionally, acknowledge your own emotional needs and reinforce self-care by practicing it. Your child will learn the value of restoration by watching you. We all want our kids to know how to relax, don't we? I have yet to meet a parent whose fondest wish for her child is that he'll grow up to be a burned-out miserable hot mess who treats himself—and those around him—badly.

How to Scaffold Yourself

To scaffold your child, you provide structure, support, and encouragement.

To scaffold yourself, stick with the same program:

A doable structure. Of course, you want to make sure your kids get the best of everything and that they have full, busy lives. But if your life has become an unending series of rushing from one place to the next, always on the verge of being late, living under the constant threat that one glitch in your schedule will ruin the day for your entire family, you have structured an unsustainable existence. Despite any misgiving you might have, scale back to a doable schedule that includes quality bonding time with your children and time-outs for yourself.

Support your own well-being. To measure whether you're being supportive and compassionate with yourself, ask, "Would I treat my child this way?" You sign up your kids for sports and fitness classes. But do *you* make time to exercise? You make sure your children are eating five veggies a day and getting adequate sleep. Why not have the same requirements for yourself? If you saw your child freaking out over his homework, you'd suggest he take a break, not force him to grind himself down to a raw nub. If your child was struggling academically, physically, or emotionally, you'd get some help from experts. What about when you are sick or struggling? Do you push yourself relentlessly, regardless?

When you ignore or disregard your own feelings, you are modeling worthlessness to your child. Kids take that in, and when they grow up, they wind up doing the same thing. Self-care is self-respect, self-esteem, self-compassion, and self-validation. Support yourself by reaching out for help if needed, eating well, sleeping well, and exercising.

Encourage effort. Reassure yourself that you're doing just fine as a mom or dad, even if your life and your child aren't "perfect" (whatever that means). So many parents feel like they're doing a terrible job at it, and I'd say that nine times out of ten, if you get angry or upset at a child, it's because you feel like you're failing as a parent. Feeling like a failure isn't the most healthy or relaxing emotion to have, or to bring into the home environment, for your sake and the child's. There will be times when you make a parenting misstep. Congratulations! You're human. Acknowledge and accept the fact that we all have our bad days, and you'll feel calmer about it. Then encourage yourself to try to do better next time.

Self-Care Checklist

The necessary supplies for building a strong, stable scaffold:

○ Exercise

○ Sleep

○ Green food

○ Affection

○ Nature walks

○ Playdates with friends

○ Alone time

○ Creative time

○ Romantic time

○ Laughter

○ Music

○ Hobbies

○ Volunteering

○ Meditation

Give Yourself a Break

Our society is unforgiving to parents, even those (and some-times especially those) who are trying their hardest. Mom sham-ing, when people bully and criticize others for their parenting choices—from breastfeeding (or not breastfeeding), letting their kids eat sugar, going back to work, deciding to stay home—is cause for so much unnecessary insecurity and sadness. Parents are afraid that if they don't do everything their peers are doing, their children will fall behind.

Your toddler might have a busier schedule than you do be-cause of society shaming. If you waver over signing up for baby yoga classes, you might notice some raised eyebrows from the moms in your playgroup. As one stressed-out mom said to me, "If Molly doesn't start Mandarin class by kindergarten, it'll be too late." This woman worked full time at a demanding job and had two other kids who were also overcommitted. Meanwhile, she hadn't been to her own doctor for a checkup in years. "It's my number one job to do everything I can for my kids," she said. "If I put myself first or took a break from my responsibilities, I'd be a bad parent."

Whenever I hear parents say, "The kid comes first," I want to ask, "What does that mean?" It's boilerplate, something they think they should say. We have to stop boiling down our lives into generalizations and take a closer look at what our families *really* need right now. If you don't have enough money to put food on the table, getting a job comes first. If the house is on fire, car-pooling to karate can wait.

A few years ago, a young couple with a toddler with autism was sitting in my office, tearful and guilt-ridden about the idea of taking a date night, something they both missed terribly. I urged them to rely on family to watch their son for one evening a week, or to hire a babysitter with training to care for a special needs child.

The mother said, "Babysitters are expensive. We can't af-ford it."

"You can't afford *not* to," I said.

For one night a week, the marriage had to come first. If the couple didn't have that time together, the stress of raising an autistic son could eventually tax the relationship, and possibly lead to a separation or divorce, two households, increased child-care expenses. Their emotional and financial lives would be a lot harder if they broke up. They really couldn't afford not to tend to their own relationship, for the sake of their son.

If you feel exhausted, taking a break to recharge comes first. Within the constraints of your hard responsibilities, adjust your schedule to include "off" time. The 24/7 work culture we're all living in would have us believe that off time doesn't exist. When you model "superbusy" only, your child learns to equate adulthood and "success" with feeling stressed out and unhappy. Show her that being successful means taking five, ten, or twenty minutes a day to meditate, read quietly, sit in the backyard, gaze into space, take a walk, or any other deliberate, nonscreen pause from the bombardment of modern life. Make sure your child knows that unplugging is important to you for your mental well-being, and that everyone deserves to have their moments to disconnect from the world and reconnect with themselves.

What does it mean to reconnect with yourself? It's not hard. Just reflect on your day, your feelings and thoughts. Look closer at what's going on in your head, what makes you happy, what's bothering you. Ideally, your child will see that you reflect, express your thoughts, and try to make adjustments. By watching you, he'll learn how to do it himself. Sitting, thinking, and evaluating is an effective process for coping in the world. If every parent and child sat down together once a day and just stared at the wall for five minutes, they'd feel more bonded and grounded.

You have to embrace the idea that you are entitled to a break. It's okay if you check out occasionally and put yourself first.

Step one: Decide what kind of break you need. Fifteen minutes to be alone? An hour to go for a walk or run? A whole day or weekend?

Self-Scaffolding with Kids Twelve and Under

Take a physical break. Younger children are extremely demanding of your time and attention. The phrase "I only looked away for a minute" is the stuff of parents' nightmares. No wonder you feel like you can't take a break, or even divert your eyes, ever.

But parents of babies and toddlers *are* entitled to have a break now and then. It's just a question of logistics. Where can you find five minutes to just sit and do nothing?

When the child naps or is playing quietly in a crib, resist the urge to "take care of a few things" and take care of yourself instead. Just lying down on your bed or sitting on a chair and breathing deeply for five minutes is enough alone time to recharge for the next hour.

Tell your child of any age that you need a break. By modeling self-awareness and valuing restoration and relaxation, you're teaching your child to recognize her own overwhelmed feelings and showing her how to cope with them.

Self-Scaffolding with Teens

Take an emotional break. Teenagers aren't as physically demanding. But they can be emotionally draining for parents. If your adolescent is struggling, academically or socially, you will feel a constant ache. You're only as happy as your least happy child. So how can you take a break from your teen-related psychic pain? "I coach parents to ask themselves, 'What's happening right at this moment? Is everything okay *right now*?'" says Dr. Emanuele. "Your child might not be as happy as she can be, but in this very moment, she is safe, cared for, well fed, and not in pain. In that moment, you can get a conceptual break." Anxiety is anticipatory dread, fears for what's going to happen, such as, "My son is going to be friendless and miserable forever." Try to ground yourself in the present, and say, "There's nothing wrong right now. The world is not going to end in the next five minutes." So, during that time, dial down the emotional onslaught.

Step two: Whatever you decide, sort out the logistics and implement it. Your parenting scaffold is not a prison. It's there to support, and you're allowed to support yourself.

However, freedom isn't free, and your breaks will depend on available resources. In a two-parent household, arranging a break will be simpler. If you can afford babysitting or summer camp, or you have people nearby to take the kids for a sleepover, great. Rely on family, a neighbor, friends—the "village"—and ask for what you need. Reciprocate in kind.

There's Not an App for That

Pamela, mother of ten-year-old Billy, laughed when her son's therapist at the Child Mind Institute brought up the subject of self-care. "I don't have time for that," she said, and she quickly ran down a list of everything she had to do for her boss, husband, kids, dogs, house. Her list ate up a good fifteen minutes of the session.

The therapist suggested Pamela take out her phone and look at her screen time usage. The woman hesitated but did it. The doctor asked, "How much time did you spend yesterday on Instagram?"

"This is embarrassing," she said.

"More than an hour?"

"I use it to unwind. It's how I unplug my brain."

The clinician let the comment hang in the air for a moment; the irony of plugging into a device to unplug her brain was not lost on our clinician. "What about TV use?" she asked.

Pamela admitted that she was so exhausted at the end of the day, she would flop on the couch and binge for a few hours. "The kids do the same thing with their shows," she said.

If you're too exhausted to do anything after work but watch TV or scroll through Facebook, your child will follow your example and rely on escapism to distract himself from any bad feelings, including boredom and burnout. Phones and screen use eat up time people would otherwise spend on self-reflection. If that rings a bell for you, perhaps reflect for two seconds right now, by asking if you are purposefully using your device to escape because you don't want to acknowledge or look at your feelings.

You would not be alone, if that were true. Using phones and Netflix to numb and distract ourselves has become the great American pastime. Plonking down in front of a screen might seem like a way to relax, but it actually taxes the brain with even more incoming stimuli and has emotional side effects. In a recent German study, researchers found that a TV binge *causes* stress because people feel guilty about having procrastinated and wasted big blocks of time.

On the other hand, when you model your ability to put down your phones, maybe your kids would do the same. Yes, even in restaurants and on long car trips. Before 2000, kids would talk to their parents at dinner. On drives, they'd stare out the window, talk, or listen to the radio. The benefits of no-screen time is that parents and kids get a chance to learn (or relearn) how to daydream, reflect, be creative, interact with each other more. Without constant distraction, people learn to cope with their emotions, to express themselves, and to connect with others.

The therapist who asked Pamela to check her phone usage time wasn't trying to shame her. The point was to make her aware of how she really spent her free time, and to start monitoring herself and acknowledge that, actually, she *did* have time to sit, meditate, or stroll—not scroll—or even create and play with her kids.

Check your own screen usage to get a real shock. And then encourage yourself to cut your Instagram use by just five minutes a day. Those few moments might be the difference between wellness and burnout.

Burnout: Not Just for Workaholics Anymore

Parental burnout is real, and it's widespread. Similar to career burnout, parental burnout strikes when you try to do too much, feel constant pressure and extreme stress, and can't seem to muster the enthusiasm or energy to do *anything*, let alone scaffold your child with love, attention, and guidance. The effects of it are disastrous: tension at home with children and partners, depression, substance abuse, and anxiety. According to a study by Belgian researchers, parental burnout is also associated with parental neglect, parental violence, and escape ideation (fantasies about running away). The more burned out you feel, the more neglectful you can become, which increases stress, which increases neglect, and so on.

Well-meaning moms and dads exhaust themselves trying to be perfect parents and turn into the opposite of what they set out to be. Researcher Moïra Mikolajczak of Université Catholique de Louvain in Belgium recently discussed her findings with the Association of Psychological Science, saying, "We were a bit surprised by the irony of the results. If you want to do the right thing too much, you can end up doing the wrong thing. Too much pressure on parents can lead them to exhaustion, which can have damaging consequences for the parent and for the children."

To determine whether the study's thousands of French- and English-speaking subjects were experiencing this phenomenon, the researchers gave them a survey called the Parental Burnout Inventory and asked them to rate their reaction to a list of twenty-two statements, from "agree strongly" to "disagree strongly." The survey was divided into three categories.

In the **emotional exhaustion** category, parents were asked to rate how they felt about statements like, "I'm in survival mode in my role as a parent," "When I get up in the morning and have to face another day with my children, I feel exhausted before I've even started," "I feel completely run down by my role as a parent," and "My role as a parent uses up all my resources."

Emotional distance queries included, "I'm no longer able to show my child how much I love him," "I sometimes have the impression that I'm looking after my children on autopilot," "I am less attentive to my children's emotions," "I don't really listen to what my children tell me," and "I do the bare minimum for my children but no more."

Personal accomplishment statements were, "I am usually able to understand what my children feel," "I look after my children's problems effectively," "Through my parental role, I feel that I have a positive influence on my children," "I am usually able to create a relaxed atmosphere with my children," and "I accomplish many worthwhile things as a parent."

You can imagine the "agree strongly" responses that would indicate burnout. Of course, there are degrees of severity and fluctuations in symptoms. Some parents might agree strongly with emotional exhaustion or emotional distance statements on Sunday night, but feel reenergized by Wednesday and have a sunnier outlook. Or they might have positive responses about their parental accomplishment that mitigate waning energy and closeness. Only

Do You Have Parental Burnout?

NORMAL	PROBLEM	DISORDER
You get irritated and frustrated with your kids when they do something obnoxious, but you can control your emotions.	You're easily irritated and annoyed with your kids and react by yelling at them and then regretting it.	You feel extreme irritation and frustration as a parent without reason, and you react with verbal or physical abuse to your child.
You feel confident in your parenting skills most of the time.	You feel okay with your parenting skills, but not great.	Several times a day, you think, *I'm a bad parent.*
		You can't muster up enthusiasm for any aspect of parenting.
You feel bonded with your children and enjoy spending time with them, even if, at times, they can be a handful.	You sometimes feel bonded with your kids, but just as often, you are going through the motions.	You are exhausted and feel resentment toward your child because of all you have to do.
		When you look at your child, you don't feel the same connection you once did.

a minority of the study subjects were at high risk for parental neglect, violence, and escape ideation. Mikolajczak and her team determined that one in twelve, roughly 8 percent, of their subjects were suffering from parental burnout. Per their review of the literature, the conservative estimate for it in the United States is 5 percent. That means 3.5 million American parents are dealing with burnout.

"In the current cultural context, there is a lot of pressure on parents," said Mikolajczak. "But being a perfect parent is impossible and attempting to be one can lead to exhaustion. Our research suggests that whatever allows parents to recharge their batteries, to avoid exhaustion, is good for children."

In a follow-up study, the Belgian team, along with scientists from Stanford University, asked subjects to agree or disagree with a new set of statements about work-family-life balance, such as: "I can easily reconcile my family life and my professional life" and "Despite my parental responsibilities, I easily manage to find time for myself." The researchers concluded that the parents who had resources to countermeasure burnout were protected against it.

We're all susceptible to parental burnout risk factors, like

Self-Scaffolding Fails

- Dressing the kids beautifully but looking like a dumpster fire yourself
- Feeding the kids better than you feed yourself
- Forgoing your own annual checkups or not having time to see the doctor if you're sick
- Surviving on little sleep and compensating with buckets of coffee
- Ignoring your own mental health problems

perfectionism, overcommitting, feelings of insecurity and incompetence as a parent, and the isolation of being a full-time stay-at-home caregiver. But by self-scaffolding—structuring a sane schedule, taking breaks, getting the support from partners and professionals, applauding yourself for your efforts regardless of outcome—you can avoid burnout and be fully present, stable, and strong to scaffold your child.

Borrowing Trouble

Dr. Emanuele had a patient, a thirteen-year-old girl I'll call Sarah, who blamed her mom for her friendlessness, her poor grades, for not getting a part in the school play. Her catchphrase was, "It's all her fault."

The mother—let's call her Rebecca—had given up her law career to stay home and raise her late-in-life daughter. During one session with the whole family in the room, Sarah all but pointed a finger at her mom and said, "*J'accuse!*"

"You're right," Rebecca agreed. "I overscheduled you, and you're stretched too thin. I should have gotten you a math tutor sooner and rehearsed with you more for that audition."

Seeing this dynamic play out, Dr. Emanuele asked Rebecca to come in for a private session to talk about the need for both Sarah and her to take responsibility for their own actions and behaviors. Rebecca seemed to believe that it was her parental duty to blame herself for Sarah's problems, absorb her hostile behavior, and carry around guilt about her unhappiness—all this on top of her regret about giving up her career for, at that time, an ungrateful child.

Your scaffold will be weakened by allowing your child, partner, parent, friends, the Internet, to throw bricks at it.

When Rebecca took on Sarah's blame, she felt crushed by it. As one part of the solution, Dr. Emanuele coached her to say,

"Sarah, you're responsible for your homework. And if you didn't get it done, that's on you." When Rebecca stopped taking the blame for all her daughter's problems, she felt stronger in her role as a parent and in her ability to scaffold her child toward personal accountability.

"Part of self-care is not owning other people's BS," says Dr. Emanuele.

Blame and shame are never more destructive than when you heap them on yourself. In the worldwide competition for Perfect Parent of the Year, we are all losers. None of us is perfect and we needn't bother aspiring to be. Remember the scaffold principle of encouragement and remind yourself of the fine efforts you are making on your family's behalf. Model accountability, pride, and responsibility to your children by owning your own feelings, actions, and behaviors and encouraging them to do the same.

Intensive Self-Care

A parent who is suffering from a major illness, a mental health crisis, a serious financial setback, or a devastating divorce will find self-scaffolding to be a particular challenge. When facing a situation like that, you have to give up on any "I can handle it" notions. Rally the family and the community and get as much support as possible.

I've often said that parenting is a marathon that feels like a sprint. Even if you're overburdened and running around like crazy day to day, you still have to think long term. So if a sick parent delegates her mom duties while she is in treatment or recovery, she's actually doing right by her kids by ensuring her/their ongoing survival.

One patient of ours, a teenage boy I'll call Jacob, sought help for his anxiety disorder. His family circumstances were the stuff of Lifetime movies. His father died tragically in a car accident and left the family of three—the mom, Jacob, and his younger sister—in financial chaos. The mother worked two jobs to pay the bills. And then, she was diagnosed with breast cancer.

The mom continued to work tremendous amounts of hours to make ends meet, and she squeezed in chemo treatments on the weekends or between jobs. Jacob stepped up to be the caregiver to his younger sister and they lived with the constant anxiety about the mom's health and the family's survival. What he talked about most in sessions was how much he missed his mother and how unmoored he was by her absence. "Even when she's there, she's not there," he said, heartbreakingly. He needed to feel an emotional, physical connection to his last remaining parent while she fought a potentially fatal disease.

It was important that Jacob express his feelings, and his therapist coached him to say to his mom, "You don't need to work quite this much. You need to slow down." His mom was locked into "I have to provide, provide, provide" mode. But Jacob very bravely spelled it out. "Provide for us by spending time with us. Put your energy into us." Unspoken but implied: "While you still can."

The mom confronted her avoidant behavior, that if she worked all the time, she didn't have to think about what was happening to her. With the support of friends and family, she scaled back her work hours and spent more time at home with her kids, to their great relief. An aunt stepped up to help with logistics, driving, and shopping. The kids' school started a Kickstarter fund to help cover costs. Resting more allowed the mom to tolerate her treatments better. The family of three passed many hours in her bed watching TV and talking, which reconnected them as a family and eased her son's anxiety.

This mom's struggle is an extreme example, but when any parent disregards self-care, it will indirectly hurt the child. Practice self-care even when you think that ignoring your needs is the only way to be a good parent.

Like Parent, Like Child

Genetically speaking, mental health disorders do show up on the family tree. An anxious parent might recognize that his anxious child needs help, but then doesn't get help for himself because he believes he can "manage" it. This belief models avoidance and a lack of self-awareness to the child. What I've often seen in therapy is that an anxious child might fixate on her parent's untreated anxiety instead of her own, and thereby thwart progress.

When one parent is anxious and the other isn't, the anxious parent's symptoms are compounded by the arrival of a child, and they increase even more if that child turns out to be anxious as well. Miscommunications between anxious Mom and nonanxious Dad—one understands the child's problem; the other harbors "he'll grow out of it" expectations—cause tension between the parents, which trickles down to the child, too.

Nonanxious parents often prefer *not* to discuss the child's anxiety with friends or family. I recommend that parents share the distress of their own childhood anxiety with their kids. Open and honest communication about the reality of anxiety is one way you and your children can practice self-care. A strong scaffold is not built on suppressed emotion. There's enough of a stigma about mental health out in the world. Destigmatize anxiety at home. Talk about your child's anxiety, autism, and depression together as a family.

For some parents, talking about their and their child's mental health at home isn't enough. Joining a community can relieve some of the stress you're all under. Self-care might include finding a support group to vent about how hard it is to raise an anxious child. Having the validation from other parents can take the edge off your own anxiety.

To find parent support groups for children with
and without special needs, go to childmind.org/groups.

All the Feels

Lisa, the mom I mentioned at the beginning of the chapter who exploded in anger at her son Max's teacher about a complicated home project for school, made what she considered to be a stunning admission during our conversation: "I was furious with Max. He left it until the last minute, and it's not the first time he springs stuff on me. And then the sulking and shrugging. Sometimes, my son can be such an . . . an . . . *asshole!*"

Every parent has a story like that. Parents tell me all the time how they lose their temper and go off on someone else. But when I ask, "Were you angry at your child?," parents are afraid to admit it. I don't think there's anything wrong with admitting that your kid infuriated you. If he has done something that deserves your anger, you should say to your child, *in a calm voice,* "I'm really angry with you about . . ." and then state the specific behavior or action.

I don't mind parents thinking their kids are assholes sometimes. Clearly, they shouldn't voice that sentiment to anyone but their spouse or a therapist. Privately, just acknowledge that ambivalence exists, that sometimes, you don't want to be hanging out with your kids, or don't always enjoy being with them. They can make you angry. They can be obnoxious. Admitting it unburdens you of any guilt you might have about these totally legitimate feelings. In therapy, I love it when parents say, "You know, I love my kid, but my God, why doesn't she *sleep?* She's the worst sleeper! It drives me nuts!"

The foundation of self-care is being self-aware. It's so rare, especially when the kids are young and your life is a blur, for you to take the time to ask, "Wait a minute, how am *I* doing?" Upon reflection, you might find that being a parent isn't what you thought it would be, that your kid is kind of a jerk, or that he thinks you're kind of a jerk, too. People run from those feelings because they seem too big and too scary. Instead, they get busy and avoid things. But as soon as they acknowledge and accept them, they feel better.

So, after Lisa finally admitted that maybe she wasn't as angry at the teacher as she was at her son, she exhaled loudly and said, "The truth comes out."

"You probably feel a lot better," I said.

She did, and she felt better still after she apologized to the teacher.

A few weeks later, the school held Parents' Night. All the Rube-Goldberg projects were on display. Max's was, as Lisa reported, the worst in the whole classroom—though perhaps his was one of the only ones done mostly by the student to who'd been given the assignment! Lisa acknowledged the state of his project without ambivalence or regret. The project might have been flimsy, but Lisa's scaffold was much stronger for it.

"But I looked at our cardboard and Scotch tape disaster with pride, because, despite everything, we pulled it together," she said. "It was supposed to teach us about how one action leads to another, and another. We both learned that lesson, but in completely unexpected ways. If you're burned out, you lash out, which brings on guilt and regret. Message received. Now I'm trying my best to avoid burnout, so Max and I can build things together."

Nail Down Those Planks!

Self-care means using the scaffold planks to feel stronger and better about being a parent.

Patience
• Instead of rushing and moving yourself and your kids through life at a breakneck pace, slow down. Structure a sustainable schedule. Maybe cancel some things. Take breaks. Relax. Restore. Even five minutes a day does wonders.

Warmth

- Forgive yourself for being an imperfect human and bask in self-love and self-encouragement for all the good you do for yourself and your family.

Awareness

- Reflect daily by asking, "What's going on in my head? What's stressing me out? What unacknowledged feelings or thoughts am I having? What is preventing me from paying attention to myself? What can I do to feel better and adapt?"

Monitoring

- Check your phone usage daily to prevent screen time from taking over your alone/romantic/nature/creative/reflection time.

3

Draw a New Blueprint

A blueprint in architecture is a technical drawing, a plan, of a structure's design. It shows where the walls, doors, windows go, as well as the underlying electrical and plumbing systems. Any construction project starts with a blueprint. It'd be impossible to raise a building without one. Most of us would be extremely wary to enter a structure that went up without a good blueprint.

As mentioned in the "Scaffolding Strategies" section in Chapter One, our brains are the blueprint for our behavior, drawn by millions of years of evolution. However, some aspects of the blueprint are outdated and don't make a lot of sense for modern life. We live in houses and apartments, but our brain blueprints were drawn for a cave with thick, solid walls that block us emotionally.

To build a scaffold that works for today's parents, we have to scrap the old, outdated blueprint, and draw a new one with a modern, open plan that's less claustrophobic, with plenty of space for additions.

Claire was going through a hard time with her "human tornado" son, Daniel. Within five minutes of entering a room, the seven-year-old would break or spill something. Claire made a habit of trailing after him, warning him to slow down and be careful. When disaster struck, she yelled at him and sent him for a time-out, which he sometimes agreed to take. "It seems like he's breaking things and running rampant just to piss me off," she said. She only saw the damage and registered the disobedience. "My son loves to give me a hard time, and I'm at the end of my rope. I'm sick of apologizing to other people for his bad behavior. My worst fear is that he's always going to be like this."

Although Claire didn't realize it (yet), her parenting style was drawn from two hardwired instincts. Both of them are preinstalled in our human brains and were once necessary for the continuation of our species, but they aren't productive for raising independent, confident children in the world we live in now. By following these ancient instincts, parents actually cause anxiety in their kids.

The two instincts that need a major upgrade are negative tracking and confirmation bias.

Negative tracking, aka only noticing what's "wrong." Vigilantly scanning the horizon for danger has kept our species alive and holds the bonds of society together. Unfortunately, focusing on the negative is an ineffective way to shape positive human behavior and form close bonds. Only seeing the bad doesn't support the development of good behaviors. If you're always on kids about what they *shouldn't* do, you're not teaching them what they *should* do. Case in point: Claire's laser focus on all Daniel's problematic behaviors and her failure to see anything good about her son.

Confirmation bias, aka believing you're always "right." The tendency to use—and twist—information to confirm opinions creates negative self-fulfilling prophecies for "bad" children, and causes anxiety in "good" children who struggle to live up to their parents' hype. Parents with a confirmation bias pigeonhole their children into types; for example, the "star," the "troublemaker," and cling to those characterizations despite contradictory evidence. Daniel is only seven, and Claire has already decided that he's going to frustrate her for the rest of her life.

To build a strong scaffold that empowers your kid's confidence and strengthens the bond between you, throw out the flawed blueprint and draw a new one that allows room for growth and prevents anxiety.

Noticing Only What's Wrong

Negative tracking is one of the central concepts that we introduce at the beginning of any behavioral parent work. When we were in an earlier stage of humanity, existing in a subsistence culture of not knowing where our food was coming from every day, parents only had the mental space to pay attention to their kids when they were endangering themselves or others. But that programming doesn't work well for fostering modern relationships.

When I lecture on the subject, I show parents a picture of around twenty kids at a playground and ask them to call out what they notice first. Invariably, the parents notice the kid picking his nose, the one who is crying, the one who is winding up to punch another. What they *don't* notice are the kids sharing nicely, the one playing quietly by herself, or the one who invites another to join the game.

So, parents often ask, should they only notice the positive and pretend the negative behaviors aren't happening? No. A strong scaffold isn't built on cotton candy and daydreams. The new blueprint design is to notice *all* behaviors, negative and positive, as opposed to just the negative. "The literature shows that if you can get to *a higher ratio* of paying attention to your child's positive behaviors—the opposite of the negative ones you zero in on—you're going to see more of what you want," says David Anderson, a clinical psychologist at the Child Mind Institute. "For example, a mother came in recently and said, 'My daughter always eats with her hands.' And, like a conscientious parent, the mom told her daughter not to do that. I asked her to change her approach, first by thinking of the opposite of the negative behavior, which is to eat nicely with utensils, and to track how often her daughter did that."

In Claire's case, she could think of the opposite of Daniel spilling things, which would be all the times he drinks a glass of juice without wasting a drop. Once you have those opposites in your mind, shift your focus to notice them—and praise your child whenever he demonstrates them. Downgrade the level of irritation about a kid getting out of bed a thousand times a night and, instead, up your level of appreciation for when she stays put.

As a guideline, shoot for a roughly 3:1 ratio of appreciation to criticism. That's very hard to do when you're used to noticing the negative only, but the long-term reward is worth the pain of biting your tongue. "The parent-child relationship is the base, with behavior management built on top. Appreciate your child when she succeeds, decrease the yelling and attention to negative behaviors, and the relationship will be stronger and warmer, and you'll see real behavioral change over time," says Dr. Anderson.

You're Never Too Old to Overlearn

Exactly *how* can you draw a new blueprint and hit that 3:1 ratio when your old habits and instincts are so ingrained?

The method to rely on is called **overlearning.** It's similar to a basketball player practicing a three-point shot over and over, thousands of times. When he's in a game and shooting against a defender, his skills might drift under pressure, but he's still more likely to sink the shot anyway because he overpracticed.

So, during your first two or three months on the new blueprint, shoot for an *even higher* ratio than 3:1 to overlearn the practice of appreciating the positive opposite behavior compared to criticizing the negative. It takes mental discipline, which is a lot to ask of parents with busy, taxing lives. But if you can do it for a while, you'll notice a change in your child's behavior. If the change is sustained over a few months, you're hitting the sweet spot. Even if your new skill drifts over time—as it probably will— you'll still engage with the strategy more than you did before in your old-blueprint, negative bias life.

The beauty of overlearning is that you're practicing new skills (noticing a range of behaviors and striving to increase appreciation for the good) at the same time that your child is improving his behavior. Both of you are drawing a new blueprint for your relationship and how you understand each other. "Parents tell me that overlearning forces them to retain the skills. Some tell me they actually hear my voice in their head, saying, 'What's the positive opposite behavior?' and 'Appreciate the effort!'" says Dr. Anderson.

Really oversell the appreciation, no matter how disingenuous it sounds to your own ears. If your kid stops eating with her hands, isn't that worth a little awkwardness? One mom told me that she got over the embarrassment by putting the word *dude* in front of her praise. "It made it okay for me, somehow. I'd say, 'Dude, thanks for keeping your snacks in the bowl. Dude, thanks for being polite to your sister,'" she said. "In any other context, saying 'dude' would be embarrassing. But in this, it helped me express appreciation."

Whatever works for you, dude.

Track Everything

For two weeks, pretend that your kids are an experiment, and you are the scientist in the lab coat with the clipboard. Choose a particular problematic behavior to study and start collecting data. Since bedtime is such a popular complaint, let's go with that. Every night, count how many times, and for what reasons, your kid gets out of bed. Record how you react. Also keep track of the times he *didn't* get out of bed.

Parents tend to fixate on the two nights a week the child broke bedtime rules, especially if it triggered an hour-long screaming match about who is the boss of whom. They forget all about the three nights the child went right to sleep, or the two nights that he complained a little but settled down quickly.

If the data shows that your child's behavior is fine most of the time, then perhaps you'll learn to relax at bedtime, instead of the usual DEFCON 3 high alert that puts everyone on edge. With data, you can look down at your tablet or clipboard and notice that the two nights your kid gave you a hard time, you yelled once and controlled your emotions once. Next week, you can strive to bring your "lost it" number down. Of the two nights your child settled quickly, he read in bed first. So next week, you should oversell how much you love to see your kid open a book.

When you track yourself and your child and use the data to learn what works and what doesn't, the bad nights become fewer and farther between and shorter in duration. With hard proof that one lost night does not mean your kid is a lost cause, you'll start to have better coping thoughts. Whether the data collection is about bedtime, playtime, or homework, it allows you and your child to pay attention to what goes right and wrong, and how to use that information for the benefit of everyone.

Kids Have a Negative Bias, Too

If you showed a group of teenagers a picture of twenty parents in a room and asked them to point out what they noticed, they would invariably point to the dad who was yelling at a kid or the mom who'd thrown her hands into the air in frustration. They wouldn't necessarily notice the mom patiently helping her son with homework, or the dad who listened respectfully as his daughter shared her troubles. Everyone is born with hardwiring in their brains to scan for aggressive or hurtful behavior. But kids' negative bias is reinforced by interactions with you, if you always respond to negative behavior. If your child wants to be

Do Not Do This at Home

Belittle your child.

An outgrowth of a negative bias is the belief that shaming, teasing, mocking, or humiliating your child is an effective model for teaching her how to behave. Absolutely wrong. A recent Canadian study of 1,400 thirteen- to fifteen-year-olds found that kids who were bullied at home by derisive parents are more likely to be bullied at school by their peers. By ridiculing their kids, parents dismantled their teens' appropriate response to anger in both directions. Springing into anger and hostility isn't a great way to make friends. Neither is having a too-high tolerance for ridicule from peers because their parents have inured them to it.

When my sons were young, I remember going to a baseball game and watching a father on the sideline yell insults about his son's athletic ability. Whenever the boy ran toward first base, the father yelled, "Is that as fast as you can go? Pick it up!" When the boy was called "out," the father mocked him relentlessly. The ridicule went on for the whole game and was agony to witness. The father might have believed in his heart that he was motivating his son to work harder. But the research shows, mocking parents damage a child's self-concept. Having a skewed sense of self leads to lasting depression and anxiety. The easiest way to prevent anxiety and depression in teens is NOT to torment them at home.

Using shame reinforces negative behavior, although some parents seem to think it does the opposite. I could only shake my head recently when I saw a news story about a father who posted a video of his son jogging to school for a week as punishment because the boy was caught being mean to kids on the bus. The father shamed and bullied his son for shaming and bullying his peers, creating a negative feedback loop from hell.

Apologies to Nick Lowe, but you should never be cruel to be kind.

Instead, be kind to be kind. Bolster a child's confidence with warmth.

noticed, she'll show you what she knows you'll zero in on, that is, being bad. A teenager who pushes your buttons is counting on getting your attention. And, if it turns into a big fight, he's opened an escape hatch from doing his homework.

In therapy and lectures, when we point out that dynamic to parents, the room gets very quiet.

A thirteen-year-old boy I'll call Stephen hated doing homework. His father, Michael, told his son's therapists that every night, the two waged a heated battle over it. Michael would ask Stephen to sit down after dinner, open his books, and get to work. Stephen would get a snack, then go to the bathroom, then "check something" online, while his father became increasingly annoyed. Michael would inevitably accuse his son of procrastination. Stephen would lash back for distracting him, for being a bad father, for sabotaging him. It just escalated from there.

The two were locked into this pattern because of the negative blueprint they were *both* using. Meanwhile, not a lot of homework got done.

You just can't reward a teen's pushing your buttons for attention with attention. Don't grant him the opportunity to escape from homework, especially if he's actually doing it most of the time. So, if a teen says some offensive things to you at the exact time he should be doing his schoolwork, do not take the bait. Instead, say, "It's inappropriate to talk to me in this way, but I like the fact that you're already halfway through your assignments."

I know it's a tall order to ask you to ignore provocative comments and bad attitude, and focus on the positive opposite, even if there's hardly any of it in evidence at the moment. It'll be just as strange to your teens, who are expecting you to yell, and then you say, "I don't like what you said, but I love how articulate you are!"

Even if your teen is savvy enough to realize you're testing a parenting strategy on him, your ignoring button pushing still works. We've led parents on this a bunch of times. After a few weeks, we ask the kid, "Do you like how Dad and Mom talked to you before, or do you prefer what they've been testing out these past few weeks?" We've never had a kid say, "I want them to go back to what they were doing before." They'd rather not fight but instead take the appreciation, regardless of how weirdly it lands.

How Quickly Does the Ink Dry on the New Blueprint?

Q: If you threw out the negative bias blueprint today, when would your child's behavior change?

A: *Three months.*

I wish it were sooner, but there is some lag time for a new behavior to become an established and normal behavior. Still, you'll see some encouraging signs along the way:

- By week two, you will have started to push past your own resistance about shifting away from negative bias.

- By week four, via overlearning, you'll have upped your appreciation-to-correction ratio to be high enough to evidence some change in your kid's behavior.

- By week six, your child will be consistently better at the target behavior.

- By week eight, you're used to the new way your child is complying more than not. (At this point, our patients' parents start asking their therapists, "What else you got for me?")

- By week twelve, new behavior—yours and your child's—has been established and solidified.

Children with clinically severe difficulties might take up to four or five months to break bad habits. For typical kids, it could be as little as eight weeks. But if you stick with the strategy for long enough to notice change, it's probably going to last. According to the research and my personal experience, the longevity of these interventions is stable. Nail down positive reinforcement for three months, your child's good behavior will still be in evidence six months, one year, three years down the road. It might feel like a long haul to the three-month mark. But once you establish change, unbiased tracking and good behavior will be the new normal.

Scaffolding Opposite Behavior for Kids

- **Structure**. Direct your thoughts to notice *everything* about your child, not just the negative. Once you can see the totality of his behavior, you will have a better understanding about what needs to change.

- **Support**. Give your child all the information he needs to make positive change, voicing appreciation for the behavior you like seeing at a 3:1 ratio or more to yelling at him about behavior you hate.

- **Encouragement**. Cheer on yourself as much as you cheer on your child. It requires a lot of mental discipline to uproot instinctual behavior, so give yourself kudos for the effort you're making.

Always Being "Right" About Your Child

My wife, Linda, and I have three sons, each two and a half years apart, who kind of look alike, were raised in the same house, and went to the same schools. But they are completely different people in terms of their temperament, deficits, and assets.

Joshua, my oldest child, was an articulate intellectual from the age of seven. When he was in second grade, we were driving around one weekend doing errands, listening to a radio show about social anxiety on NPR. When we pulled up to the house, he said, "Don't turn the car off. I want to hear the end of the program."

So we sat in the car in the driveway until it was over. Then he said, "Dad, you don't really understand what they were talking about. You and Adam [my middle son] can just talk to anyone without thinking about it. Mom and me, we have to think about what we're going to say first."

His having that kind of self-awareness so young made me proud. And he was absolutely right. When Joshua and his mother walk into a room, they think, *Who is going to talk to me?* When Adam and I walk into a room, we scan the crowd and think, *Who am I going to talk to?*

Joshua did me the service that day of telling me who he is. And I scaffolded him by listening and believing him. I didn't say, as many parents do when their child brings up an anxiety, "Just relax and be yourself. You'll be fine." If the child is really given the freedom to "just be yourself," his parents wouldn't dismiss his anxiety. The parental scaffold takes shape around the child's building as he figures out who he is. It doesn't confine and compress the child based on who the parents think he is.

Confirmation bias is usually referenced to a political context about ideological echo chambers and people living in "bubbles." What you believe is confirmed by the five hundred people in your Facebook feed, the news media you allow into your life, the state you live in. But you might be doing the same "bubble" thinking about your children as well. You might have subconsciously drawn a blueprint for your child based on a number of factors, like her personality at two, your personality, and who you'd like your child to be. Once the fantasy blueprint is dry, it's extremely difficult to edit or redraw it, ever. Whenever I hear a parent like Claire say, "Daniel is a troublemaker," a red flag starts waving in my mind. Claire believes that she's 100 percent correct in her assessment of her son, and nothing can shake her sense that she's "right." No matter how Daniel behaves, Claire will "spin" it to confirm her established opinion.

More times than I can count, parents come in with their child for an assessment and say, "I don't know what's going on. Lily has always been such a happy child." Not to say that Lily has never been happy. As a toddler, perhaps she was. But as she matured, her brain changed. Hormones were activated. Life happened. If the child's anxiety or depression is severe enough to bring her to me, she's clearly not *always* happy. And yet, parents really struggle with seeing their child for who she really is versus their fantasy version.

Confirmation bias is a dangerous parental blind spot. Thinking you're "right" about your child can lead you to mishandle problems that need to be scaffolded. Insisting that a child is not who they say they are—"Just relax, you'll be fine"—also damages the parent-child relationship. By not listening and refusing to break out of your bubble, you're teaching your child not to count on you for support.

Believe in the Moment

Say your child fails two math tests in a row. If he gets As on the next two math tests, would that be enough for you to change your opinion that your kid struggles with math?

Probably not, although it should. First, your brain blueprint led you to anticipate and look for problems (negative bias), and then you sought to confirm the negative impression. Once opinions are formed, it takes an abundance of contradictory evidence to change them. Humans have a tough time reformulating our interpretation of anyone who tries to do or be something different.

So if you already think, *My kid is bad at math,* you might become anxious and anticipatory about the subject. Even if your child succeeds, you might not be able to let go of your anxiety about it. Hiring an expensive tutor for a kid who does just fine in math because he once failed a test is an example of overscaffolding, or doing too much when doing nothing would empower growth and build strength.

When a boy I'll call Viktor was in middle school, he was not conscientious about his studies and was very vocal about his disdain for the school and his teachers. His parents had a terrible time just getting him out the door in the morning, literally dragging him to catch the bus, which he intentionally missed constantly. The family spent a fortune on Uber to get him to school on time.

Somehow, Viktor got through middle school. And then, in high school, something clicked. Inspired by his new teachers, he cared about his classes and wanted to show up on time. Once he began participating, he made friends and felt peer pressure—the good kind—to care about school and join some clubs. What's more, he put pressure on himself to succeed.

It took a significant period of time for his parents to believe Viktor had changed. For the duration of his freshman year in high school, they continued to yell at him every morning about not being late. They didn't seem to realize he hadn't missed the bus once. The nightly homework nag session continued, even though he'd become an intrinsically motivated self-starter. By sophomore year, they acknowledged that he was doing well, but they lived in constant fear of his backsliding out of his "honeymoon period" of success. Viktor's mom suggested he'd been pretending to care for two years in order to "get something" from them. It wasn't that he'd genuinely turned a new leaf. They were living in anticipation of him reverting back to the kid they "knew" him to be.

This particular kid overcame his parents' subjective bias that he would always be a slacker and went on to graduate at the head of his class, go to a top college, get a good job, and become an independent adult. Unfortunately, to this day, ten years later, his parents still worry that it'll all come to a disastrous end when he backslides.

Viktor sustained his success, despite his parents' lack of faith in him. You should know that he is a rare exception. For most families, the only way to see sustained change for a long period of time is for parents to believe in their kid, to reinforce all the good stuff that's going on, and not to insist that any success is a fluke. As we have all experienced, success is not an unwavering straight line to the moon. There will be zigs, zags, downturns, and backslides. But kids (and adults) can recover more quickly

Do This at Home

Act like you believe.

When parents see evidence of a change, they're wary that it won't last. That wariness is only natural, but it demonstrates a fundamental lack of trust, which isn't healthy in family relationships.

Trust takes time. I get it. The road behind you might be littered with broken promises and dashed hopes. But your job as a parent is to meet your kid wherever she is now. Your best bet to keep positive momentum going is to encourage and support her current, good behavior. The possibility of backsliding is real, and you might have to deal with that when it comes. But in the meantime, be present in the moment and react to what you see before you. Even if you don't really believe the change is real, act like you do.

The father of a teenage daughter with substance abuse issues told her therapist, "Why should I make the effort? I've been duped so many times. She said she was doing better, and we all prayed that she was, but it turned out to be lies." He couldn't bring himself to believe.

No doubt about it: Humans are hard work. We're complicated. Children and adolescents don't always follow through with what parents think or know is the best thing for them. But if children have opportunities to do so, they're more likely to change. Encourage the child to keep trying, and support her with resources and assurance that you will love her even if she fails.

and get back on track if they feel that the people around them believe in them and support them.

Self-Fulfilling Prophecy

If a child is told over and over that she's a troublemaker, a bad student, or a lazy person, she may eventually start thinking, *Maybe I am a loser.*

I specialize in children and adolescents with ADHD, and even though it's a brain-based mental health disorder, these kids are told frequently from an early age that it's not biological, that they just have to try harder. If they're not treated by late elementary school, these kids do start to believe that they are lazy, difficult, and not invested in school, and they behave accordingly.

The bias becomes a child's self-fulfilling prophecy. Even when ADHD kids get effective treatment—be it a mix of supports, from tutors to therapists, and possibly medication to bring them focus—and their teachers and parents notice and acknowledge improvement, the kids are still saying, "I'm such a procrastinator" and "I'm so lazy." It's kind of tragic. External and internal biases are so hard to overcome.

Your biases influence how you treat your child, for good or ill. This phenomenon, called the Pygmalion effect, was proved back in 1964 by a Harvard professor named Robert Rosenthal who did a fascinating experiment on elementary-school students and teachers in San Francisco. He created a fake IQ test, put the Harvard stamp on it, informed the teachers that this new test could predict academic success, and administered it to eighteen classrooms of kids. Totally at random, he chose 20 percent of the students and told the teachers that he predicted their intelligence quotients were going to "bloom." Over the next two years, Dr. Rosenthal tracked the students' real IQ scores. Compared to the untapped 80 percent, the "bloomers'" scores soared. To explain this, Dr. Rosenthal determined that the teachers gave the chosen students more time, special attention, and encouragement, which translated into IQ gains. Expectation became reality.

For further proof, all you need to do is look back to your own past. What beliefs did your parents or teachers have about you that you carried through childhood, adolescence, and maybe into adulthood? How would your life have been different if you weren't burdened by their expectations?

Remember that a strong parental scaffold blueprint is an "open plan," open to the possibilities, open to new information, open to discovery. It's designed for flexibility and strength, to best support your children to become the best version of themselves.

Open Plan Scaffolding with Teens

- **Structure**. Plan your life to be emotionally available to your teen, so that when he tells you who he is and what he needs, you can really listen to him.

- **Support**. Meet your child where he is, not where you think he should be. Further support him with warmth and positive reinforcement in the here and now.

- **Encouragement**. Expectation creates reality, so don't tell your teen what he can't do. Encourage him to make his best effort and to keep trying if he fails.

Claire, mother of "human tornado" Daniel, spent every minute she was with him watching and waiting for him to be destructive. She was so primed to track negative behavior, she missed anything positive and was convinced that her son would never be "good." Claire expressed this opinion to her son and referred to him as a "troublemaker" to her family and friends daily. It was almost as if she were enlisting her social circles to confirm her bias and reinforce it when they were with Daniel.

After I explained how negative tracking and confirmation bias were damaging Daniel's positive behavioral change, Claire was appalled. Her hypervigilance and criticism were creating a self-fulfilling prophecy. Daniel, in his need for attention, lived up to her expectations.

Along with introducing the concept of appreciating opposite behavior and tracking target skills, I suggested that Claire have Daniel assessed for ADHD. "His behavior might not be his fault,"

Is It Rambunctiousness or ADHD?

NORMAL	PROBLEM	DISORDER
Your child is active and loves to run around, climb, and play, but when you tell him it's time to leave the playground or shift to quiet activity, he can do it.	Your child is very active and prefers running around and climbing to any other activities.	Your child makes careless mistakes.
		He is easily distracted.
	When it's time to leave the playground, he puts up an argument and sulks for a while after.	She doesn't seem to be listening when spoken to directly.
Your child is inquisitive and asks a lot of questions. She's able to pay attention to your answers.		He has difficulty following instructions.
	Your child struggles to sit still at a long dinner, or to pay attention when the grown-ups are talking.	He has trouble organizing.
		He avoids or dislikes sustained effort.
When your child is reading or doing puzzles, she can concentrate for a while until she gets bored and wants to do something else.		She is forgetful, always losing things.
	He's impatient with any activity that he's not really interested in.	She fidgets or squirms or taps.
		He has trouble staying in one place or waiting his turn.
Your child can follow directions and keep track of his possessions.	Your child has a hard time paying attention in class and, when bored, can be disruptive.	He runs and climbs excessively.
		She has trouble playing quietly.
		She is extremely impatient.
		He always seems to be "on the go" or "driven by a motor."
		She talks excessively, interrupts, or blurts out answers.

I said. It had never occurred to her that Daniel, her little hellion, her troublemaker, wasn't running rampant on purpose to try her patience. She consented to have Daniel tested.

Not too surprisingly, we determined that Daniel had a severe case of ADHD. Like most parents, Claire had mixed feelings about the diagnosis. On the one hand, she was relieved that a medical professional recognized that her child was not "normal." On the other hand, she had doubts about treatment options for her son. From what she'd heard around school and in headlines she'd read, American children were being overprescribed by doctors who wanted to zombify rambunctious kids. Overdiagnosis and overmedication are hotly debated in the pediatric psychology and psychiatry field. But that discussion doesn't mean a child who has symptoms is faking it or just needs to "calm down."

In this case, I outlined a treatment plan that absolutely included stimulant medication. Claire asked to think about it. "I've heard bad things about Ritalin and Adderall. I'm going to do some research on my own first," she said.

Though I think careful consideration is important, Claire's aversion to medicating her son brings up an unescapable facet of confirmation bias in the digital age: using Google and other search engines to reinforce prejudices that affect parenting choices.

Search Bias

Neurobiologically speaking, when you find something that reinforces your worldview, you get a dopamine surge in the reward center of your brain. It feels good to get that confirmation, and it's only natural to seek out more of it. Unchecked, it can be like an addiction that's hard to change. The Internet is full of things that will reinforce what you already believe, which makes you feel good, so why challenge yourself by looking at other viewpoints? Even the way people type their question into Google will give them the answer they want, like, "Is ADHD a myth?" and "Do vaccines cause autism?" No one types, "What is the most reliable evidence-based information about a causal link between vaccines and autism?"

A major concern in the field of child and adolescent psychiatry and psychology is working with parents to look at the scientific evidence and not listen to unreliable sources for their information. Vaccinations and autism is one area of concern. Another is the side effects, aka the "black box warnings," about prescription medications. Parents might have a friend, or a friend of a friend, or have heard a story, or read an article, about a link between suicidal thoughts and antidepressant medications. I speak to parents about search bias and misinformation every day. A study might make headlines, and parents become afraid about treating their children's mental health issues with medications, regardless of the validity of the story or how it was reported.

Not long ago, the media extensively covered a study that said that one in five depressed subjects had suicidal thoughts despite being on antidepressant medication. Some of our depressed patients' parents read headlines about the study and freaked out. One mother, an anxious woman herself, said, "I'm afraid to treat my son because of what might happen." This was one study, a controversial one. The fact is, other studies actually showed that when doctors prescribed less medication, suicide rates increased. From our perspective, parents need to be afraid of what might happen if they *don't* treat their child.

Parental resistance to medication or therapy—many are more fearful about treatment than the disorder itself—comes from a societal stigma about mental health issues. They might have had bad experiences in the past with their child's or their own interventions. Many can't seem to navigate the health-care system and can't get the access or attention they need. At the Child

Mind Institute, our mission is to educate—and, in some cases, reeducate—parents about the goals of treatment. Misinformation compounds the anxiety and other disorders we're treating. The evidence says that a kid with anxiety or depression benefits from medication. We monitor the patient closely for side effects and to see if he or she is getting better, and we work with parents and educators on a team approach.

"What made me decide to treat Daniel for ADHD was the realization that I didn't know my own son," said Claire. "I knew the problems, but not the person. After years of thinking about him in a negative way and knowing that our relationship wasn't what it could be, I was ready to try something different." Daniel started treatment a year ago and can now read at grade level, sit still in class, and isn't as accident prone. "When he does spill something, I don't yell anymore. I help him clean up and praise his efforts," she said. "And then we go back to whatever we were talking about or doing together. He's a great kid, I'm proud to say. And now I feel excited about watching his life unfold."

The Wonder of Discovery

Childhood is a time of wonder, when kids can and should believe anything is possible. The wonder of parenting is looking at this person you've created, and asking, "Who *is* she?"

Now that I'm a grandparent, I know that wonders never cease. I look at my grandson and think, *He is such a beautiful boy.* (Yes, another boy!) My opinion of his beauty is validated when people stop his parents on the street and say the same thing.

Now, as friends of ours start to have grandchildren, they tell me how beautiful theirs happen to be, and how people stop them on the street to say how gorgeous the children are. I make all the right noises when they show me photos, but sometimes I'm really thinking, *This is not a beautiful child. He's kind of funny looking.*

Those new grandparents are in thrall, just as I am, by what their children have produced. And it'll take a while before they figure out that their allegedly stunning bundles shouldn't audition for diaper TV commercials.

I would never begrudge a grandparent or parent the adoring fog of babyhood. But once it clears, we need to start the process of objectively recognizing a child's assets and deficits.

My wife and I have no idea who our grandson is. Will he be like his mom, his dad, his grandparents, or none of the above? Right now, he's only fifteen pounds. It'll be many years before he's grown, and he'll reveal himself to us gradually while he, and we, solve the mystery of who he is. While he builds himself, we'll all be on our scaffold, supporting and helping, guiding and marveling.

Nail Down Those Planks!

When inking your new blueprint for raising your child, remember to draw upon your planks.

Patience
- It can take up to three months to establish new behaviors after you start positive opposite reinforcement. But stick with it. Once the changes set in, they become the new normal.

Warmth
- Never tease your child. Period. Full stop. Be the person who your child can count on for kindness and compassion.

Awareness
- Listen to yourself talk, and ask, "Am I only seeing what's wrong, or focusing on always being right?" If so, acknowledge your bias blueprint and strive to redraw it.

Dispassion

- Anger and hostility lock parents and kids into negative patterns. If you feel your blood pressure rising, know that nothing positive will come next.

Monitoring

- Track all your child's behaviors, negative and positive, to find out if his bedtime or homework routine, for example, are really as bad as you think.

4

Lay a Solid Foundation

The parent-child relationship is the foundation, the base, upon which you will build your scaffold. If the foundation is poured from a concrete mixture of emotional availability, positive reinforcement, clear messaging, and consistent rules, your child will rise and grow securely from that solid base. If the foundation is poured from a shoddy mixture of emotional distance, negative reinforcement, ambiguous messaging, and inconsistent rules, your child will struggle to rise and grow from a shifty, insecure base.

Stacy, forty-two, a professional woman with a corporate job, was deeply concerned about her eleven-year-old daughter Maya's weight. Childhood obesity is a serious problem, affecting one in five American kids between six and nineteen. Among girls, there is a significant correlation between obesity and depression. I understood Stacy's concern, but Maya was not obese. She carried some extra weight, but nothing to be alarmed about.

"I've done so much research and put so much into it," said Stacy. "Maya eats salads, steps on the scale every day, and gets in at least five thousand steps, but I know she's sneaking food at her friends' houses and gets up in the middle of the night to snack.

I kind of resent it that she's sabotaging my efforts. I'm doing all this for her, and it's like she's working against me."

I asked, "Have you talked to Maya about how she feels?"

"Does it matter? If I let her make her own choices, she'd be twenty pounds heavier."

I believed Stacy wanted the best for her daughter. She expressed concern about Maya's health and that she'd be teased at school. However, in her effort to spare Maya pain and embarrassment, Stacy was causing it at every weigh-in and mealtime. She believed her vigilance would make her daughter happy, but Maya was probably miserable.

On the surface, it would appear that Stacy was scaffolding her daughter. She provided instruction and resources, monitored Maya's progress, and gave her structure via schedules and routines. "I encourage her every day," she said. "I tell her 'you got this!' and 'you can do it!' But she just rolls her eyes at me."

Stacy hoped I could explain the psychology behind Maya's overeating and give her strategies for fixing her daughter's problem. The real problem, however, was their parent-child relationship. The mother was trying to build a scaffold on sand. She and her daughter were interacting daily, but they weren't connecting at all.

The Groundwork

Each parent-child relationship is unique, but invariably, it can improve by following the concepts of a program known as Parent Management Training (PMT), which was developed in the 1960s by pioneering child psychologists including Constance Hanf and Gerald Patterson. Notice that the phrase isn't "child management," it's "parent management," and as such refers to how you change your behavior for the benefit of your child and your relationship. Each concept that follows aligns with the core scaffolding pillars of structure, support, and encouragement.

Presence. This one is easy to understand, and not as easy to do, given the demands of modern life. When you are physically in the room with your child, be mentally in the room with her, too. Don't check email or recall a conversation with your boss. If you find your eyes glazing over while playing with your kid or hearing about her day, shake it off, and refocus on where you are, what you're doing, and whom you're with.

Emotional availability. Be available to lend emotional support and guidance. If your child trusts you enough to share his feelings, give him your undivided attention, validate his emotions, and allow him to vent. Praise his ability to express himself, and never tell him his feelings are "bad" or "wrong." Children respond to sincerity. Ideally, you *are* authentic when you validate and explore your kid's emotions. Otherwise, fake it till you make it. Even if you're new or rusty at speaking openly about feelings, kids still prefer you to make a sincere effort than not bothering to try.

Emotional regulation. Showing anger as a parenting tool doesn't work. It trains kids not to listen to you until and unless you go nuclear. A classic example is calling a kid to dinner with a calm voice that she ignores ten times and only responds when you scream and threaten to throw all her toys in the garbage if she doesn't come to the table *right now*. It's not that you should never get angry. That's not reality. If you react, you react. You're only human. But be aware that anger has a diminishing effectiveness over time. Eventually, it has no effect at all.

Attachment rituals. In therapy, we can get a quick snapshot of a child's attachment to a parent by asking, "What do you do with your daddy?" If she says, "We have breakfast at the diner every Sunday," or "We watch Monty Python movies," we know she has at least one attachment ritual, one thing they do consistently together that is "theirs." If the child says, "Nothing. He works all day and plays golf every weekend," then that relationship needs attention. With teenagers who are peeling away from the family to spend more time with friends, you'll need to beef up a dwindling inventory of things to do together, and then make them happen.

Nonjudgmental quality time. We also call this "special time" to practice skills and promote the idea of your child following your lead and giving her positive attention. Whatever you do together, don't tell her she's "doing it wrong," or take over the art project or puzzle. That would be judgmental. Like attachment rituals, special time needs to happen consistently. You can't show interest in her one day and ignore her the next, or every effort you make will appear robotic and manipulative, especially to teens.

These techniques work for teachers who have to keep a dozen or more kids under control and playing nicely together. It will work for you. In effect, PMT concepts are about parents being there physically and emotionally and having fun with their kids. It seems so simple, and yet when many moms and dads confront the reality of how they interact with their children, they realize that they aren't as present, available, calm, and kind as they could be. Parenting can often feel like "all work, no fun," when you're stressed out and view spending time with the kids as effortful duty. But when you make even the slightest effort to shift your perspectives toward positive attending, children respond, and suddenly, there's a lot less anger, frustration, nagging, and hostility at home, and more laughter and harmony.

The Magic of Positive Reinforcement

Using sincere, specific language that calls positive attention to admirable behavior is called "labeled praise." You will help a child if you attach words to what you value and celebrate.

There has been some blowback in recent years about over-praising, that a constant feed of "amazing!" and "awesome!" will turn kids (or adults) into "praise addicts." The logic here is that every compliment gives a child's brain a hit of dopamine, and over time, she will become addicted to it. Her motivation is to receive praise, not do a task for its own sake, or for the gratification of accomplishment. Unless she can expect to be flooded with superlatives, a praise addict sees no reason to do anything at all.

I agree that filling children's heads with empty flattery is as beneficial as filling their stomachs with junk food. On the other hand, *meaningful* praise is pure emotional sustenance for kids who, from birth, look to their parents and caregivers for approval and affirmation that what they're doing is right and good. When they accomplish something new that's a little scary and took serious effort—like learning to walk, making a friend, decoding to read—they want to share their joy and receive validating applause from you. I know many midlife adults who still crave their parents' approval; just as many still suffer emotional distress if it's withheld.

Some guidelines about praise include the following.

It has to be sincere. Kids can sniff out a fake better than any adult. If she has any sense that you don't really believe what you're saying, the praise loses all value and the child won't trust your words, even when you're being honest.

The language has to be highly specific. Saying a vague "Great job!" doesn't resonate as profoundly as "Great job coming to the dinner table right when I called," "You were very nice to your brother today even when he was throwing your toys around," and "Thanks so much for helping me clean the dishes." Be clear about what you like seeing so the child knows *exactly* what made you happy.

Praise the behavior, not the accomplishment. This is crucial. Praising positive behavior is foundational for your scaffold and your child's self-esteem. Say a gifted test taker gets an A on a calculus test without studying. If you said, "Great job! You're crushing it!," you are telling the child that she's amazing for slacking off and getting away with it. An A is a good thing, but it's not worthy of praise unless the student worked for it.

On the other hand, say a kid studies for hours and gets a C.

Not every kid is an A or B student, and a child who puts in hours of effort to get that C deserves a mountain of praise. You should say, "Great job working so hard to prepare for the test!"

As we all know, the skills we really need to succeed in life are determination and resilience. Calculating cosines and integers? Not so much. (Apologies to rocket scientists.) Praise the effort, not the grade. No effort, hold the applause.

Every time a child demonstrates perseverance, expressiveness, compromise, or hard work, tell him that you've noticed and are thrilled about it. As a result, your child will increase the positive behavior you've praised. You'll boost their self-esteem and strengthen your bond. Build a solid parenting scaffold on a foundation of labeled praise.

As for unspecific praise, there's no harm in yelling "Great job!" from the sidelines of the soccer field. But know that it won't make much of an impact on anyone but the other parents around you.

Another important point is to use labeled praise to validate a child's feelings. For example, if a child confides in you about a bullying incident, say, "Good job telling me about it and sharing that you're upset," and he will be comforted about divulging. If he can name his feelings and talk about them, he'll be able to cope effectively in the world. If you went the other way, and immediately pumped him for more information about what happened— any parent's first instinct—he'll feel anxious and ashamed, and the lines of communication will slam shut.

If you'd like your child to improve on a particular skill or behavior, focus your labeled praise on one or two things at a time for emphasis. Once she's mastered the behavior, move on to the next item on the list.

To put it in adult terms, if your boss complimented a specific aspect of your work, you would be motivated to continue doing it well from that point on. If the boss trashed it, you would be less motivated to do that task ever again. You might fob it off on someone else or make excuses, anything but do the hard work to improve.

Even Criticism Can Be Framed Positively

Giving positive reinforcement *does not mean* that you can't criticize a child. You have to point out when he's doing something you don't like. **Scaffold by giving kids corrective feedback** that doesn't feel like a slam or a slap. It should feel like a gentle nudge.

Give feedback about the behavior, not the child. Like labeled praise, corrective feedback needs to be as specific as possible. A child shouldn't have to parse words or infer anything. State clearly what you do not approve of, couched with affirmation that the criticism is not a character assassination. For example, "I love you, but I don't love when you make fun of your sister."

Ask the child to participate in reaching conclusions. Say your child comes home with a bad grade on a test. You aren't surprised because, despite your asking him to study, he played video games instead. Engage in a conversation about how your child feels about the grade and why he thinks he got it. No matter what excuses he might come up with, keep steering the conversation to the "how" and "why." Give him an opportunity to figure out what went wrong himself and praise him when he does. If he's stumped, you can say what you observed, like, "I noticed you on the computer a lot, but didn't see much studying at all." Deliver the observation dispassionately. You're not accusing him of lying or slacking off; you're merely stating a fact. And then, with warmth and authority, say, "I know you are capable of more."

Include clear direction. What, *exactly*, do you expect from your child? Be as specific and clear as you can be so there is no confusion. Feedback is not about issuing orders. You're not a drill sergeant. But you are the authority figure, and your children look to you for direction. In the case of a parent giving feedback to a child who chronically resists bedtime routines, preemptively direct his behavior, like, "It's time for bed. Change into your PJs. Choose a book. Get in bed. I'll be there in five minutes." To an older kid who doesn't reliably follow the rules about checking in, say, "You can go to the party, but please be home by midnight. If there is any reason you can't be home by then, you must call or text to let us know by 11:45."

Give plenty of guidance. Corrective feedback has to include guidance. Criticizing behavior with a positive spin is great, but to effect change, you have to spell that out, too. For example, with the kid who played games instead of studying, explain to him how he can change his behavior for a better outcome, such as, "Remember last time we talked about how you played games instead of studying? This time, I'd like to see you hitting the books." Offer to help by quizzing him on the material.

Catch Your Child Being Good

Some parents might feel like all they do is praise, instruct, and guide their child over every behavior and expectation. It can be tedious, but it's better than the alternative!

Rachel Busman, the senior director of the anxiety center at the Child Mind Institute, has a nine-year-old son, and she gives him "*a lot* of feedback, but that's how kids learn," she said. "If you observe a behavior you want to see more of, say so. Whenever my son does something I like, I say, 'Thanks for hanging up your coat' or 'I love how you got ready for bed so nicely.' I also point out whenever I see something I don't like. 'Bedtime is at 8:30, and I don't like seeing you out of bed at 8:45.' At no point do I ever say that he's bad or naughty. That's not helpful, especially with anxious or sensitive kids, who might dissolve into 'You're being mean! You don't like me!'"

Deciphering your child's response to feedback is an opportunity for you to learn. "If a child says, 'You don't like me!' the parent needs to follow up and repeat the feedback that they love the child but are not happy with the behavior," said Dr. Busman. "The 'you hate me' line might be a child's attempt to disengage from the conversation or turn it into a power struggle. Do not fall into that trap. Stay focused on correcting the behavior. Be brief with your instructions. If possible, limit them to a sentence or two. Think talking points, not a lecture." Holding forth or nagging does not lead to compliance. If you calmly communicated the feedback and instructions once, you've done your job. You might have to repeat them ad nauseam, always succinctly and dispassionately.

Catch your kid making corrections, and then give him labeled praise for how well he took your feedback. Say, "I love it that you're studying hard and that you asked me to quiz you." "I love it that you're in bed on time." "Thanks so much for checking in when I asked you to."

Follow up praise by asking for their feedback of your parenting, like, "How do you feel about doing what I asked you to do?" so they can express and name their feelings about the process, good or bad. You might not love what they say, but the important thing is that they have the opportunity to express themselves, and that you validate their feelings, as in, "I'm glad you told me that you feel upset about strict bedtime rules. I hear you. We are going to stick with the same bedtime for now." Whatever they say, as the parent, you have the authority to continue to set the rules and instruct and guide your kids.

Their noncompliance is not about you. If your child keeps repeating the behavior you have tried to correct, don't assume she's intentionally ignoring you or that there's a hidden message or secret hostility behind it. It's not about you. It's about a kid being forgetful or distracted or just not appreciating the importance of the task, despite your (calmly) explaining it many, many times (briefly and consistently).

The wrong response to repeated noncompliance? Going ballistic, as in, "I've told you a thousand times! Put your dirty dishes in the sink!"

You can communicate your frustration and get their attention with "I mean business" eye contact and a calm-yet-deadly-serious tone. Don't scream. Don't smile. Say something like, "I'm not happy that I have to keep telling you to put your dishes in the sink. It makes me feel bad that you aren't doing what I've asked." Kids should be aware when their parents are really displeased and understand that bad behavior causes a negative reaction, even from the people who love them most.

Stay positive by framing the language. Say what you want to see, not what you *don't*. "I want to see you studying" instead of "Don't waste time playing games." Or "I want you to keep your hands to yourself" instead of "Don't hit other kids." Excessive "don't"-ing can be shaming, and shame is a poor motivator.

If a particular behavior keeps recurring, it could be helpful to find out if there is anything getting in the way. If the child is seven and older—an age when he or she is capable of explaining— parents can ask what's happening, why your instructions aren't being followed.

"My son and I have been having the same conversation about bedtime for a while and I've gotten sick of telling him to turn his light out at 8:30, probably as sick as he is to hear it," says Dr. Busman. "I'd made myself superclear, and yet every night, bedtime wasn't happening. When I asked why, he said, 'Mommy, you're not listening. It takes longer to do my homework now, and I only get ten minutes to read before lights out. I used to get twenty.' I told him that he made an interesting point and praised him for expressing himself so well."

Did he get another ten minutes to read, though?

"My son was making a great argument, but ten minutes can turn into fifteen, and then we're right back to having the same conversation again," she says. "Sometimes, you have to say no.

I told him, 'I hear you, but lights-out is at 8:30. It's hard and it stinks, but that's my decision. I love you, good night.'"

There's no reason you can't engage your child, listen to her opinion, and have a democratic negotiation. But in the end, you have the authority. Do your best to hear and validate her feelings. Then make your decision and stand by it until a renegotiation is appropriate.

Scaffolding Compliance with Kids

- **Structure.** Establish a feedback routine of calling it like you see it, when you see it. Don't save up a list of corrections to deliver all at once at bedtime. Your means of delivery should be consistent and productive: brief, clear, calm. Allow kids to negotiate for themselves, and to abide by your decision.

- **Support.** Give plenty of guidance so kids know what to do with your feedback. Support their ability to learn from mistakes by giving them the freedom to correct themselves. Validate their feelings by acknowledging them. You don't have to agree with their feedback about you, but you do have to listen.

- **Encouragement.** Saying "thank you" is a simple-yet-profound way to encourage your child to keep doing well and to keep trying and adjusting.

It's Not Bribery, It's Behavioral Contracting

Relationships have moods, just like people. Sometimes, a relationship is happy and joyful. Sometimes, it's problematic and downright vexing. The mood of the parent-child relationship will change depending on your interactions and interventions. As kids turn into teens, that mood might be sullen and hostile, most of the time. The "catch them being good" principle might fail you when you're sitting across the dinner table from a teenager who can barely maintain a neutral facial expression or engage in conversation without calling your questions "dumb" and "stupid." You can manage faint praise by saying, "Thank you for your presence at dinner and your willingness to talk to us about what you're studying in history." Or you can try another approach: Offer her $5 extra spending money for the weekend if she talks to you politely at dinner all week.

When we suggest this, parents often say, "I'm supposed to bribe my kid? That's insane!"

Let's adjust the terminology. Bribery is reactive. If your child didn't do what he was supposed to do and you then offered him money not to repeat the behavior, that would be a bribe. I don't advise parents do that. What I do recommend is that you identify a situation ahead of time and then, proactively, offer a small reward or money to ensure the behavior you'd like to see. This scaffolding strategy that encourages a child to uphold house rules and engage in good behavior is called *behavioral contracting*.

For example, say you were taking your teenager to visit his elderly grandparents at the nursing home, an activity she might not be too excited about doing. Before you leave home, settle on the terms of the contract, the behavior you want to see and the reward at the end; for example, "I expect you to talk to Grandpa about your studies and activities, to shake hands with the people you meet, to try to smile, and to be patient about how long we stay. If you can do all that, I'll give you $10." If the kid sticks to the contract, she gets the money. If not, she doesn't.

What she learns is that, by upholding her end of the bargain, she will be glad she did. Future reward—be it a treat, a small toy, an extra half hour of screen time, or cash—is otherwise known as an *external reinforcer*. External reinforcers give children, and adults, a motivational incentive to follow through. If your boss told you that upping a particular aspect of your work would result in a raise or bonus, your boss is using an external reinforcer to motivate you. The promise of future reward incentivizes hard work and good behavior.

Our brains are hardwired to seek out rewards. People spend all day long thinking about the little gifts we give ourselves once we've earned them. For some, the reward for a hard day's work might be a happy hour beverage at the bar, a spa treatment, a yoga class, a purchase. It's psychologically sound to encourage yourself, and your kids, to associate being good with goodies.

That said, the rewards themselves have to match the effort. A small effort deserves a small reward, maybe just praise. A major effort deserves a larger reward, within the context and comfort of the family culture. In some families, giving a child $50 for bumping up a C to a B, or a B to an A, is normal and appropriate. In others, that might be over the top.

Forget the idea that kids should do right just for the sake of it, aka *internal motivation*. You might not want to pull external strings to make a child do something he should feel good about doing because it's healthy, will improve his skills, or make him more independent. But what you want for him might not be very high on his priority list. Teens might have internal motivators but only for things they personally care about, like extra privileges. Sorry to tell you, Moms and Dads, but what you want from your teen, like general politeness, is probably not that important to him.

Try to remember being fifteen, feeling acutely awkward all the time, and having to be polite to your parents' dinner guests who really do say stupid things. Adults forget how hard it is to be a kid and to control your impulses, to "behave," or to do anything you don't really want to do. By using behavioral contracting and offering external motivators, you will help kids do things that, eventually, they are happy about doing, and at that point, their internal motivation will eventually kick in and they will do it for their own sake. Once that process takes place over time, you can scale back the reward in that area and use the tool of external motivators to encourage other, new skills or behaviors.

It sounds transactional, but we prefer to call it functional. Every human behavior has either an internal reward or an external reinforcer associated with it. Instead of fighting human nature, figure out how to make the transactional aspects of parenting work for you.

What's your reward for all this skillful parenting effort? A great relationship with your child? An independent adult child? Praise? A twenty?

If you expect your kids to say "thank you," you might have to wait a while. Yes, you changed a thousand diapers and have spent a fortune on their clothes, food, and classes. Maybe you would have taken an annual vacation in Maui for the last fifteen years, if not for your sullen teenager who is only polite to keep his phone and get his allowance! But know that it is the rare under-eighteen-year-old who can express gratitude for the sacrifices you've made for him. The two major gratitude phases occur when the kids grow up and live independently for the first time or have children of their own. So any sincere praise you get before they go to college will come in fits and starts. Take their positive behavior as its own reward and consider that transaction a bargain.

Scaffolding Compliance with Teens

- **Structure.** Establish a routine of contracting good behavior. What starts out as an external motivator will teach them skills that, ultimately, are their own intrinsic reward.

- **Support.** By linking good behavior with rewards, you are supporting your child to develop life skills he might be reluctant to engage in otherwise.

- **Encouragement.** Cut them some slack for not saying "thank you." Teens' brains aren't developed fully yet for gratitude.

When They Just Don't Listen

"A couple of years ago when Dylan was five, we went shopping and I refused to buy him a toy. He had a tantrum that was so violent and loud, the security guard at the store had to help me get him off the floor and out of the building," said Amy, mom of seven-year-old Dylan, who came in for an assessment. "He screamed all the way home in the car, and I nearly had an accident while driving. The next time he went shopping with me and grabbed a toy off the shelf, I let him. I know it was the wrong thing to do, but I was terrified he'd freak out again. Ever since then, Dylan knows he has my number and he refuses to do anything I say. If I ask him to hang up his jacket or put away his toys, he flings his things around the house. I've gotten used to picking up after him because it's just easier than having a fight. The only times I get really angry are when he breaks his young sister's toys, which he seems to do just out of spite. And God forbid I don't do exactly what he wants! If I don't cook him the dinner he asked for, he either refuses to eat or he throws the food on the floor. Honestly, there are times when I hate my son. And if you asked him, he'd probably say he hates me right back."

The words Amy kept using to describe Dylan's behavior were "defiant" and "oppositional." Her instincts were correct. We diagnosed the boy with oppositional defiant disorder (ODD), which affects roughly 3 percent of children, more often boys than girls before adolescence and in equal numbers after.

Kids who have defiant behavioral issues push parents toward the extremes of permissiveness in the hope that a larger amount of control will get the kid to listen. But a permissive strategy only reinforces the bad behavior. After Amy went through that nightmare with the security guard, she seemed to realize that she and Dylan were stuck in a bad pattern that started with his screaming and ended with her complete capitulation. Every time she yelled back or gave in, their behavioral rut got a little bit deeper. Along the way, Dylan learned that throwing a tantrum was the best way to get what he wanted.

A hallmark of ODD is that it takes a huge toll on the family. Every member is affected by it. Amy mentioned the son's seemingly spiteful acts against his little sister. My guess was that Dylan resented her for taking time and attention away from him, and he acted on his feelings with anger. You can't blame Amy, although she helped to create the situation. You can't blame the boy, either. Through no conscious effort of the child, he learns through repeated trials that defiance is a way to continue getting what he wants.

Is It ODD?

NORMAL	PROBLEM	DISORDER
The child talks back sometimes but goes along with the decision of an authority figure.	The child talks back with an angry or aggressive tone, but ultimately does what he's told by an authority figure.	The child is unusually angry and irritable.
The child tests the rules in a healthy way but follows them for the most part.	The child breaks the rules sometimes. If he faces consequences for his actions, he will learn from his mistakes.	The child frequently loses his or her temper.
The child might be annoying but doesn't necessarily intend to be.		He is easily annoyed.
		He argues with authority figures.
His tantrums last several minutes.	The child takes some pleasure in being a disrupter.	He refuses to follow rules.
		He deliberately annoys people.
		He blames others for mistakes.
	His tantrums can last ten minutes.	He is vindictive.
		The child demonstrates these symptoms for at least six months.

To get to a diagnosis, our therapist asked Amy if Dylan was as difficult at school as he was at home. "Not really," she said. "He can be annoying to the other kids, and he has had tantrums there. But it's not nearly as bad as it is with me."

That's a tell. Kids who have ODD are likely to be more

oppositional with people they know well, partly because the pathways are so well worn. At school, where he has less control in general over his environment, being oppositional and defiant might not pay off as much.

Although it can be hurtful to moms and dads that their child is only awful with them, it can also be a positive indicator that the child is capable of change. Even kids with diagnosed behavior disorders like ODD or ADHD (or both; the two disorders often go together) respond well to the Parent Management Training strategies I've described earlier in this chapter, like using positive reinforcement, being emotionally available, and setting clear expectations for behavior.

We worked with Amy and Dylan using a combination of behavioral modification—for parents and child—and medication. One strategy that really worked for this family was Amy's ignoring bad behavior and praising the good. When Dylan threw his dinner on the floor, she didn't yell at him to clean it up or prepare him a new meal. She left the food where it was and said nothing. When the boy realized he wasn't going to get his way and took a bite, she praised it by saying, "I appreciate you eating the dinner I made." If he acted out in public when she denied him a toy or treat, she got him into a private place as quickly as possible and allowed the tantrum to wind down. But she didn't yell or beg him to stop. When he'd quieted, she said, "Thank you for calming yourself down. That's a great skill to have."

After a few months of therapy and by the magic of positive reinforcement, his symptoms were improving steadily. Most important, mother and child were able to rewrite their relationship to have happy moments as well as challenging ones, and build their bond from a new, solid foundation.

The Golden Rule

Stacy, the mom who was worried about her teenager Maya's weight, came to realize that all their mother-daughter time was judgmental, not what anyone would call "quality." She wasn't correcting her daughter's behavior; she was trying to control it. Every conversation they had was about how Maya was failing. The only rituals they shared were Stacy's forcing Maya to step on the scale and count carbs. As for emotional availability, Stacy never asked Maya about her feelings at all; she did show her own anger and frustration about her daughter's noncompliance.

If asked, "Would you physically harm your child if she didn't do what you wanted her to do?," Stacy would probably be offended by the very question. But according to a 2011 study by psychologists at the University of Michigan in Ann Arbor, when a person feels intense social rejection—in the study, a romantic breakup, but any situation when someone feels personally dismissed—it activates the same regions of the brain as physical pain. Emotional distress "hurts." I'm not saying that Stacy's criticism and dismissal of her daughter's feelings were like punching her in the gut. But to Maya, the sensations were the same.

To scaffold her daughter, Stacy needed to manage her behavior, and to treat Maya the way she would want to be treated, with love, compassion, and kindness. It wasn't natural at first for Stacy to catch Maya being good. But when she started looking for positive behaviors to praise, she found so many. Maya was a generous friend, showed remarkable focus when reading and drawing, diligently labored over her homework, and took wonderful care of the family's pet dog, and the list goes on. "Maya is a great kid," she said. "I mean, I knew that. But I took all her positive traits and behaviors for granted. They were a given. Now that I'm focusing on them and calling them out, Maya seems suspicious of me, and that fills me with shame."

I encouraged Stacy to keep at it. I usually find that it takes about a month for kids to process their parents' shift toward positivity. Then they come in for a session and say, "Mom is being so nice to me. It's strange . . . but I like it."

The next time I saw Stacy was a few months later, and I was happy to hear that her relationship with Maya had greatly improved. "The biggest change happened when we started walking the dog together after dinner," she said. "Maya had always done that by herself, which I pushed so she'd get more steps. I tagged along one evening—to get some of that nonjudgmental quality time. The conversation was awkward at first, but then we talked about the dog, the things we saw, nothing in particular."

The twenty-minute walk turned into an hour. Mom resisted pointing out that they were logging thousands of extra steps. "Any discussion of food or fitness was put aside," she said. "If it came up, I could see Maya shut down." By spending that time together, mother and daughter got to know each other. Eventually, Maya opened up about how she felt about her weight and her mother's vigilance. "She told me that every time I made her get on the scale, she felt like crying, and my heart just broke. I realized risk of depression and low self-esteem were a lot more important than some far-off threat of her having a heart attack at fifty," she said.

Stacy redirected her energies toward building her daughter's confidence with labeled praise and positive attending. Increasingly, Maya opened up about her feelings on their walks, and Stacy scaffolded her daughter with validation and support. The mood at home went from excruciating to easy, and the pair grew close. Maya didn't feel the need to flee home for her friends' houses where she habitually binged on junk food. As a result, she wound up losing a bit of weight. Most important, her outlook was lightened considerably, all because of changes Stacy made in her *own* behavior, not in behavior she demanded be changed by her daughter.

"I wasn't helping her before," she said. "Now, I know I am, and that feels great."

Nail Down Those Planks!

A solid parent-child relationship is the base on which your child will grow and learn independence and resilience. To secure the base, practice your planks.

Patience

• Even if you have to repeat yourself a thousand times, keep giving your child corrective feedback until she gets it. Then move on to the next skill, and the next.

Warmth

• Reinforce positive behavior with praise and rewards.

• By being emotionally available and present, you'll validate your child's feelings and encourage her to open up and share them.

Awareness

• Check yourself before your helpful feedback turns into harsh criticism.

• Take a close look at your schedule and make sure to include daily quality family time.

Dispassion

• Frame feedback by saying what you like and always deliver it with a calm, clear voice. Anger and nagging do not lead to compliance.

5

Hold Steady

Even if you have secured yourself, drawn a beautiful blueprint, and poured a solid foundation, there will be times in life when your scaffold, as well as the child's building, is rocked by circumstances beyond your control.

When the world is quaking beneath you, break out your emotional skills toolbox, and tighten every bolt and screw on every level of the scaffold. If it's rattled by those unfortunate, unforeseeable circumstances, your kids will be vulnerable and exposed to emotions and experiences they aren't developmentally equipped to deal with. But if you hold steady and batten down the scaffold, you can guide kids through the tumultuous times of life, so they emerge from them confident, safe, and secure, and ready to face the next one.

When I was a kid, I went to sleepaway camp every summer. The camp was pretty conventional. We played sports, learned to swim, did arts and crafts, and put on a show at the end. Sounds fun, I know, but I hated it. Along with the separation anxiety of being away from home for eight weeks, I lacked the necessary skills for camp success, like knowing how to catch a baseball. I clearly remember standing at second base, thinking, *Can't the runners just go from first to third? Do I have to get involved every single time?* When I was mercifully moved to the outfield, I just stood there, daydreaming, not paying any attention to the action on the infield.

My father was a jock, a college soccer star, and he wanted me to love sports like he did. He couldn't understand why I wasn't a natural athlete and decided early on that he didn't have the patience to teach me how to improve; he gave up on trying to help me with anything athletic. The hit-catch-throw gap in my skill set certainly caused some problems for me later in adolescence. If I'd played sports, my life would have been easier socially in junior high or high school, no question.

When I became a dad, I wanted my three sons to acquire the skills I lacked, so I made sure they learned how to swim and played tennis, soccer, and baseball. I never had fantasies that they'd go from Little League to the major leagues. And I in no way needed them to be very good at it! I just hoped that sports proficiency would make their lives easier.

My wife, Linda, and I decided to send Joshua to sleepaway camp when he was eight. Linda had loved camp when she was a kid. She's naturally athletic and never got homesick. Maybe her camp-love would pass down to him? Since he knew how to catch a baseball, I thought the odds were in his favor.

At parents' visiting weekend, Joshua ran into our arms and hugged us a bit too tightly. I asked, "How's camp?"

He said, "I want to come home."

One look in his eyes and I knew that he hated camp just as much as I did. I'd done my scaffolding due diligence. I'd stacked the odds. Surprised and disappointed, I thought, *But . . . but . . . you can play baseball! I gave you the toolbox!*

Seeking privacy to get into this conversation, we took a walk in the woods. "So tell me," I said. "Why do you want to come home?"

"I'm unhappy. There's no one here to love me," he replied. And just like that, the separation anxiety I'd experienced as a kid at camp came rushing back tenfold because, this time, I felt it on behalf of my precious child. Tears welled. I couldn't help it.

Joshua said, "Dad, don't *cry*."

How can any feeling person not cry when his eight-year-old son tells him he feels unloved? I said, "It's okay to cry when you're upset, and I'm upset!"

Except . . . crying in front of Josh didn't make me feel any better. I'm sure it made him feel worse. Yes, it's fine, recommended, to let the tears flow if you're unhappy. But it's not okay to compound a child's sadness with your own. My son came to me with a problem—he felt unloved—and I responded to it by burdening him with my feelings. Since I had a bad history with camp and was ambivalent about sending him into a situation I'd despised, I had plenty of guilt, too, and a sprinkling of ancient hurt about having disappointed my own father by not being the athlete he would have preferred.

No parent is perfect; not you, not I. In this chapter about tightening the screws of your scaffold to hold steady, even if your child's world is falling apart, my "Josh at camp" story is the bad example!

When Parents Freak Out, They Freak Out Their Kids

As parents, we all feel our children's pain. When they ache, we ache. Their hurt hurts us. When they don't get invited to the party or make the team, our hearts break. When they're suffering from anxiety or depression, we would gladly take their pain entirely as our own to give them some relief. Although commiserating and sharing pain is beneficial in a friend context, you are not your child's friend. Regardless of how intense emotions fell into your lap, the onus is on you to control them. It's *never* your child's job to scaffold your feelings. It's overwhelming, unfair, codependent, and gives the kid too much power. The best way to

help a troubled kid is to model and reinforce emotional processing and self-control to teach her how to cope with her feelings of
rejection, insecurity, worry, and sadness.

Parents often say, "I would never dump my feelings on my
child!" without realizing the subtle ways they do it all the time.
Say a child does badly on a test and you say, "Swear to me you'll
do better next time." The kid can't guarantee a future outcome!
You're asking your daughter or son to lie in order to make you
feel better about her or his failure. Plus, the kid will worry that
only success is acceptable in this house. What if she or he can't
live up to that?

The child is suddenly dealing with stressors, worries, and responsibilities beyond their capacity to handle.

Little Big Problems

Melvin, the father of an eight-year-old boy we'll call Scott, told
one of our therapists about going with Scott to a classmate's
birthday party at a local play space. "At home, his social anxiety
isn't on display. I wanted to see it with my own eyes when he was
with his peers," said Melvin. "We walked in and all the kids were
running around on the trampolines, playing in the foam pit, having loads of fun. Scott started running around but steered away
from the other kids. They avoided him, too. It was like he had
a force field around him. He seemed to be having an okay time,
it was just that he was on his own planet. He turned back and
waved at me, and my heart shattered."

Melvin was determined to coach his son into having friends.
So he took to shooting video of Scott at birthday parties, playing
it back, and discussing what he could have said or done to get
another kid to play with him. "It didn't work," said Melvin. "He
hated the videos and got angry and upset with me for forcing the
conversation. But I insisted that if he listened to me, he'd make

friends and have a great time at the next party. In hindsight, I realized that by trying to psych him up to override his anxiety, I added to it and turned myself into a liar."

If you suspect a situation is going to be challenging for your child, I recommend highlighting his ability to just get through it. Instead of putting pressure on him by saying, "It's gonna be great!" take the realist approach and say, "It could be fun. It might not be. But it's always worth giving it a try."

Concentrate your efforts on what you can do before the event or situation to help it go well. Scaffolding might mean shopping with your child for a new party dress that makes her feel confident or arranging a playdate with the party's host beforehand to establish some rapport. Focus on the fact that she's going to face a challenge and that there are things you can do to help her get through it. In the long run, whether an eight-year-old has a good or bad time at a party doesn't really matter. But what does matter is your supporting her ability to cope with it, either way.

Melvin's "let's review the tape" approach might work for a football coach's postgame analysis. But in this case, it was asking Scott to relive uncomfortable or even low-grade traumatic experiences, which is more likely to cause anxiety than provide insight. Not to say you shouldn't do a postparty evaluation, as long as you do a lot more listening than talking. In therapy, if a patient casually mentions something that seems to be completely random, we make a note of it. Those casual mentions almost always circle around to be relevant. For example, if a girl talks about how pretty the host's new dress was but fails to mention how her own new dress went over, that might be worth further exploration. As always, scaffold with reassurance, by saying, "Well, I love your dress and think it looks great on you," to get her to open up.

Whenever you feel a sense of panic or helplessness about your child's predicament, you have to pause and remind yourself that your pain has to take a backseat to your child's. An acquaintance of mine told me the story of getting an out-of-the-blue phone call from a nearby hospital. "My thirteen-year-old daughter was hit by a taxi while crossing the street and was rushed to the emergency room," she said. "I was shell-shocked." When the mom arrived, she found her daughter in tremendous pain with a broken leg. Seeing her child in agony sent her own fight-or-flight response into overdrive. Instead of sitting by her daughter's bedside and consoling her, she started chasing down every nurse, doctor, or technician she could find and demanding attention.

The mother's first instinct was to seek immediate help. If a parent sees her child suffering, it's only natural to spring into action to stop it. However, when parents freak out about their children's pain—and their own—they are not helping. The girl had been all alone in the ER. What she needed even more than a pill was the comfort of her mother's presence and her soothing reassurance that everything was going to be okay. By the time Mom returned to her daughter's bed, the girl was inconsolable. Mom thought she was helping her daughter, but by giving in to her own distress, she made things worse.

Facing Crises with Control

It's not about your feelings. It's about scaffolding your child to process hers. When children express difficult emotions and parents react with distress, the child learns to feel anxiety about expressing herself and hides her feelings. But if you react with sympathy and nurturance to your kid's distress, the child learns to express herself openly without shame and becomes more sympathetic to others. The key to your child's success in future adult interactions depends on your ability to hold steady in your interactions now.

However, in some situations, *not* freaking out would be patently absurd. And yet, the best thing you can do for a child who has experienced a tragic event is to be a stable force.

One of our teenage patients was raped by a teacher. Her experience was traumatic; we treated her for PTSD over several months. Eventually, she was able to say, "It was not my fault. I didn't do anything wrong." By living with that understanding, her intrusive thoughts and nightmares decreased.

Unfortunately, her mother's progress lagged far behind. She felt terrible guilt that she didn't prevent the rape, even though there was no way she could have. She was convinced her daughter's life was ruined, and that any contact with boys—including her male friends—would further traumatize her. Dating and relationships were out of the question. In sessions with both mother and daughter, the mom cried and talked about how the rape and ensuing guilt had affected her. Every time she cried, "It's all my fault," and the girl replied, "I don't blame you," the parent forced her child into the role of comforter, and out of her own recovery. The mother's ongoing crisis prolonged the pain for her daughter.

"Even when families are in crisis, in a situation that can only be described as 'out of control,' parents still need to maintain emotional control in front of their kids," says Jamie Howard, director of the Trauma and Resilience Service at the Child Mind Institute.

Dr. Howard has led parents and teachers through some ghastly experiences. Since the mass murder of twenty-eight people at Sandy Hook Elementary School in Newtown, Connecticut, in December 2012, the Child Mind Institute's therapists have worked with hundreds of patients, parents, and educators who have been touched by school shootings. For some parents and teachers, we've recommended they get PTSD counseling for themselves that always includes training for how to appear dispassionate in front of their kids and students.

The fear of being shot at school is an anxiety truly unique to Millennials and Generation Z students—and their parents. "Through all the work we've done in this area, what we've found is that children take cues from adults about how to feel," says Dr.

Howard. "I have a lot of parents who get very upset about how active shooter drills at school are affecting their children. But when I ask the kids about it, they don't report feeling scared by the drills. For them, active shooter drills are no different from fire drills. It's just another part of their week. The reality for kids is that their parents are more terrified than they are." The kids who do freak out—manifested in nightmares and reluctance or refusal to go to school—usually have parents who obsess at home about the latest incident.

"With parents, we focus on competence," says Dr. Howard. "How can people increase their ability to stay safe? What steps should they take? What do they need to learn or practice?" Working through a **competence protocol** reduces anxiety in fear-provoking situations that involves the larger community: a school shooting, a health outbreak, a crime spree, a hurricane warning. A competence protocol in brief:

- **Be ready.** Every discussion should focus on how to stay safe, and not on how unsafe and dangerous the world is. The odds of your child being killed by a school shooter are one in two million, according to a 2019 study by the Centers for Disease Control and Prevention. Tell your kids, "Chances are, you'll never be involved in a school shooting. But if it does happen, you know where the exits are. You do the drills. You'll know what to do."

- **Send a consistent message.** Avoid confusion by contacting the school, getting information about how the administration presents the facts about school shootings and their safety plan, and present it the same way at home.

- **Act unfazed.** If a child comes home and says, "We did an active shooter drill today," respond dispassionately, but not dismissively. A condescending "That's nice, dear," sounds like you don't care. You can show you care without flying off the handle. Keep it positive by saying, "The drill sounds useful. It's great to practice lots of different ways to stay safe."

- **Be reasonable.** Preparation is an adaptive function of anxiety. Anxiety drives us to prepare. It becomes a disorder when anxiety overrides the adaptive part. People start to believe that nothing they do will prevent disaster, and they experience disproportionate worry about low-probability events or things that wouldn't be that bad if they did happen. If the preparation is taken too far, it doesn't alleviate anxiety. It exacerbates it. In a panicked state, you won't find solutions to problems because you're not thinking clearly, which helps no one.

What Happened to Feeling All the Feels?

After I cautioned one mother to modulate her anxiety in front of her kids, she said, "Am I supposed to role model emotional expressiveness or not? Get your story straight, Dr. Koplewicz."

Being upset or angry is part of life. We have all experienced fear, dread, sadness, frustration, confusion, panic, and we all need to teach our children that scary feelings will be a part of their lives for their whole lives. What matters is how we deal with them. Show your kids that emotions don't control you. You control yourself while experiencing them.

"You don't want to role model being a robot," says Dr. Howard. "A common situation that comes up often at the Child Mind Institute is how to handle grief, like when a child's grandparent is dying or has died. The child's mom or dad is losing *their* mom or dad. It's totally expected that the parents would feel grief. So go ahead and cry. If your child seems alarmed by the sight of your grief, say, 'I'm feeling sad. I'm going to miss Grandma. That's why I'm crying right now. But I'm not going to feel sad forever.'"

Scaffold by role modeling an appropriate (not dramatic) authentic expression of emotion, and by teaching a child the mechanics of the emotion itself. The mechanics of grief, for example, are that people are sad about a loss. It's normal and healthy to feel that way. Eventually, the sadness will fade, and they'll feel good again.

Coincidentally, while Dr. Howard and I were discussing the topic of role modeling grief, she learned that her own mother had been rushed to the hospital with pneumonia. "My daughter is four and she's clearly alarmed, as am I," she says. "I was nervous about Mom, and she picked up on it. I wasn't going to pretend to be unaffected, but I wasn't going to start wailing, either. So I said to my daughter, 'I really wish Grandma weren't sick, and the hospital is not a fun place to be. But it's where the medicine, doctors, and nurses are. They're working really hard to make her feel better. I'll be happy when she gets home and can rest in her own bed.'"

Even a four-year-old can tell that Mommy is upset and distracted. Being "not okay" is perfectly okay, if it makes sense in context. Grandma's in the hospital? Of course, it's concerning and that's what can and should be expressed.

What's unduly frightening for a child is a parent's intense expression of emotion without explanation. If you said to a child after a grandparent is rushed to the hospital, "Grandma's going to be fine!" while hysterically crying, the child would be, understandably, confused. Confusion causes anxiety in children, just as it does in adults. The difference is, kids don't know how to cope with conflicting messaging. If the adult who's in charge of their safety and survival expresses emotions with too much intensity to fit the given situation, kids of all ages will feel overwhelmed by the experience and either freak out or shut down.

It's also upsetting for kids when parents try not to show any emotion at all. Many of us were raised in households where the philosophy of "not in front of the kids!" was religiously enforced. Researchers at Washington State University studied the impact of parents hiding their emotions from children. They asked 109 parents (roughly half moms and half dads) to do a stress-inducing task, speaking in public and receiving negative feedback, followed immediately by going into a room and building a LEGOs structure with their child. Half of the parents were asked to intentionally hide the stress of having been booed by the audience from their child; half were told to just "act naturally."

Sara Waters, assistant professor in the Department of Human Development at WSU, told *Science Daily,* "The act of trying to suppress their stress made parents less positive partners during the LEGO task. They offered less guidance. But it wasn't just the parents who responded. Those kids were less responsive and positive to their parents. It's almost like the parents were transmitting those emotions."

A far healthier approach than suppression is to allow kids to see that you face hardships, feel distress, and then cope and resolve the conflict. "Let them see the whole trajectory," Waters told *Science Daily.* "That helps kids learn to regulate their own emotions and solve problems. They see that problems can get resolved. It's best to let the kids know you feel angry"—or sad, afraid, confused, disappointed—"and tell them what you're going

Scaffolding Emotional Control with Kids

- **Structure.** Focus on competence whenever possible to ease a child's—and your own—discomfort about "out of control" situations. Like fire and shooter drills at school, preparation and emotional checking-in should be done regularly.

- **Support.** Bolster children's coping skills by modeling your own ability to deal with difficult emotions and by explaining the mechanics of how feelings work.

- **Encouragement.** If you freak out, they freak out. Encourage kids to express themselves openly by reacting to whatever they share with dispassion.

to do about it to make the situation better." The exception to the rule is that high-conflict fights between parents should stay behind closed doors.

Freaky Friday (and Saturday, Sunday, Monday . . .)

If your kids are exposed to your extreme emotional expressions and are forced to comfort you too often, they will adapt by developing unhealthy amounts of adult behavior. We see it happen in families with mentally ill, drug-addicted, alcoholic, disabled, and divorcing parents. In dire circumstances, kids are taken out of a normal childhood existence because of what they've seen, heard, or had to do for the parents to keep the family going. The child becomes the caregiver, and the parent becomes the cared for. This role reversal is called *parentification*, and it's highly destructive for the relationship and the child's emotional development.

Psychologically speaking, the two variations of parentification are instrumental and emotional. *Instrumental parentification* happens when the child is enlisted to do adult tasks that go far beyond what we think of as chores. One family we consulted had fallen into a deep financial hole and couldn't afford round-the-clock care for the grandfather with dementia. So they required their twelve-year-old daughter to become a de facto home health-care worker, feeding and bathing her grandpa, an eighty-seven-year-old man. Kids who are expected to get jobs to pay the family's bills, or to look after their younger siblings the way a mother or father would, are being instrumentally parentified to varying degrees. Not to suggest that a teenager shouldn't have babysitting duties for younger siblings in a pinch or on Saturday nights. But chronically enlisting a kid to do work that should be provided by the parent causes her to grow up too fast.

Emotional parentification might be even more insidious. The parent turns to the child to be his or her confidant or confessor.

We see this all the time when parents are going through an acrimonious divorce. One parent tries to get the kid on his or her side, by revealing personal, sexual, or emotional spousal experiences. No child should be a mediator between her parents. Nor should he have to listen to Mom's dating stories, Dad's financial worries, boost parents' egos, or monitor their drinking.

You can't just skip childhood and be okay. Kids need to have years and years to feel carefree, to be silly and creative, to make low-stakes mistakes, to not carry the heavy burdens of adulthood. No kid should be crushed under the weight of her parents' feelings and responsibilities. When parents force a child to concern herself with their problems, it's overwhelming and damaging. The child is knocked out of her own developmental progress and will miss out on learning essential life skills. Meaning, while she is conscripted to be a wee Cinderella, she fails to learn how to trust, make friends, study, share, become self-aware, believe in her self-worth, find a purpose, and carve out an identity.

We had a patient, a sixteen-year-old girl I'll call Sasha, whose mother had metastatic breast cancer. Sasha became very clingy with her father, a man who expressed a lot of self-pity about his situation. She was worried about her mom's health, but she put her energy into shoring up her dad, not so that he could better care for his sick wife, but so that he wouldn't fall apart himself. Sasha was going to lose her mother to a terminal disease, and then all she'd be left with was her erratic father. She took on the responsibility of maintaining that relationship but, because he was so stressed out and self-pitying, he didn't appreciate or notice it. The mother was too ill to do anything.

So concerned by her father's distress, Sasha agreed to whatever he asked even if it made her unhappy, like transferring schools and quitting therapy. Before she left our care, she was already showing the effects of parentification in her increased anxiety and unhealthy coping behaviors. She started seeing a boy who was not good to her and acting out with drugs and alcohol. Later in life, she would most likely have to deal with codependency and people-pleasing/self-negating behavior. The parentification risks for kids are serious and long lasting: anxiety, depression, eating disorders, substance abuse, distrust, ambivalence, a destructive sense of entitlement, getting involved in harmful relationships.

Parentification is like forcing a kid to forget about adding stories to his own building, and instead, to erect a scaffold outside of your scaffold to support you.

You are the instructor, the guide, the support for your kid. It should never be the other way around.

Parentification in Action

An emotionally damaging role reversal goes well beyond asking kids to do chores around the house or help out when needed. Responsibilities that put a child at risk:

- Helping an alcoholic parent take a bath, get in bed, or clean up when sick

- Monitoring a parent's drinking or spending

- Being a parent's confidant and shoulder to cry on

- Cooking, cleaning, and caring for younger kids for absent or negligent parents

- Paying household bills

- Demanding he or she weigh in on adult matters, like the parents' finances, marriage, and sex lives

The Provocative Teen

I've already talked about how teenagers push their parents' buttons to escape from doing something they don't want to do, like homework. But that's only one reason a teenager comes off as intentionally provocative.

You might have heard or read about the epidemic of anxiety among the younger generations. Generation Z (born between 1996 and 2012) has been called "the loneliest" and the most "stressed" generation, and the most likely to report being in poor mental health. Why? Kids today are under a lot of pressure and that is a cause of the high rates of anxiety we're seeing now. They act irritable because they have a ton of work or social problems. Since teens can't yell at their teachers and friends, the easiest solution is to take things out on the parents. Whatever they're upset about, you might become the target of their anger, frustration, and fear.

A classic catch-22 parenting conundrum: You don't want your teen to go nuclear on someone else because it could be damaging to that relationship, so you make yourself available to be the target, even if it risks damaging your relationship. The sacrifices we make!

If you remain perfectly calm while your teen unloads on you—which we recommend—the venting process won't be as satisfying for the kid. It feels good to argue with someone who argues back, right? But don't. You might wonder if it is doing your teen a disservice not to give him a good fight. Certainly, it's all too tempting to argue back and call it "helping my teen get his feelings out in the open." But that is a bad short- and long-term strategy. Scaffolding isn't about teaching a teen how to pick and win a fight. It's about teaching him how to work through his feelings and resolve them without inflicting collateral damage.

Here is a two-step "hold steady" protocol for teens.

First, *validate*. Make sure your teen knows you have heard him by repeating back what he just said to you, for example, "I get it. You're superfrustrated. The test was really hard. I'm really sorry. It doesn't sound fair." Or "I get it. You want to stay out later than your curfew to be with your friends. But you can't because I don't think it's safe."

One phrase in particular is completely invalidating and will inflame a teen's already prickly mood: "Because I said so." It's like waving a red cape at a bull, or an open invitation to wage a battle of wills. Instead, be thoughtful about how you come up with your rules. You should be able to define and justify them. A vague demand to obey your authority is useless to older teens. It's their developmental job to question authority.

Second, *vacate*. Role model stepping away from escalation, which just might be a lifesaving skill. You'll know it's time to leave the room when the conversation starts repeating. Unless someone with emotional control—you—stopped it, the discussion could keep circling forever. Say, "Listen, I need to go start making dinner now" or "I've got to go check on your sister's homework now." You're not stonewalling; you're taking a break, an effective strategy to reset the conversation.

This approach works miracles in couples therapy, too. John Gottman, PhD, an American psychologist and an expert on marriage stability, has conducted experiments about conflict resolution for forty years. In one study, he hooked up couples to heart rate monitors and asked them to engage in touchy conversations about their problems. As the discussions got heated, the participants' heart rates skyrocketed. Some of the couples were told by a technician that their monitoring equipment wasn't working and were asked to stop talking until it was fixed. During that time, the couples read magazines or twiddled their thumbs, anything quiet and calming. When their heart and respiration rates had returned to baseline after twenty minutes, and they were told to resume talking, their conversations were far more constructive than the couples who kept arguing without a break.

Breaks work for parents and teens just as well. Model stepping back when you're at an impasse. It can be very helpful and prevent either of you from saying something you regret later.

When Parents "Can't Deal"

Some kids have horrible struggles socially and emotionally, and parents simply can't bear to watch. Instead of committing the scaffolding sins of intense overreaction, some parents underreact in the extreme.

Avoidance as a coping strategy for dealing with difficult emotions does not work. Child psychologist, director of the Anxiety Wellness Center in Cary, North Carolina, professor at the University of North Carolina at Chapel Hill, and author Aureen Pinto Wagner, PhD, wrote about the Worry Hill, a "vicious cycle of avoidance," and shows how ineffective it really is. When exposed to anxiety, you climb a figurative hill to its peak intensity. You can either tolerate the anxiety and go down the other side of it as it dissipates—over time, you will become habituated to anxiety and its effects will diminish—or, when you climb the anxiety hill to its peak, you avoid the feelings via escapism. The anxiety will dissipate quickly, but avoidance prevents habituation. Every anxiety episode will reach the same high peak, without diminishing over time. You never crest the Worry Hill. You just keep climbing the slope of anxiety, over and over again. To cope with discomforting emotions, you have to learn to tolerate them. By escaping, that learning never takes place.

Maggie started coming to the Child Mind Institute as a teenager for depression. Lauren, her mother and a very anxious person, got tearful about Maggie's depressive episodes. Seeing how fragile Lauren was, Maggie felt too afraid to talk to her about her depression. The situation was complicated by Lauren's drinking, another thing Maggie was afraid to talk about with her. Their relationship was defined by all the things they avoided talking about. Lauren wanted to be there for her daughter (in theory at least), but in her alcoholism and avoidance, she missed every opportunity to support Maggie.

The flip side of being too fragile to deal is being too angry. We were treating a fourteen-year-old boy for anxiety. Let's call him

Tom. His father, a superintense Wall Street master-of-the-universe type, would rage at Tom if he didn't do well in sports or get straight As. Dad believed that Tom's failure reflected poorly on him. (FYI: This man had a lot to learn about scaffolding!) Tom told his therapist that he was afraid to do anything but sit at the table with his laptop open, because it made his dad happy to see him doing homework. In truth, Tom was watching TV on his computer, but his father didn't realize that. Tom used all his energy and time strategizing ways to manage Dad's anger, when Tom himself had a lot of other things to strategize about how to do, like manage his own anxiety. Our therapist did insist on a private consultation with Tom's dad to tell him to ease up on his son, that his anger wasn't helping. No happy ending there. The father raged at the therapist.

These are extreme examples, of course, and both the fragile mom and the angry dad needed interventions of their own. But most parents can relate to not wanting to listen to their kids' problems or not feeling "up" to supporting them sometimes. We

Scaffolding Emotional Control with Teens

- **Structure**. Require them to do chores, but don't turn them into miniadults with grown-up responsibilities. And never confide in teens as if they were your friends, or risk parentification.

- **Support**. Be the person in their lives they can safely vent to. Validate their feelings and if the conversation starts circling back on itself, vacate the room to reset, and pick it up again later.

- **Encouragement**. Holding steady is the only way to encourage teens to share their difficult feelings. If you react with sadness, anger, or avoidance, they'll bottle up.

have our own problems to deal with on top of theirs. No one said parenting was for the weak willed. To be steadfast, you'll need planned breaks for self-care and to rely on your network of emotional supporters—your partner, friends, and family. Kids need our support and encouragement to get through the pain and pressure of adolescence. Climbing down off your scaffold and leaving them to deal with their feelings alone is not an option.

The Anxious Parent

Dr. Howard had generalized anxiety disorder (GAD) as a kid, but never went to therapy for it back then. "I'm still dealing with it. When I walk into the playground with my daughter, sometimes I feel overwhelmed by noticing all the ways she could hurt herself and having to keep track of her with so many kids running around in different directions," she says. "Some anxiety is good to protect her from harm, but the amount I feel can be unreasonable."

Well aware that anxiety is hereditary, she's sensitive about how she expresses it in front of her daughter. "A playground is supposed to be fun. I make sure to say things like, 'Look at all the stuff! What are you going to do first?' to mediate the experience and help myself out." In effect, she's convincing herself and her daughter at the same time.

Kids look to their parents to interpret situations. If an anxious parent's interpretation is unreasonable (seeing only how steep the slide is or how high the swings go) and doesn't fit the facts (the playground is safe and well maintained), it trickles down to the child. If an anxious parent can interpret a situation based on the facts, she's modeling being reasonable.

To scaffold reasonable responses to stress and anxiety, it helps to know if you and/or your child has GAD. If so, then treatment and therapy are called for. If not, do what Dr. Howard does, and ask yourself, *Am I being reasonable? Is my worry reasonable? How can I present my state of mind in a reasonable way that won't unduly upset my child?*

Is It GAD?

NORMAL	PROBLEM	DISORDER
You/your child experiences worry in the head, not the body; no physical symptoms.	You/your child experiences worries that seem outsize for the events that triggered them.	You/your child worries incessantly about everything, but particularly over performance in school/work or other activities, or the ability to meet expectations.
You/your child has concerns that are objectively reasonable, temporary, and based on specific real-life tangible events.	You/your child feels anxious in a general way, not necessarily tied to anything specific.	You/your child frequently seeks reassurance in an attempt to assuage fears and worries.
You/your child can diminish worry by coming up with solutions to the problem.	You/your child has a hard time calming down, even after the cause of the anxiety has been resolved.	You/your child is rigid, irritable, and restless due to anxiety.
		You/your child has physical symptoms, including fatigue, stomachaches, and headaches.
		Your/your child has exaggerated fears that tend to focus on tangible, real-life issues.
		Unlike adults, children with GAD may not recognize that their fears are outsize.

So how did Linda and I handle it when Joshua told us he felt unloved at camp?

After my initial upset, I approached it like a problem to be solved. We met with the camp director to talk about our son's distress. Attention was paid; accommodations were made. Joshua got through the rest of the summer, but when we picked him up and drove home, he told us that he'd forced himself to bear camp and had been miserable the whole time.

I wasn't too quick to let go of the idea that Joshua could and would love camp, so my wife and I explored other options. We researched other camps and collected a nice stack of brochures to show him. But when we presented them to Joshua with great enthusiasm, he wasn't interested and rejected them all.

He wasn't disturbed by not wanting to go to camp, so why was I? I had to take a closer look at my motivation. I was uncomfortable with his not keeping up with a timetable in my head about when kids should be ready to do things. But I gave myself a little talk about allowing Joshua to grow and develop on his own schedule, not mine. I'd given the same talk to other parents and needed to take my own advice. My discomfort with his life pace did not help my son. It hurt him. Forcing him to go back to camp would have been a bad idea.

The next summer, he went to a day camp, which he loved. The year after that, he went to a two-week sleepaway tennis camp, also a success. Eventually, he went away for an eight-week camp and, a few years after that, on a teen tour for a whole summer. By looking past my own discomfort, I was able to move alongside my son at his pace and give him positive, empowering experiences.

Nail Down Those Planks!

Few things are harder than watching your child suffer, but you have to hold steady, and tolerate your own discomfort, to scaffold their growth.

Patience
• Even though you feel your child's pain deeply, wait to vent your distress until you are away from your child. The goal is to guide and support him first and to model self-control. If you need to vent or find comfort, turn to other adults.

Warmth

• Be affectionate and attentive when your child is upset.

• Listen more than you talk.

• Validate her feelings.

Awareness

• Be conscious of whether you are overreacting, trying to suppress your emotions, or avoiding dealing with what's going on. None of those approaches is helpful for you or your child.

Dispassion

• Modulate your intense emotional expressiveness so your child isn't confused or frightened.

• Never react to your child's emotional expression with distress, or he'll learn to hide and internalize his negative feelings.

Monitoring

• Check in with your child about how she feels. Don't assume that one scaffolding session of providing comfort and modeling control is enough.

6

Stay on Their Level

Imagine being on the ground floor of a house and trying to talk to someone on the roof. Not so easy. The person on the roof will have to "talk down" to you, or yell. He or she might decide it's too much trouble to talk at all. The distance between you is just too great to allow for easy, open communication.

Now picture the child's building, and the parent's scaffold around that building, being on the same level. You will be able to speak directly from a short distance apart, look each other in the eye, use the same language and tone, and talk about subjects that put you on equal footing.

To establish and maintain open lines of communication with your child and teenager, keep your scaffold on the same level as theirs. And stay "on the level," too, by being honest and authentic.

One of our patients at the Child Mind Institute is a fifteen-year-old girl named Gwen. She plays the guitar, is an excellent artist, and rereads Daphne du Maurier's *Rebecca* every Christmas. We diagnosed and treated her for mild depression. The precipitating event that brought her to us was a conversation Gwen and her mother had a few days after one of her classmates committed suicide. "Gwen didn't really know him," said Katherine, her mom. "They were in different grades and didn't have any social overlap. He was a so-called popular kid, and Gwen is more artsy, on the fringe. What terrified me was that, when I asked her how she felt about the suicide, as we were instructed to do by the school's administration, Gwen said, 'It's really sad. He seemed like a nice person. But if he were really that depressed, then maybe he's better off.' The next day, I called about making an appointment with a therapist. The real problem was that we didn't know how she was feeling or thinking. She seemed okay. If she'd come to us and said, 'I'm depressed' or 'I have no friends,' we would have acted immediately. In hindsight, I realize that she didn't talk to me about her feelings at fifteen, because we didn't do it when she was ten, or five, or ever. That's not how my husband and I were raised. I remember, when I was a little kid and crying over something or other, my mom told me to go to my room and not to come out until I had a smile on my face. I was taught to fake it. It kills me to think that I might have done that to Gwen. I never taught her to express her feelings."

A foundational brick in your parental scaffold is giving your children an emotional vocabulary. Along with teaching them nouns like "cow" and "house," teach them to identify feelings as well. A child who can say, "I feel sad," "I feel disappointed," "I feel angry" is gathering social, emotional intelligence that she'll use for the rest of her life. Labeling an emotion also helps to manage its effects in the moment. For a 2007 UCLA study, researchers showed participants photos of people's faces displaying anger, fear, and sadness, while their brains were being imaged in an fMRI machine. When people saw anger or fear, their body's emotional alarm system, originating in the amygdala region of the brain, went off. But when the people verbalized the emotion, just by saying "angry" or "afraid" when they saw the photos, the activity in the amygdala decreased.

Once a child learns how to label his emotion, the "what," the next step is to consider "why" it happened, and then "how" to deal with it. This "what," "why," "how" process is the way each and every one of us solves problems in life.

If we do nothing more in our scaffolding, we lay a foundation of emotional awareness and analytic strength for our children to take with them into adulthood. It's only possible, though, if you are listening, talking, and connecting with your children at every age and stage along the way. Our job as scaffolders is to guide kids to understand themselves, and if the lines of communication with you are blocked or strained, that job will be much harder.

Kids and teens won't necessarily make it easy for you to communicate with them, especially teenagers who fiercely protect their privacy, or kids who are too confused or embarrassed to talk about how they feel. When met with resistance, you might shut down communication, misunderstand your kids' messages, or miss opportunities to connect.

Anyone who has endured the nonstop chatter of a four-year-old or been frustrated by a sullen teen whose conversation consists of single-syllable grunts already knows that communicating with your child can be frustrating. But by using the scaffolding planks of patience, warmth, awareness, dispassion, and monitoring, you can begin the fascinating, funny, revealing, nurturing, sometimes hard, always rewarding, conversation with your kids that keeps getting deeper and richer throughout their childhood and adolescence and into adulthood.

How to begin this lifelong conversation?

Small Talk

It can be hard for loving parents to get their mentally healthy kids to freely share their thoughts and feelings. Imagine being a therapist in a first session with an anxious or depressed kid. By the time the patient gets to our office, she's probably been suffering for months or years with her symptoms, rituals, and avoidances. Her academic and social lives are in shambles. She might have seen other doctors and is already cynical about the therapeutic process. We often hear parents say that the Child Mind Institute is their last hope. So how on earth do we get a child in a state of acute crisis to open up to a complete stranger?

We have ways of making kids talk. Here are some of our tricks of the therapy trade to use in your home environment on your nonclinical, but not particularly articulate or open kids:

• **Use language they understand.** Break down topics into simple components and tackle them one at a time. For example, with preschool kids, if you want to know how your son's playdate went, ask questions like "What were the best and worst parts of the playdate?," which will bring open-ended, multiple-word answers. Questions like "Did you have fun at your playdate?" or "What did you eat there?" will get you one-word answers that won't help you much. Avoid conceptual questions like "Do you think you and Dan will become good friends?," which will probably be met with confused silence.

• **Use a consistent tone.** Don't speak to a six-year-old the same way you'd speak to a sixteen-year-old, but don't infantilize the child, either. To gauge the right tone that a child will respond to, use the same one that his friends, teachers, and coaches use. By studying how your child talks "in the wild," you can pick up frames of reference and adapt the same tone at home.

• **Avoid bulls**t.** Kids don't have the same filter that adults do. "I could say something pretty boneheaded right now and the adult in the room would overlook it out of politeness. But a child will ask, 'Why'd you say that?' Kids will call you out on it," says Jerry Bubrick, director of our Obsessive-Compulsive Disorder Service. "A conversation can end or be sidelined by BS, so don't bother trying it."

- **Ask about their interests.** If they love sports, talk about your teams. If they're into fashion, have a working knowledge of brands. When kids feel confident with the subject matter, their guard comes down.

- **Give to get.** "One school of thought is that a doctor shouldn't disclose details about his or her personal life with patients," says Dr. Bubrick. "With adult patients, I agree. But that doesn't always work with kids. They have to understand a little bit about who you are. So I talk a lot about my past anxieties, like my fear of dogs. Kids with anxieties trust that I'll understand them, and they feel comfortable enough to tell me what they're afraid of." Prove that you can relate to your child by sharing a similar feeling or experience. But shift back to the child quickly, or it'll feel like a lecture.

- **Present casually.** "Normally, in sessions with kids, my tie is loose, my collar is unbuttoned, my sleeves are rolled up," he says. "I'm not the doctor, I'm Jerry." As a parent, you are the authority figure. But a relaxed presentation makes you less intimidating.

- **When they tell you who they are, listen.** "One of my patients has been called Johnnie his whole life. At fourteen, he announced that he wanted to be called Jonathan," says Dr. Bubrick. "Everyone in his life made the switch, except his mother. She couldn't break the habit. He would say in therapy that his mom didn't take him seriously because she used his 'baby name.' And if she didn't take him seriously, why should he talk to her?" Your child has grown in many ways since his "oopsie" and "ouchie" days. Stay on his level by keeping up with his vernacular. You don't have to speak his language—it might sound "totes ridic" coming out of your mouth—but you do have to understand it.

The Big Talks

The time will come when small talk is not going to cut it. You will have Big Talks with your child, probably sooner than you'd like, about sex, death, divorce, drugs, climate change, among other subjects.

Parents often ask us, "What should we tell our kids about . . . ?" Some parents of young kids are determined not to say a word about anything that's just too scary. Others believe in telling their children everything.

Neither strategy is right.

"I have a patient, a seven-year-old boy, who had a death in the family," says Dr. Rachel Busman. "His ninety-three-year-old great-grandmother died. It was sad, but not a world crisis. The boy was asking questions like, 'Where did Gram go?' 'What's going to happen to her house?' 'What will happen to her body?'"

From a developmental and clinical perspective, it's completely normal for a child to be curious about death, the afterlife, decomposition. But his mother was so disturbed that her son kept asking about Grannie's bones, she shut down the entire discussion by saying, "We're not talking about it."

In this case, the mother's scaffold lagged behind her son. He was growing and she wasn't emotionally prepared to keep up with him. "Refusing to answer a kid's appropriate questions is a major parenting misstep," said Dr. Busman. "Big experiences, like burying a loved one, give the parent an opportunity to build trust, advance the child's understanding, and encourage his inquisitive mind. Shutting down the entire subject is frustrating and more frightening to the child than a straight answer. He might be thinking, *Why isn't she telling me? It must be really bad!* Even if the parent is distraught and can't deal with a litany of questions, she can say, 'We have a lot to talk about, and I'm going to answer all your questions, but right now, I need to deal with other things.'" Stalling is better than refusing to talk, but only if you keep your promise.

If you are too anxious to talk about one thing, you're probably going to be hedgy about lots of things. People tend to be creatures of habit. You might just be a closed-off and temperamentally up-tight person who shies away from difficult conversations. You can't necessarily change your personality, but you can recognize that your natural preference might not be ideal for your child's social, emotional education. Be aware of your reluctance, and work to overcome it to inform and support (scaffold) your child's growth. Establish a back-and-forth, question-and-answer, call-and-response that your child can count on. He should be able to come to you with all the hard questions in his life.

We've found, for parents who are uncomfortable "going there," it helps to prepare for the discussion first. Get information from a reliable source—your pediatrician or a therapist—about how to discuss the subject and what to say. When you're better informed, you'll feel less anxious about going there.

We tell our kids, "If you're ever in trouble, come to me!" and "If your friend is drunk and can't drive, call me and I'll pick you up." The message is, "We are prepared and available at a moment's notice to help you." So when the child *does* call at 3:00 a.m. to ask for a ride home, and you immediately start yelling, "What the hell were you thinking?" the emotional contract between you is violated. If you want your kid to trust you, you have to keep your promises, listen to his story without judgment. Later on, you can discuss what happened in a calm voice.

The same dynamic is at play when a child asks you a hard question that, for whatever reason, makes you too angry or uncomfortable to answer. A second grader's asking, "Is Grannie in heaven?" is a warm-up to getting a 3:00 a.m. call when he's in high school. A strong scaffold is unshakable; it isn't rattled by a healthy questioning and honest discussion about the truths and realities of life we all face.

Your ambivalence sends the message to the child that you can't handle the truth. Your child will learn very quickly that you can be counted on to refuse to answer him, or to yell at him for even asking. Just as quickly, he will learn that, if he wants answers, he will have to go elsewhere for them.

The last thing any of us wants is for our kids to learn about death, sex, drugs, and religion on the Internet.

If your child is old enough to ask you anything, you need to give her an answer. It doesn't need to be a dissertation. You only need to answer the questions she asks. And the amount of detail you give her depends on the child's age, experience, and temperament, and your personal preferences. Again, ask your pediatrician or therapist for guidelines.

A friend of mine told me recently, "When my daughter was around six or seven, she asked, 'Where do babies come from?' I was totally prepared with my answer and gave her a little lecture about the sperm meeting the egg and developing into a human. My daughter thought about that for a minute and then said, 'But how does the sperm get out of the body?' I blinked a few times and said, 'Ask me when you're eighteen.'"

Dr. Busman says, "Be as truthful as possible. When my sister was pregnant, her eleven-year-old asked, 'How is the baby going to come out?' My sister hemmed a bit and said, 'I'm going to go to the hospital and the doctor's going to help me.' That answer didn't satisfy my nephew. 'But where is it going to come out?' Finally, she said, 'My vagina. The baby is going to come out of my vagina.' The boy considered this and said, 'Oh. Okay,' and then went into the other room to play a video game." If you give a kid an honest answer, he might not fully comprehend it, but he will understand intuitively that you were truthful with him. And in many cases, that's what the child wants even more than a technical answer. Children look to you, with trust, for honesty. If they don't understand what you tell them, they'll just drop it for now, and pick it back up later when they've had a chance to think about it and are ready to learn more. Kids are inundated with information everywhere they look. As parents, we'd rather they ask us to clear up misconceptions and supply information that's consistent with our values.

After any important talk, you should always follow up with, "Do you have any more questions?" Keep asking it. It's not like the sex talk or the drug talk is a one-and-done. It's the start of an ongoing, far-reaching dialogue. Kids will hear and see things constantly that raise questions—"I can't tell you how many corrections I've had to make about what my patients have heard on the school bus," said Dr. Busman—and hopefully, they will come to you again and again as they gather experience and knowledge.

> For guidelines about how to have Big Talks about a variety of subjects, go to childmind.org/bigtalks.

Side by Side

You might be thinking right now that you do try to get your kid to talk to you, but he's always doing something else, like playing video games. You are not alone! Many parents tell us that they have to wrench the controller out of their kids' hands, yelling, "Turn off the computer! Why are you playing that game anyway? It's rotting your brain!" If your child does wind up turning off the computer, he probably won't be in the right frame of mind to have a friendly chat with the person who just yelled at him.

According to a recent study, eight- to ten-year-olds spend eight hours per day on a variety of media outlets; older kids and teens are glued to screens for eleven hours per day. That is too much, per the recommendation of the American Academy of Pediatrics. Kids' media exposure should be limited to one hour per day on school days, and two hours on weekends or vacations.

Along with monitoring how much time kids spend on their devices, pay attention to *how* and *why* they are always online. Children seem to get it, that Internet addiction is a real threat. However, only a small subset is actually impaired by their attachment to their devices. The Child Mind Institute surveyed five hundred kids between seven and fifteen for a study on the impact of social media and gaming on mental health, with an interest in finding links between problematic Internet use (PIU) and mental health disorders. To measure PIU, the scale, similar to other addiction assessments, asks questions like intensity and dysfunction, not just "how long."

For example, we asked kids, "How often do others in your life complain to you about the amount of time you spend online?" "How often do you lose sleep due to being online?" and "How often do you choose to spend more time online over going out with others?"

As it turned out, we did find links between PIU and depressive disorders and ADHD, as well as impairment in normal functioning in children's academic, social, and home lives. If you are concerned with your kids' online attachment, you can monitor their screen use by participating in it with them, aka "parental mediation." By sitting right there, you can support a child's mindfulness about his use by saying, "It's been an hour! Wow, that time flew. Let's stretch our legs for a bit, do something else now."

Also, establish house rules. No media entertainment should be allowed until all homework and chores are completed. Screen time should be balanced with developmentally integral activities like hanging out with friends, participating in extracurriculars, spending quality time with family, and getting enough sleep. If your clear and established media rules are broken, your child should be subject to consequences.

But during the kid's nightly hour of gaming fun, it wouldn't kill you to pick up a controlling device and play *Minecraft* or *Fortnite* with your child. In fact, the side-by-side shared activity presents a rich bonding opportunity that you would otherwise miss if you didn't get next to him on the couch.

Play with your kid. Do something fun that he enjoys. You might like it, too. You'll have a common interest, and a chance to pepper in the conversation with self-esteem-building praise, like, "You're really good at this!" You might want to just sit back and watch him play and talk about what's happening on the game. It shows you're sympathetic to your child's life and interests.

Watch their TV shows, listen to their music, and read their books. Consider it scaffolding due diligence. You'll have a better idea what they're absorbing and can approve or disapprove of the values it represents. A seat on the couch next to your child solidifies trust and confidence in the relationship and gives you stuff to talk about. No more stilted dinner conversations. The biggest bonus of logging hours on Disney+: When your child needs to talk about something that's not media related between levels of a game or episodes of the show, you'll already be next to her and ready to listen.

Scaffolding Open Communication for Kids

- **Structure.** Include time to talk to your child every day, either after school, before bedtime, or during TV/gaming hour. Find opportunities to talk early on. Reading to him before bed is a great way to start your ongoing dialogue. Establish a routine of taking a walk around the park every Saturday. Talk in the car on the drive to piano lessons.

- **Support.** Help kids emotionally by teaching them to label their feelings.

- **Encouragement.** Cultivate conversations by answering their questions quickly, honestly, and reliably, so that they'll get used to coming to you for information.

The Chatty Child

If a child does all the talking, it's not really a dialogue of thoughts, feelings, and information. It's a monologue. "My daughter Olive, four, will not shut up," said a friend of mine. "She asks the same questions over and over again and talks about her feelings constantly. She recaps every episode of her favorite shows ad nauseam and talks over movies at home and in the theater. It's embarrassing to be shushed in public. I know I sound selfish but just once, I'd like to read a book without being interrupted or have a quiet moment. It's too much."

Another mom described her seven-year-old son's constant blurting. "I don't mind it at home but it's disruptive at school," she said. "His teacher is trying to address the whole class, and Xavier pipes in with comments that get the other kids laughing, and then the classroom is thrown into chaos. We have all asked him repeatedly not to interrupt the teacher, but it's like he can't help himself."

Most preschoolers—four and under—are chatterboxes, like Olive. They're having new experiences all the time, and they learn to process and assimilate what they've seen and done by talking about it. By age five, however, most kids pick up on social cues and figure out when it's okay to talk, and when it's not. The kindergarten teacher's hand goes up, and the child knows to be silent. Appropriate communication is one of the most important lessons of preschool—going around the circle to talk, raising your hand to speak, using inside voices, respecting quiet time, saying "please," "thank you" and "I'm sorry," learning to "use your words" and "talk it out" after a tiff.

By first or second grade, if a child continues to interrupt, blurts whatever pops into his head, talks incessantly, doesn't allow others to speak, he might have a behavioral, neurological, or genetic issue. Xavier, the kindergarten blurter just discussed, a patient of ours, has been diagnosed with ADHD. For excessive, impulsive talkers diagnosed with ADHD, we recommend medication if appropriate, parent training, and behavioral therapy. Following are a couple tips for anyone who'd like their child to learn when to stop talking.

Signaling. With your child, choose a signal for you to send him that means he should stop talking, like putting your finger to your lips or a gentle touch on his shoulder.

Labeled praise. Tell him, "Great job noticing the signal and stopping talking" or "Great job letting other kids talk."

Is It Just Chattiness?

NORMAL	PROBLEM	DISORDER
A naturally loquacious child who enjoys conversation and is excited to share her perspective about the world learns by seven to pick up social cues about when talking is appropriate, when it isn't, that everyone gets a turn to talk, that she shouldn't launch into lengthy chats with complete strangers.	A child who talks too much to get attention or to be intentionally disruptive, who hasn't learned to edit his comments and figured out boundaries about whom he should talk to and what he can discuss in public.	Impulsive blurts and incessant chatter can be symptoms of ADHD. Pressurized speech, when a child can't stop talking even when alone, can be a symptom of autism, Asperger's, or bipolar disorder. Constantly asking for reassurance and validation could indicate an anxiety disorder. Talking excessively and indiscriminately with friends and strangers alike with no filter might indicate a rare genetic syndrome called Williams syndrome.

The Reticent Child

Genetically introverted kids (and adults, for that matter) prefer to keep their own company and are reluctant to share their thoughts and feelings. It's only an issue if they avoid all social interactions and never learn necessary life skills. Usually, a shy child just needs a chance to get used to a new classroom and warm up to a new student or teacher. Once they relax, they can participate in every aspect of school and have conversations with other kids or adults.

Children who suffer from selective mutism (SM) are not silent due to shyness. Their anxiety is far more severe. At home, SM kids engage in perfectly normal interactions with siblings and parents. But at school, they don't talk with the other kids, raise their hand in class, ask for permission to go to the bathroom or to see the doctor if they get hurt. Selective mutism and social anxiety can co-occur or not. Children with both anxiety disorders are paralyzed by any interaction. You'll see them hiding behind their mom, or sitting alone in a corner, never engaging or talking. A kid who runs around and interacts with the other children in the playground isn't socially anxious. But if he never speaks, he does have selective mutism.

The disorder is rare, affecting fewer than 1 percent of kids. It's usually diagnosed when children start school. It's partially genetic. Of our neighbor's three daughters, two were very quiet as children and one, I'll call her Jennifer, was selectively mute. On the Thanksgivings that we cohosted, we would go around the table and share why we were grateful, and it was always difficult for the girls—and awkward for the rest of us to watch them struggle. When it was Jennifer's turn, she would turn beet red and her eyes would tear. The first few years of this, I thought, *We do this every year. Why aren't her parents rehearsing with her?*

One year, I interceded. When Jennifer's family arrived at our house, I pulled her aside and said, "Just whisper to me what you were thankful for this year. Was it playing field hockey? Getting your braces off?" She would share her thoughts with me. Then I said, "When we go around the table, I'm going to ask you if you'd like to speak. If you decide that you don't want to do it, just shake your head and I'll say, 'Jennifer and I discussed this before dinner, and she told me she's thankful for her friendships.'" That way, she could participate, and not have her holiday ruined by anxiety.

Another year, Jennifer's sister Abby was in a wheelchair with a cast on her leg. We'd invited over a couple who didn't know that family. The man said to Abby, "Hello, little girl. What happened to your foot?" She just stared at him. Her father stood behind and said nothing. The man asked, "What's wrong with her? Does she talk?"

Her father replied, "She's just shy."

In that situation, deflection was certainly better than letting a stranger be rude to his child. Some parents of selectively mute children are the ones asking, "What's *wrong* with you?" as if hostility and shaming will change an anxiety disorder. What does help is behavioral training called "brave talking," or teaching a child to unlearn silence and practice talking in a safe environment with gradual exposure to speaking around other people in new places, labeled praise, and lots of incentives. For example, in our program Brave Buddies, headed by Dr. Busman, kids are exposed to experiences that stimulate anxiety over the course of a week. Gradually they learn to tolerate their anxiety and speak (use "brave words") in more and more challenging situations. It culminates with a trip to the ice cream shop, where "brave talking" is rewarded with ice cream. "Treatment is all about helping them develop stress tolerance," says Dr. Busman. "The goal isn't to get rid of all anxiety, but to learn to tolerate it, and be able to talk despite it." The same could be said of any difficult conversation between you and your kids, and between adults, as well.

By the way, Jennifer, Abby, and their other reticent sister grew up, graduated from college, and are now quite chatty. They missed out on some socializing along the way, but with intervention at a young age, they overcame their problems.

Is It Just Shyness?

NORMAL	PROBLEM	DISORDER
Your child needs some transitional time to adjust to new people and environments before she can talk freely.	Your child habitually avoids interaction because of social anxiety. Shyness is affecting her academic progress.	Your child has no problem talking at home but does not speak a word at school or elsewhere and might be paralyzed by social interaction.

The Sullen Teen

When my sons were teenagers, I talked to them about everything, and my wife and I were lucky enough that they opened up to us. Although I'm sure they had their secrets, we gave them every opportunity to confide in us, and fortunately, they usually did. When I asked some of their friends if they shared the details of their lives with their moms and dads or turned to them for advice, most laughed and said, "I don't tell my parents *anything*. They have no idea what's going on with me, and that's the way I like it."

Do not make the mistake of believing that a teen who doesn't talk to you just wants his space.

"I make the parallel between a sullen teen and a stray dog," said Dr. Bubrick. "You see a dog on the street. You know it's hungry. You know it's scared. You approach it, but it barks and growls, and your first reaction is not to go near it. But if you don't befriend the dog, it'll probably go hungry or get sick. So instead of backing off, you can just stand there. Maybe you can put your hand out and slowly take a step forward. If the dog growls again, stand there for a minute, and then take another step with your hand out. Eventually, the dog understands that you're not a threat. Once it trusts you, it's yours."

Leaving out a dish of food for the dog, or the teen, helps, too.

The kids who bat away your conversational salvos still need to express themselves, but they're wary. Like the stray dog, teens are fearful for a reason. If you come on too strong by asking personal questions or bringing up touchy subjects, the teen will feel interrogated. Even if you defend yourself by saying, "I'm just trying to make pleasant conversation," your teen will still think you're trying to force him to spill his secrets. And then, forget it. He'll lock the vault.

Your teens don't actually want or need you to back off entirely, even if they say they do. However, it's frustrating to be rebuffed by them, and all too easy to say, "Okay, you want space, you got it," and slip into not paying too close attention, especially if they don't seem to want it. You might go in the opposite direction and apply *even more* pressure to force your teen to open up. Both extremes are ineffective.

Having counseled thousands of closed-off kids, I can say that neither strategy will work. For one thing, kids might not know how to talk about their feelings. For another, teen secrecy is a function of their development. An adolescent's job is to test the limits of his world, and when a parent demands, "Talk to me!," a teen's instant reaction is to do the opposite. At a certain point in healthy development, teens will rattle your scaffolding and see it as confining, not supportive.

To get *any* response from your teen, avoid personal or prejudicial subjects, and keep it neutral. Safe subjects:

- The weather
- Local news
- Movie reviews
- Vacation plans
- Color choice for a new living room rug

- Their shows and games
- How quickly bananas turn brown on the counter
- The many uses of TikTok

The goal is to get your teen talking about literally *anything,* in person, or by engaging him online by commenting or liking his Instagram pictures or tweets. It doesn't matter if the exchange or conversation is real or deep. With every exchange, you're assuring your teen that you are harmless, nonjudgmental, and available. You're not trying to spy on him, "fix" him, or preach at him. All you want is to hear words, any words, emerge from his lips, which you will affirm by doing more listening than talking. Once your teen is convinced that you are not going to jump down her throat or dig for personal information—a process that might take a while, so be patient—she'll feel comfortable enough to open the vault and tell you what's really going on in her life. You might find yourself having a perfectly innocuous chat about something cute the cat did, and your teen might suddenly shift the topic to something important that might be upsetting him.

Conversation Killers

Two opening lines that DO NOT WORK with teens, and one that does.

"So, how was your day?"

Does this one work for you? Ever? No one wants to answer that! It seems like it's an open-ended question, but it's really a conversational dead end.

Here's how it's likely to go:

You: *So, how was your day?*

The kid: *Fine.*

You: *Just "fine"?*

The kid: *It was good.*

You: *How was it good?*

The kid: *I don't know. Just fine. A normal day.*

You: *You've got to give me a little more than that.*

The kid: *What do you want from me?*

You: *Don't use that tone . . .*

[An argument ensues. The kid runs into her room and slams the door. The parent fumes in the kitchen. And . . . scene.]

It's only natural to have an expectation of how the conversation should go. You'll ask The Question, and your child will launch into a charming, funny, descriptive narrative of his entire day like on an episode of *Full House* that ends with the child saying, "Thanks so much for listening and being such a loving parent! I appreciate you." Anything shy of the sitcom ideal, and you might feel rejected and angry if your child doesn't follow the script after you serve up your stellar opening line.

A far better idea would be to throw out the script entirely. Drop any expectation of how a conversation should go. And meet your child on his level by talking about something specific that he cares about, like the computer game he's obsessed with at the moment, or the latest Lizzo video. Kids don't know how to make small talk. Recruit them into conversation by appealing to *their* interests, something they feel confident about, even smarter than you about. Remember the details of their lives. Of course, listening to them talk about the nuances between emo and goth can be tedious. But if you don't, they won't open up to you about something that might be more interesting to you, like the ins and outs of their social lives, how they feel, what's upsetting them, what makes them feel proud of themselves.

"When I was your age . . ." Hearkening back to how you dealt in the past with your child's present concerns becomes a whirlwind of pressure. When you say, "I never worried about [fill in the blank] when I was a kid," your child would be totally justified in replying, "But when you went to high school, there were no computers." Think back to how you used to groan when your parents told you about walking five miles to school in the snow. To stay on the kid's level, you have to get off your high horse and appreciate that her world is different from how yours was at her age. Try to keep up with the changes!

And now, an opening line that DOES work:

"Have you heard the one about . . ."

This "kills" in a good way. Tell Dad jokes and use humor to get a kid talking, responding, and to lift him out of a bad mood.

"Laughter is a medicine. We see kids who are anxious and sad. They need to have a lot of laughter in their lives so that they're not caught up in their anxiety and sadness. Their darker thoughts impact functioning, affect their mood, and define how they feel about themselves," says Dr. Bubrick. Their disorders are the downward spiral; laughter is the "up" elevator. "Using humor is a powerful countermeasure."

The value of laughter and smiling as a way to offset negative emotions has been hotly debated by scientists for decades. But, as of 2017, it has been proven to be scientific fact. According to a meta-analysis by researchers at the University of Tennessee of 138 studies spanning 50 years of 11,000 individuals, smiling *does* make you feel slightly happier. It's not going to be a miracle cure for the severely depressed, but if you can bring a smile to your child's face, in whatever stupid way possible, jokes, funny voices, silly walks, it can improve your child's mood.

One effective style of humor is irreverence. "I had a fifteen-year-old boy in session yesterday who had an obsession that he was going to physically harm his family," says Dr. Bubrick. "Those thoughts freaked him out, understandably, and I had to come up with a way to release some of the pressure he felt. We were scheduled to meet again the next day. I said, 'Just in case you hurt your parents tonight, let's make sure you pay up for the week today.' He burst out laughing. This kid was not used to hearing that kind of humor in the face of something so scary, and it was diffusing."

When a child is anxious, you get caught up in it and can only talk to the anxiety. But your "real" child is still in there, and he wants to be acknowledged and spoken to like he's a normal kid. Treat the anxiety separately from the child. The anxiety is serious and needs to be handled with the appropriate gravity. But with the child, you can still joke around. It's a balancing act. On one side of the seesaw is the heaviness of the anxiety. On the other side is the lightness of laughter. Dr. Bubrick prescribes families to watch *The Office* together, and for parents to laugh at every joke. They're role modeling to the child how to reduce stress and anxiety in a healthy way, to use laughter to make yourself feel better.

A couple caveats:

Know your audience. If your family has a great sense of humor already, then adding in a bit of irreverence will probably be successful. If injecting irreverent humor feels disingenuous, it can undermine the intervention. The child might think you aren't taking him seriously. The child will feel misunderstood and frustrated, which will increase his feelings of isolation and anxiety.

Never tease your child. Sarcasm, as a humor tool, has to be applied *very* carefully. This comes up in couples counseling as well. Saying to your partner "Thanks for doing the dishes" is productive. If you add "It only took you a thousand reminders this time!" you spoil it. Children are even less able to separate the praise part ("You and your brother played nicely together all afternoon") from the sarcastic tack-on ("I'm shocked you lasted five minutes!"). All they feel is the contamination at the end. If you're used to being sarcastic, you might not realize how uncomfortable it makes your child. As an alternative, find your earnest voice. It's not easy to get used to earnestness if you're not programmed this way. You might find speaking from the heart to be embarrassing. Start small and practice making statements of praise and biting off the jab at the end.

Scaffolding Open Communication for Teens

- **Structure.** Carve out quality time with them, which will be a challenge for busy adolescents. If it's not possible to schedule time together every day, establish an hour every week or weekend that is sacrosanct. No canceling! (That goes for you, too.)

- **Support.** Respect their need for privacy by not pressuring them to tell you about their personal lives.

- **Encouragement.** Help them to confide in you by waiting for them to be ready, not being judgmental and critical when they do, and praising them for sharing.

Back to the story of Katherine and Gwen, the mother and daughter who were having problems communicating with each other in the aftermath of a classmate's suicide. Katherine told me, "I try not to pry about Gwen's feelings, but it's all I can think about. Does she feel okay? Is she still depressed? What can I do to help her?"

I reassured Katherine that she'd already scaffolded her daughter by getting her into therapy and working with her doctor on a treatment plan. The best thing to do now was to wait for Gwen to feel comfortable enough to talk to her parents about her feelings (or not), to keep a close eye on Gwen's behaviors for signs of depression, and to control her own emotions about her daughter's emotional state.

Katherine asked Gwen for only one thing: to spend some time together every day. They got into a routine of post-homework TV time and chatting about neutral subjects. "Gwen got into *The Great British Baking Show* on Netflix, and I sat side by side with her while we watched episodes. We talked about trying to bake our own bread," said Katherine. "I was thinking of it as a fun project for us, and then Gwen said she'd like to give a sample of our baked goods to her music teacher at school. Then she shocked me by saying, 'She's my only friend. Whenever I have a free period, I go to the music room to play guitar and hang with her.'"

Katherine had no idea how isolated and lonely her daughter was. She wouldn't have found out if she'd asked point-blank about her social life. But by talking about baking, the truth came out. "Hearing it was like a punch in the gut," she said. "I felt awful for Gwen, but also so grateful to the music teacher for being there for her. I knew that I had to stay calm, not get emotional, not pry, so I asked, 'Does the teacher play guitar, too?' And then we were talking about her favorite songs, and how much her guitar skills had improved lately. I dared to make a joke and said, 'Well, I guess being friendless is good for something,' . . . *and she laughed*. It was the first time my daughter and I had laughed together in months."

It felt like a breakthrough. Gwen finally let her mother into her life. Later on, Gwen shared in therapy that she'd been afraid to tell her mom how lonely she was. Once she did, some of her fear and shame diminished, and Gwen felt better. A conversation that started out being about nothing turned into a deepening of trust in their relationship. Katherine scaffolded her daughter to open up just by being there, listening, and remaining calm. It'd be a while before Gwen learned to talk about her emotions freely, but it was a good start for both of them.

Nail Down Those Planks!

To scaffold open communication, parents have to stay on their kids' level and be honest and authentic. The end game of any interaction with your child is strengthening trust and modeling respectfulness. Remember to use your planks.

Patience

• Talk about impersonal subjects, and casually ask for their opinion.

• Get *any* neutral conversation going and wait patiently for your child to bounce into what is really on her mind. It might take a while.

• Wait for your child to ask for your opinion before you give it.

Warmth

• Use irreverent humor when appropriate.

• Be interested in your child's hobbies and pastimes.

• Don't criticize his taste in music, games, and shows.

• Praise her for her curiosity when she asks a lot of questions, and then answer them.

Awareness

• Listen closely to what your child says to any opening that you can then gently push a bit wider.

• Praise him whenever he expresses his emotions and encourage him to think about why he feels the way he does.

• Be aware of your own anxiety and discomfort about communications and overcome them for your child's sake.

Dispassion

• Be a neutral, nonthreatening, noncontrolling visible presence.

• Don't ask open-ended questions—e.g., "How was your day?"—that might be perceived as prying and manipulative.

Monitoring

• Get a frame of reference about how best to talk to your child by observing her "in the wild" with peers and other adults. What does she talk about? How does she interact? Work within that frame to get to know your child better.

• Check in with him daily with specific queries that lend themselves to replies. "Tell me about practice" is much better than "How was practice?"

7

Empower Growth

As a child learns new skills, his building will grow. Since learning means trying and sometimes failing, the child's construction is a process of installing and reinstalling new parts. The scaffold is always there to catch pieces of the building when they fall and help gather materials and choose tools for new additions. Some kids' buildings will expand straight upward, in multiple stories one on top of the other, like a skyscraper. For others, the building expands outward, like a sprawling ranch house. The style of your child's construction is not up to you. You can't force a kid who has the talents and affinity to become a bungalow to grow into a mansion, or vice versa. The parental scaffold should accommodate the shape the child is taking. Any effort from the parents to block or control growth will stunt it.

A friend of mine, Annie, an elementary-school teacher, had always been involved in her son Ben's learning. She taught him to read at five and helped him with rudimentary math in first grade. They both enjoyed homework hour as he advanced through school. But what began as a bonding ritual turned into a bad habit by fourth grade. Annie was "helping" Ben do all his homework every night. "More than helping. I was giving him the answers," she said. "I knew he needed to do his own work, but when I left him to it, he'd struggle over it for hours. It was torture to watch. I felt compelled to jump in. By the time he was in middle school, our pattern was locked. There was no expectation on either of our parts that he'd do it on his own. If I'm going to be completely honest, I was doing it all. I wrote his papers. I did his assignments. He was present but didn't contribute much."

None of Ben's teachers realized what was going on. "His in-class test scores were poor, but his teachers just thought he was 'bad at tests.' They cut Ben slack because his homework assignments were so good." As bizarre as it seems, Ben was considered to be a top student.

"As a teacher, I constantly warn parents about the danger of doing too much for their kids," she said. "And then I would go home and ignore my own advice. His homework took longer and longer; I had no time for my husband and my younger daughter. Our homework habit was hurting every other aspect of my life, but what could I do? If I refused to do it, we'd be exposed. It'd be humiliating for him and could damage his college chances."

When parents do too much for their kids, they block growth. Annie is an extreme example, but her means of "helping" her son prevented him from learning, except the lesson that he was incapable of doing his homework for himself. He was taught, night after night, to be dependent on his mother.

I've talked a lot about the power of positive reinforcement. Even with the best intentions, parents who do too much for their kids are flooding them with negative reinforcement, to believe in their own incompetence and to be terrified of anything that challenges them.

If you want to raise future independent, competent adults who aren't afraid to take on challenges, do less for them as children. Not to do nothing. But to stand back on your scaffold, support with instruction, encourage them to try, allow them to fail, and guide them to look at what happened so they don't repeat mistakes.

Besides the one-in-a-billion exceptions of Derek Jeter and Beyoncé, every person in the world experiences failure, over and over again. Failure is a given. What really matters is how people handle it. If you scaffold kids to take failure and rejection in stride, they'll grow emotional armor that will protect them throughout their lives.

The Parental Consultancy

When our kids are young, our job is to be fixers, protectors, and social secretaries. We childproof the house so they can't get under the sink and block the stairs so they don't fall down. We set up playdates and throw their parties. We call their teachers when there's a problem. But at some point along the way, the parents' job changes, without warning or indication, and we become consultants. Our job then is to help them find solutions for themselves.

Shifting from "fixer" to consultant is a major change, and you might have a hard time with that. As parents, we're socialized for the fixer/protector role, to step in and take care of the problem. If your kid falls down and scrapes his knee, your instinct is to put a Band-Aid on it, and say, "It's okay, sweetie. I'll make it better." Then they go back to playing and you feel good about having done your job as a fixer well.

However, you can't put a Band-Aid on a social rejection or a failure experience. There is no instant fix when a twelve-year-old girl is suddenly cast out of her friend group, or when an eight-year-old boy struggles to memorize math tables and starts to believe he's stupid. You can't protect a child from the trials of life. But you can give your kid armor by teaching him to advocate for himself, and thereby develop the grit he needs to survive and succeed.

Among our patient population of anxious parents with anxious children, moms and dads tend to stay in fix-it mode longer and may never shift into consultants. As soon as a child expresses anxiety, the parents instantly start rattling off a list of solutions, like "do your calming strategies" and "let's talk it through." The parent is basically standing at the ready with an open toolbox, handing the child his tools. The child learns to depend on the parent to solve problems, as in, "I'll ask Mom. She'll know what to do."

If your child gets a poor grade on a test, for example, a fix-it parent would say, "You should call the teacher to talk about what happened. You should meet with your friend who's great at math and get some tutoring. You should study harder." You should, you should, you should. Listen to how you talk to your child. When you hear that phrase, be aware that you are in fix-it mode, essentially choosing and handing him tools.

To scaffold, parents support and encourage the child to learn how to select the right tool for the particular task all by himself. He might choose wrong, and then you can guide him to evaluate why that particular tool wasn't the best choice. Next time, he'll try something new.

It's not that you are letting him hang out there on his own. You are standing by and collaborating with him to come up with his own solutions. Instead of his depending on you for answers, you will guide him to come up with ideas about how he can do it for himself.

As always, start with emotional availability, nonjudgment, and validation. Say, "I'm sorry that happened. It sounds like it's been really hard for you. I get where you're coming from." Follow that up with guidance, by saying, "I have a couple thoughts on how to handle this, but why don't you tell me your thoughts first and then we can compare notes and see which idea sounds like the best next step?" In collaboration, the two of you will come up with solutions. But the child or teen has to think and advocate for herself.

Your child might say "Just tell me what to do!" at first, but once he gets used to a feeling of agency and having some power and control, he will actually prefer to make his own mistakes, learn his own lessons, and find his own solutions. As hard as it might be for you to relinquish control, know that by doing so, you are setting up a framework for your child's future independence. The choice seems obvious. Or you can stay in fix-it mode and welcome your child to live on your couch until he's forty.

The Growth Zone

A psychological state is often called "a zone." In the active construction site that is your child's development, it helps to be aware of her various zones, as well as which are the safe and unsafe areas.

The Comfort Zone. This is a no-anxiety, no-stress figurative place where a person feels safe and secure, believes he's in control, and can do any social, emotional, behavioral, or academic task easily, without help from parents or teachers. In the Comfort Zone, a child can build confidence and self-esteem. He is secure doing the activity; he enjoys it because he's proficient. It might feel good to hang out here; it might be a bit boring, too. Since growth comes from learning new things, and learning requires you to be vulnerable in your ignorance and inexperience, the child will have to leave the Comfort Zone in order to grow.

The Growth Zone. Maximal learning and growth happen in the area just outside the Comfort Zone, when the child is reaching and stretching to acquire new skills. Russian educational psychologist Lev Vygotsky called it "the zone of proximal development" (ZPD) in the 1920s. The ZPD is where a child cannot do a particular skill without the guidance and support of an adult. With that interaction, the child acquires knowledge and goes forth to reach mastery. Once mastery has been achieved, the child and instructor can move on to the next skill that is as yet slightly out of reach.

Dr. Vygotsky believed that educating children in the

ZPD—just beyond their current capacity, not too far from where they already are—inspires kids to become independent problem solvers and self-motivated learners. As mentioned earlier, American psychologist Jerome Bruner picked up where Vygotsky left off, using the word *scaffolding* in this educational context of collaborative learning. The theory holds up in the context of scaffolding a child's emotional, social, and behavior learning as well. *Learning, aka growth, an ongoing process of reaching for more, is always empowered by parent-child collaboration.* You're in it together, but once your child learns what he needs to learn, he can move on, and up, to the next level, while you cheer him on from the near distance of the scaffold.

The Danger Zone. If the task or activity is so far out of the child's reach and capacity that she can't solve the problem or learn the skill in collaboration with a parent, the child will enter the Danger Zone, where she's at risk for anxiety, stress, and anger. When a child throws down the puzzle or toy and storms away in frustration, she's in the Danger Zone, and will drag you into it with her if you react to her upsetting feelings with some of your own. The only thing learned here is low self-esteem. Try to stay out of the Danger Zone as you scaffold your child to acquire new skills. The plank of patience is crucial here. All things come in good time, including growth.

Failure *Is* an Option

Apologies to Yoda fans, but I disagree with his Jedi philosophy, "Do or do not. There is no try."

There *is* try. And there is the potential for success or failure, or degrees of both, every time you try. As adults, we know that the first time we try racquetball or acting in community theater, that we might discover previously untapped brilliance, or we might fall flat on our faces. To pursue our desires and curiosities, we will probably experience embarrassment, frustration, and confusion on the way to the joy and satisfaction of success. The other option is a life of inertia. You're either growing (trying, failing, learning), or you're stuck.

For your kids, you scaffold their current and future growth by teaching them to take risks, despite the very real possibility of going splat.

Labeled praise plays a major part here. If you want your kids to be more proactive and prosocial, you have to praise them when they try. Be careful about what you praise, though. If you praise success, your kids learn to think that failure is bad. But failure isn't good or bad. It's just one possible outcome.

This shift in perspective is necessary but hard to make in our "winner takes all" culture. In America, parents are fearful of their own, and their child's, rejection and failure, and they seek to avoid them at all costs. We've socialized to being afraid of something that is just a fact of life.

It is important to understand logically that process—how we scaffold a child to work hard, be kind and compassionate, express himself—is more important than outcome. We lose sight of that when kids get stressed out about getting the grade, making the team, achieving social status.

Emily, a fourteen-year-old girl with severe anxiety disorder, always became extremely worried in the days leading up to her midterm and final exams. Her mother Diana's reaction to her daughter's stress was to tell Emily to study harder, but that wasn't helpful. Obsessive studying was a symptom of Emily's anxiety, not a coping, calming strategy. It was like giving a drug addict permission to smoke more crack.

We coached Diana to scaffold Emily with nonjudgmental validation and by presenting failure as just a thing that sometimes happens, to say to her daughter, "I hear you. You're worried that you're going to fail. Maybe you will, and that's okay."

With the "death threat" of failure off the table, Emily could turn her deficit (anxiety) into an asset (productivity). She still prepared twice as much as her peers and always met with teachers for reassurance. But by telling herself failure was fine, by releasing that valve, the destructive "I can't do this!" anxiety was gone.

Diana had to send the same message many times. Her patience wore thin during her daughter's college career whenever midterms and finals rolled around. But eventually, the message sunk in, and Emily, now a young woman, flings herself into intimidating job opportunities. "Failure isn't fatal," she said. "I'll just try again."

Make Failure Fun

Failure is an opportunity. I hesitate to say people should celebrate it. You don't need to throw a party when your child blows it big-time. But I do believe that parents can take the fear out of failure by teaching kids at a very young age that it can be fun.

I do this with my grandson, Jackson. Yesterday, I read *Goodnight, Moon* to him six times, repeatedly asking, "Where's the red balloon?" When he pointed to the balloon, I said, "That's good!" By the fourth reading, I continued to ask, "Where's the red balloon?" even on the pages where the drawing was dark and the balloon wasn't visible and on the pages where it didn't appear at all. He would look for the image and try to turn back the page, and we'd laugh. Sometimes, he'd point to the wrong image. I encouraged him to try again, always praising him regardless, so that he wasn't afraid to guess wrong.

I will keep up this "no wrong guesses" strategy as he gets older and is learning to recognize letters. I'll ask him to point to the word *room* or *cow,* always praising, right or wrong. We have learning disabilities in our family, and we weren't aware of the extent of our son Adam's issues for too long. But the fear of having a disability delays treatment, and a child or parent who is unaware or afraid of the problem is not collaborating on finding solutions. So my "no wrong guess" game with Jackson, and using funny voices, doing whatever I can to make reading fun, will become a way for me to assess whether he's decoding the language or not. My son and daughter-in-law are on alert. If it turns out he has a learning disability, they will know as early as possible, and I know they will scaffold him by getting him support from experts and by encouraging his effort and progress.

Swooping In

Hovering within reach of our kids to help them when they face the slightest hurdle is the stuff of "helicopter parenting." The practice of taking care of problems for your kids has been called "concierge parenting." Clearing away all their obstacles is called "snowplow parenting." All these behaviors are of a piece. A parent's fear of failure and rejection on the child's behalf leads to the parent riding to the rescue to save the day, by doing his homework, calling teachers and coaches, taking care of every tiny thing for their kids.

Our umbrella term for these parenting styles is "swooping in." A well-known example of swooping in was the 2019 college admissions scandal known in the media as Operation Varsity Blues. The gist of it was that a number of parents (many high profile, including the actors Lori Loughlin and Felicity Huffman) were accused of paying their children's way into college. They hired a firm run by a college consultant named William Singer, who set up various frauds, like having ACT and SAT proctors change students' answers before submitting their exams, creating fake histories of sports stardom on their applications, and bribing school employees to gain children's acceptance into top American colleges and universities. When the news came out, it seemed that the entire country was outraged and disgusted by the unscrupulous behavior of these wealthy parents, a bona fide "eat the rich" cultural moment. Some of the parents have since been sentenced, paid huge fines, and gone to jail. And what of the kids who were supposed to benefit from their parents' fraud (some participated; some had no clue)? Now they know their parents didn't believe they could succeed on their own. To put it mildly, that's got to hurt.

The irony of swooping in is that parents believe they're helping their kids by preventing pain. But what they're actually preventing is growth.

Say your daughter doesn't get the part she wanted in the school play. Do not swoop in by calling the drama teacher, demanding an explanation, telling the child that the casting was rigged, that she's so much more talented than the kid who got the part, and then discourage the child from auditioning again because the whole process was inherently unfair and just too awful to repeat. That's a recipe for getting your child to stay in the Comfort Zone, where it's safe.

Nine times out of ten, parents who simply can't stand to see their children fail are using hypercontrol to quiet their own anxieties about the uncertainty of life. They have a fragile sense of self and demonstrate parenting behaviors that, unfortunately, cause the same fragility in their children. Annie, who did her son Ben's homework for a decade, wasn't supported by her own parents in her academic life. "I wouldn't call it neglect per se," she told me. "But they never went to Parents' Night or asked to see my report cards. They didn't help me with college or loan applications." She vowed that her children would never feel as unsupported as she did, but she went too far in the opposite direction and raised a dependent child.

To scaffold a child through a school play rejection, validate her disappointment, then encourage her to express her feelings and consult with her on coping strategies. Begin with one crucial question: "Why?" as in, "Why do you think it happened?" Make a list of possible "whys."

Your kid didn't rehearse enough before the audition.

Maybe her acting isn't as good as she'd like it to be.

She had an off day.

The other kid was better.

Once you have the "whys," you can take corrective steps. If your daughter realizes that she didn't know her lines as well as she could have, she knows to go into the next audition with the pages memorized. If she acknowledges that the kid who got the part was just better, then she can work toward improving her acting skills with classes or practice, or by asking which role would better suit her personal talents.

Asking "why" also puts emotional distance between the rejection and the child's interpretation of it. What you want to steer clear of is the child or teen having a global negative interpretation of events—turning one failure into how they view their entire life and identity—which contributes to anxiety and depression. Failing a test turns into "I'm stupid!" Not making the team becomes "I suck at everything!" Not being asked to the prom means "No one will ever like me!" Not getting the part can turn into "I'm never putting myself out there again." As long as you and your child are talking about "why" specifics, she's less likely to turn

Scaffolding Growth for Kids

- **Structure.** By age seven, parents can begin to shift from fix-and-protect mode to consulting their kids about how to solve their own problems. Making the change is hard for parents, but kids prefer to have agency and some control over their own lives.

- **Support.** Validate their feelings after they fail. Collaborate with them in the Growth Zone, as they learn new skills. Always be mindful of whether kids get stuck in the Comfort Zone and gently guide them to take on the next challenge.

- **Encouragement.** Reinforce effort and problem-solving with praise. Role model maintaining an even keel during life's trials. Cheer them on when they take risks, regardless of how it plays out, to teach them that failure is just something that happens.

one failure into her life story. By thinking through causes and reasons, she'll learn to use logic to solve problems, a coping strategy that will empower emotional control.

Take the "I" Out of Child

One father whom I'll call Aidan came in to talk to me about his daughter Donna's sudden decision to quit soccer. She'd been a star player for years, and no one was as proud of her as her dad. Aidan never missed a game. He had been on his high school team and was in heaven to be able to share his love of the sport with his gifted daughter.

The summer before her sophomore year in high school, Donna tearfully announced to her parents that she didn't want to play soccer anymore. Both parents were concerned; soccer had been her "thing" since she was six. Why the change of heart? "We were completely blindsided," said Aidan. "Ten years of schlepping to away games, cheering on the sidelines, watching her talent grow. And then, she pulls the plug? Her timing couldn't have been worse. College recruiters were just starting to notice her. Maybe she's being bullied by the other girls? She must be depressed. Why *else* would she want to quit?"

A mental health disorder was the best reason the father could come up with to explain why his sixteen-year-old daughter didn't want to do the same exact thing she'd been doing for the last ten years of her life.

"Is it possible she doesn't really like soccer?" I asked. "Or that she just wants to try something else?"

Aidan looked at me like I was crazy. But he admitted that he'd never once discussed with Donna how she felt about the sport. He'd prefer to keep her locked in the Comfort Zone, where *he* felt safe and secure, rather than allow her the freedom to venture into the Growth Zone of trying new things, stretching and maybe failing, but always learning. Playing the same game with the same coach and the same team was stifling her and blocking potential growth that might be found elsewhere.

"Have you asked her what she'd like to do instead of soccer?" I asked.

"She wants to join the show choir. She saw some movie or TV show, and now she wants to sing. I can tell you, Dr. Koplewicz, I've heard this kid in the car. She can't sing. She's throwing away her future!"

The reality is, it's about as likely she'd become a professional soccer player as a professional singer. But, in the here and now, where all scaffolding takes place, your job is to be emotionally available and to listen nonjudgmentally when your child is brave enough to tell you what she needs.

With gentle prodding, Aidan examined his personal reasons for pushing sports and realized he was trying to relive his own experiences as a star athlete through Donna. He also had his eye on a sports scholarship. In session, Donna expressed how hard it was to disappoint her father, but that she was really sick of playing the game—both the sport itself and pretending to love it as much as her dad did.

Major self-awareness reminder here: Your child is not a mini you. Empower her growth by letting her choose her activities and

Selfish Reasons Parents Push Their Kids

- To make them pad their résumés for college applications
- To repeat their own past victories
- To avoid their own past mistakes
- To reach goals they didn't when they were kids
- Out of fear or concern that the child isn't keeping up
- Out of embarrassment that their kid isn't doing the "right" thing

learn who she is, what she cares about, what makes her feel confident. Use your authority and awareness of what's in her best interests by asking, "Will the activity enrich *her* life?" "Will it make *him* happy?" "Will it build *his* self-esteem?" "Will it make *her* grittier?"

It's essential that you separate your own goals and expectations from the reality of who your child is. To do so, Stephanie Lee, an ADHD and behavioral disorders specialist at the Child Mind Institute, advises parents to sit down and write a list of goals for their child. Then she has them ask themselves if each goal is really about their child or about themselves. In other words, are their goals important to the parent or truly to the child?

"Parents might set the goal that their child be 'confident,' and after a little reflection, they realize that this might be their stated goal because they weren't a confident child themselves. Or they might write 'accomplished,' and come to realize that they've set this goal because they feel their child's accomplishments will be a good reflection on them. 'Happy' might be a stated goal because they're anxious or depressed," says Dr. Lee.

A better goal for the child is "growth." Scaffold a kid through validation, reassurance, and collaborative problem-solving to teach him the skills he needs to face a challenge or setback himself. If he can do that, the end result will be his feeling confident, becoming accomplished, and being happy.

Monitoring Pushback

Maria was good at math, and her mom, Carmen, suggested that Maria join the math club. "I thought it made perfect sense," said Carmen. "She was interested in it, and she'd hang out with kids who shared a common interest. No-brainer. But Maria acted like I'd suggested she jump off the roof!"

Often, we have parents who complain that their child refuses to try activities that would promote growth and seem like a natural fit. In this case, Carmen and Maria had a heart-to-heart and it turned out Maria was afraid that if she joined the math club, she'd be thought of as an even bigger geek than she already was. "I scaffolded her via validation and encouragement and said it was fine if she didn't want to join the club, but that living in fear of what others think was only hurting her. Maria rolled her eyes, but I think she got it," said Carmen. "Once we talked about it and she opened up about her fears, they kind of went away, and she did join the club in the end."

Often, when a child feels railroaded by a parent's "suggestion" (which feels more like a mandate to the child), there's some miscommunication afoot. The parent may have already signed the child up for the activity and refusing to go is the child's only tangible way to assert some level of control. These scenarios aren't always easy to untangle, but we get there.

Other times, however, a child's adamant refusal to do something that is objectively a good idea is a sign of something else going on. We had a seventh grader who was a computer whiz, coding well beyond his grade level. His computer science teacher begged him to join the coding club. His parents thought it was a great idea, too. Their son didn't have any friends, and this seemed like a good way to build some relationships. But the boy refused. Our task was to determine if his refusal was about control, fear, or an indication of a larger problem. We assessed him as having undiagnosed social anxiety. In therapy, he learned how to calm his knee-jerk reaction to the idea of participating in a group, to desensitize, and eventually he did join the club, where he made friends and had fun. If his parents hadn't taken a closer look at his pushback, they might not have figured out that the boy had a real emotional limitation that required intervention.

If your suggestions are met with *strong* resistance, there might be something deeper going on. If you determine the problem is distaste or disinterest, keep suggesting new avenues for growth. Your child might roll his eyes time and again but keep trying to spark an interest. And if he comes to you with an idea that you absolutely hate—"I want to learn how to play the drums!"—try to accommodate him and give the interest a chance to stick or fizzle out.

Are They Just Unmotivated?

DISTASTE	DISINTEREST	DISORDER
Your child doesn't like the activity.	Your child doesn't care about the activity.	Your child reacts strongly against the activity with inappropriate intensity by throwing tantrums, crying.
Signs of distaste are exaggerated eye rolls and fake puking noises.	Signs of disinterest are shrugs and nonresponses.	He might push back because he simply can't handle another activity and is at risk for or suffering from burnout.
The activity might be something the child once enjoyed. Preferences change as kids get older, and what she once liked could be a huge turnoff now.	Disinterest might be due to lack of proficiency. A nonathletic kid will be indifferent to sports.	
	It might be due to social pressures; the activity isn't considered "cool."	Intense reaction against joining clubs or groups within his area of interest might indicate a social anxiety disorder.
Keep searching to find activities the child will like and be excited about pursuing.	If you sense that social pressure is overriding a child's preferences and interests, scaffold him to follow his curiosity wherever it leads.	His refusal to participate in academic clubs or groups might indicate a learning disability he's afraid will be exposed.

You Can't Force Growth

Gardeners know that you can force a plant to bloom by manipulating its exposure to light. Not true for kids. They cannot be manipulated into growth in any one direction or on a specific schedule. In fact, if you try to rush a child to develop more quickly than she's ready to, you'll delay progress. Every child is different and has unique experiences. You can't expect yours to develop on any specific timelines. You might get that intuitively and still worry about your child "keeping up." We discourage comparing, because of the "each kid grows at her own pace" reality. It's important to monitor your child's development, though, so you can promote healthy growth and be cognizant of any concerning delays. Strive for a balance of the following.

One part information. Basic benchmark ranges can be found online. But always go a bit further than Google to gather information. Rely on experts—pediatricians, therapists, and teachers— who know your child and have a breadth of knowledge about normal ranges of development.

One part instinct. Listen to your gut about your own child. If all his peers are ready for a certain skill or activity, but you don't think your child is, trust that instinct. If you sense a problem, pay attention to that voice, and seek professional insight.

One part influence. Be mindful about how you are influencing growth by trying to push or hold back your child based on your own prejudices and personal history.

Dr. Rachel Busman told me a story that illustrates this well. "My husband and I are huge readers, and we wanted to encourage our nine-year-old son to enjoy reading, too," she said. "I liked the idea of his keeping a books log, and I had a pretty good idea of what he should be reading, how long it should take him to finish a book, how many books a month. The whole process seemed harder than I thought, and then it occurred to me to ask the teacher. As parents, we forget that we can do that. I told her that I thought our son should be reading chapter books, one after another. But the teacher said, 'Kids like to reread books. And that's good for them for comprehension and decoding.' I thought, *Huh. That's why you're the teacher and I'm not.*"

As an ambitious parent, Dr. Busman wanted to push her son to read new, increasingly challenging books. But his reading skills would bound forward by his rereading the same book. Her takeaway: "Parents need to know what they don't know and turn to trusted sources of information," she said. The teacher had a long history of leading hundreds of kids to read. Even someone as informed about what's going on in a kid's brain as Dr. Busman wasn't the best source on that subject.

But who knows your child better than you in other ways? Any ten-year-old might be capable of reading *Harry Potter*, but you might know that the wizarding world would be too intense for your son and leave those books on the shelf for now.

For general information about mental, emotional, and physical benchmarks, go to childmind.org/milestones or to the American Academy of Pediatrics parenting portal www.healthychild.org.

At the Institute over the years, we've seen parents trying to force growth by making children take on experiences they weren't ready for to keep up with peers, appear accomplished, or pad résumés for college. One family sent their daughter to China for a summer, when being so far from home was traumatic for her. One father, a medical doctor, insisted his teenage son intern at a hospital. But the boy felt faint at the sight of blood and came home crying every evening.

"I had one eight-year-old patient who was overprogrammed with activities, multiple tutoring sessions, occupational therapy for handwriting, and physical therapy, each week. I thought his schedule was excessive," says Dr. Busman. "Obviously, if a child needs OT, PT, and tutoring, I wouldn't object. But in this case, I felt his schedule was getting in the way of his emotional development. I told his mother, 'Your child is really overprogrammed and I'm worried that he needs time to be a kid, to just play and be.' She didn't want to hear it. She believed with all her heart that her son needed to 'get ahead,' and that this was the way to do it." What happened, though, was the child burned out at ten, became anxious, had to drop everything, and even left school for a semester. By pushing her son to "get ahead," the boy fell behind.

"Sometimes parents want their kids to reach for the top, but the top isn't appropriate for every kid. My great-grandmother used to say, 'There's an ass for every seat,'" says Dr. Busman.

"Not every kid is bound for the Ivy League, no matter how rigorously he's been tutored. Wouldn't you rather have your child go to a school that's academically, socially, emotionally, and temperamentally a good fit? I have a patient who is starting to look at NYC high schools, and as an exercise, I asked her and her mom to write down what they liked about the schools they'd toured. The mother liked the prestige of the schools. The daughter noted the feel. She described one school as 'a homey place.' It felt cozy to her. The people were nice. She felt comfortable there, which made it a great fit emotionally. School is not just a place to learn academics. You learn life lessons there, too."

When you push for prestige over emotional fit—in schools, activities, friendships, and the pace and direction of their growth—there is a predictable damaging impact on kids. They feel anxious, stressed out, and turn to escapist behaviors to cope, none of which empowers growth. However, when kids feel that "cozy" quality at school, in their activities and friendships, they are secure enough to take risks, explore, and experience—to grow.

The Big Picture

"When a teenager is dealing with any failure, parents can scaffold them by putting it into perspective," says Mark Reinecke, clinical director of the Child Mind Institute in the San Francisco Bay Area. "Kids think it's going to be terrible if they get a C in trigonometry, because then they won't get into Princeton." (FYI: They're probably right. Princeton has a 6 percent acceptance rate.) "So what can parents do to give their kids perspective? Ask them, 'Just wondering, but do you think you could be happy if you *don't* go to Princeton?'" For that matter, parents can ask themselves, "Do you think you'll be happy if your child doesn't get into Princeton?" A lot of the pressure kids feel about prestige college acceptance comes from their parents.

Princeton University researchers—economist Angus Deaton and Nobel Prize–winning psychologist Daniel Kahneman—explored this very question. They did a study about whether high income (what many parents and students associate with an Ivy League degree) determined happiness and life satisfaction, surveying 450,000 people over two years, and found that most of them, 85 percent, reported to feel happy day to day, regardless of income. The high earners acknowledged that having money made life easier, but abundance of wealth did not make the individuals any happier. If they had enough to cover their monthly bills and some expendable cash for fun, their life satisfaction rates were equal to the wealthiest among them.

"That trig test? It doesn't matter. Getting into a top college? Not nearly as important as you might think," says Dr. Reinecke. "You can be miserable or happy, no matter where you go. If you're happy and optimistic now, you're probably going to be happy and optimistic later. The opposite is also true. College choice doesn't make a bit of difference about those trajectories."

Having a long-term perspective might be a hard sell to a teenager who is steeped in the competitive crunch of the college process. Your soapy stories about the blessing of unanswered prayers—the jobs that didn't work out that opened the door to opportunities that did, the bad boyfriends who broke your heart and freed you up to meet your future husband—will probably not inspire a teen who is in *agony* right now about a boy's not texting her back. But keep trying to instill in them a healthy perspective, and the grace not to freak out about every test, game, party, or outfit. Having a long, broad view in the face of failure is critical. That's what you want for yourself, and what you want for your child. If the kid can sit still long enough to listen to your stories, she might be fidgeting, but the information is getting in. The thing about teens is that they do listen. They look to you for guidance, even if they are groaning the whole time.

Role model taking the long view. If you are balanced and calm in the face of the storm, your kids will learn from you that a stressful event, a loss, a failure, a social humiliation, requires evaluation (the "why") but that, in the long term, it brings growth and learning. Mistakes will be made. But if you and your child avoid catastrophizing—making problems bigger than they really are—and realizing what seems important today may not be important a year from now, you can move forward.

To nudge teens toward a big picture perspective, "Stay Socratic," says Dr. Reinecke. "Put your comments in the form of a question, as in, 'I'm just wondering, five years from now, do you think any of this is going to matter?' If the teen says no, reinforce that belief by saying, 'I think you're right.' If the teen says yes, ask more questions to force her to explain why and how." Scaffold by having the conversation, and guiding teens to question, evaluate, and take an objective, philosophical approach to life's ups and downs.

Scaffolding Growth for Teens

- **Structure.** Provide structure by being available to talk through failures. Do not organize your life around making theirs pain-free. Swooping in is structurally unsound. It trains teens to be dependent and incompetent, the opposite of what you want.

- **Support.** It's not about what you want for them, but what they want for themselves. Support them as they pursue their own goals and interests.

- **Encouragement.** Reinforce adolescents to take the long view during this time of high drama and tension, when their failures and problems seem huge, but won't matter a year from now.

When Annie, the teacher who'd been doing her son's homework since kindergarten, realized that Ben was completely unprepared for college and life, because of her actions, she sat him down at the table and said, "We can't go on. We have to change."

They each wrote down ideas of how to break the pattern they were stuck in and collaborated equally on a solution for the first time in their lives. Their plan involved a lot of tutors, which the family could ill afford. But they acknowledged that the expense would pay off in the long term. Annie needed to spend more time with her husband and daughter, and to have some time for herself. Ben had to learn how to budget his time and compose a paper on his own if he were going to thrive in college and afterward.

"The biggest change was in my relationship with Ben," said Annie. "For years, I was an enabler and coconspirator. I love him, but I associated him with bad feelings. When I stopped doing his homework, we did things together that had nothing to do with school and were fun. The tutors were good, but Ben's grades suddenly dropped. My new role was to encourage him emotionally, which felt so much healthier for both of us."

By the time Ben went to college—a fine state university—he was prepared to do the work and was successful there. "His first report card was mainly Bs and Cs, but he'd earned them," said Annie. "Other kids might see that as failure. But for Ben, he got to finally experience the joy of accomplishing something on his own."

Annie felt more guilt for depriving him of that happiness for so long. "But growth isn't exclusive to kids," she said. "I learned from my mistakes, too, and am being extra careful about doing too much for my daughter."

One of the great and humbling discoveries of parenting is that, while we're empowering our kids' growth, we're also learning that we, too, still have a lot to learn.

Nail Down Those Planks!

Growth is a process of trying, failing, learning, and trying again. Parents can empower growth with their planks.

Patience

• It can feel like torture to watch a child struggle and fail when you know you could take away the pain by doing things for him. Your patience will be tested when you nudge him out of the Comfort Zone, and gain as you collaborate in the Growth Zone, again and again. But the reward for being patient is a self-reliant, self-motivated learner.

Warmth

• Be the shoulder to cry on. If your child is sad about a failure, let her be sad and validate those feelings. And then, with warmth and compassion, move the discussion gently toward "whys" and empowering problem-solving.

Awareness

• Always be aware that what you want for your child might be more about you and your past, more than what's in the child's best interest. Whenever you feel the urge to push, reflect on why you feel so strongly about it.

• When parents swoop in, it's usually because of their own fears about the uncertainty of life. If that rings any bells, check yourself before you swoop. Life is uncertain. Better to teach kids about that reality than reinforce a damaging illusion.

Dispassion

• Failure hurts. Rejection stings. But to role model that failure and rejection are just outcomes, and not cause for a global negative interpretation like "I suck at everything!," you have to take your own stumbles in stride. Fall down, stand up, brush off, onward. No histrionics or self-pity.

Monitoring

• Take a closer look at a kid's pushback against growth opportunities that seem like a good fit. A hard limitation might indicate a deeper problem that needs professional intervention.

• Check in with your reliable sources of information, instinct, and influence about whether your child is growing at a strong pace for him, but resist comparing his growth to his peers.

8

Build Strength

The child's building is going up, and the parental scaffold is rising along with it at a close but clear distance. All good! But the building has to be fortified to protect and promote all that impressive growth. By installing internal steel beams—like courage, confidence, resilience, and tenacity—the child will have more than just a building to "live" in. He'll have a fortress that will withstand bad weather and difficult times. Even if he does take some fire from external forces, he'll have internal strength to cope with whatever the world throws at him. From your scaffold, you reinforce those steel beams with guidance and support and modeling strength.

Early on in our friendship, Mark Reinecke, the clinical director of the Child Mind Institute in the San Francisco Bay Area, told me about raising his now young adult daughter. "Gracie was anxious. I don't know if she was temperamentally anxious with a genetic predisposition, but she was certainly an anxious toddler and little kid," he said. "Frankly, she was often sick growing up. There was a level of threat and danger that surrounded the pregnancy and she was critically ill as an infant. Childhood illness has an influence on the way a parent feels about his baby. She was fragile and she grew up in a dangerous world. We weren't sure if she was going to make it. So she grew up as an anxious child, very fearful, always in Mom's shadow, clinging to her leg. She was timid. She wouldn't explore out into the world.

"So one day when she was about six, I was playing with her in the front yard of our house," he continued. "She was going back and forth on one of those little Razor scooters. She says, 'Daddy, look at me, look at me!'

"I encouraged her, saying, 'That's great, Gracie! Look at you go!'"

And then, Gracie's grandma, Dr. Reinecke's mother-in-law, came out of the house. "We love Grandma. Grandma's wonderful," he said. "She took one look at Gracie on the scooter and said to me, 'You know, she really needs to be wearing a helmet, shin guards, knee guards, and wrist guards so if she falls, she won't break anything.'"

Dr. Reinecke wasn't too quick to agree. "I said, 'Grandma, that thing is one inch off the ground. If she just steps off it, she'll be fine. I don't think there's much risk here.' She looked at me and said, 'You're her father. Why would you accept any risk?'"

That well-intended (if judgy) comment was a turning point for Dr. Reinecke. "A chill went up my back because, all of a sudden, the situation was clear," he said. "Grandma grew up very poor in North Carolina during the Great Depression. Her mindset was 'just hope for the best.' I realized at that moment that her anxious, fearful mindset had passed down from her to my wife, and now it was being transmitted to our daughter. I remember walking into the house, going right up to my wife, and saying, 'The intergenerational transmission of anxiety ends here!' It was very much the kind of declaration that only a child psychologist would make. My wife and I sat down, talked it out, and vowed that we were going to raise a brave child."

And how did Dr. Reinecke and his wife do that?

"By role modeling and reinforcing courage, resilience, and confidence," he said. Along with letting her watch multiple viewings of the ultimate brave girl movie, Disney's *Mulan*, Gracie's parents encouraged their daughter to do courageous things, seek out challenges, and never give up. And she didn't have to wear wrist and knee guards when she was just tooling around on the scooter in the driveway, even if she risked bruising an elbow.

They'll Be Fine

You might want to lock your children in the house and shield them from any risk. But by putting aside your own anxieties and being willing to let your child stumble and fall, you might have a life-defining, incredible moment of parenting clarity like Dr. Reinecke did, about not pouring your own fears into your child.

The greatest risk to an overprotected child is not a bruised elbow. It's her social and emotional development and her academic success.

For a 2018 study, researchers at the University of Minnesota followed over four hundred kids from diverse backgrounds over eight years, checking in with them at ages two, five, and ten. The scientists collected data from the participants' teachers, self-reports, and by observing the children playing and interacting with their parents in a lab. The "helicopter parents" tended to control their kids' every move, telling them what to play with and how to do it. The lead researcher, Nicole Perry, PhD, described the interactions as "too strict and demanding" in an article published by the American Psychological Association. "The kids reacted in a variety of ways. Some became defiant, others were apathetic, and some showed frustration." The study found that, by five, the overprotected, overcontrolled kids showed poor emotional and behavioral regulation. What's more, the kids who had impulse control at five indicated fewer emotional problems, better social skills, and a higher level of academic productivity at ten.

"Children with helicopter parents may be less able to deal with the challenging demands of growing up, especially with navigating the complex school environment," said Dr. Perry. "Children who cannot regulate their emotions and behavior effectively are more likely to act out in the classroom, to have a harder time making friends, and to struggle in school. Our findings underscore the importance of educating often well-intentioned parents about supporting children's autonomy with handling emotional challenges."

The goal of scaffolding is to raise children to be independent, resilient, confident adults. That process begins with allowing even two-year-olds to have some autonomy about what and how they play. School-age kids should be given the opportunity to work out emotional, social issues on their own before you or a teacher steps in to referee. The question should always be, "Can my child do this on her own?" If you're not sure, let her try and you'll find out.

Courage in Three Steps

Where does the courage to, say, ride a bike come from?

It starts with desire. The child has to *want* to ride a bike. If the desire is there, onward. If the desire isn't there, then forcing her to climb on and start pedaling is an exercise in obedience, not courage. Instead of making demands, ask why the child doesn't want to do it, and explore gently what she might be afraid of. You can model and reinforce that we all have to approach and master things we fear.

Next, a sense of competency. Does the child have the competency to ride a bike or not? Are her legs long enough to reach the pedals? If she doesn't have the competency yet, you can scaffold your child by teaching her. For just about every life skill, you need someone to show you how to do it, whether it's reading, apologizing, hitting a tennis ball, or playing the piano. If a child hops on a bike and falls down, it's not a personal failure, it's a deficit of competence. If you can explain the difference to your kids, they'll be more likely to get back on the bike and try again.

Finally, expectation. Learning to ride is a predictable process that looks like this: pedal, fall down, get up, repeat. If your child goes into it with the healthy expectation that it takes some time and practice to get it right, he won't fear failure or avoid doing it.

No one should be expected to be perfect from the get-go at anything. You can role model and reinforce comfort with imperfection to show your kids small acts of courage every day. For example, you can introduce yourself to a new neighbor, or make a new recipe, or install an Amazon Firestick into the TV. Take things on. Test yourself in front of your child. Screw up and persist.

One should not have the expectation that life will be easy or should be perfect. We see a lot of parents who think that their kids should be expert bike riders at five, get straight As, play the violin, and be the most popular kid in school. Having unrealistically high expectations and perfectionistic standards is a setup for making kids feel miserable when things do not turn out the way you expect. That misery squelches the desire to try something new and hinders your child's gaining competency of it, effectively blocking courage before it can start.

A Lifetime of Resilience in Fifteen Minutes

Back in 1970, Austrian-born American psychologist Walter Mischel asked a few dozen three- to five-year-olds from a preschool class at Stanford to, one by one, come into a room and sit down at a table with a single treat of his or her choosing (a pretzel, an Oreo, or a marshmallow) on a plate in front of them. The researchers told each child, "You can have one treat now, or two if you wait fifteen minutes." Then the adult left the child alone in the room with the treat. If the child simply couldn't wait, he or she was told to ring a bell to summon the adult, and then was permitted to eat the treat. The kids who could wait were found to have better impulse control.

The truly remarkable findings came in Dr. Mischel's 1989 follow-up study with the original subjects. The kids (now young adults) who delayed gratification for the whole fifteen minutes turned out to be more successful in a whole range of social, academic, and emotional dimensions years later. They scored higher on the SATs, used fewer drugs, had happier social lives, and were more adept at handling stress and frustration. In a 2013 follow-up, the now middle-aged delayed-gratification individuals had lower BMIs than their bell-ringing counterparts.

The study became famously known as *The Marshmallow Test,* also the title of a book by Dr. Mischel that revealed all he'd learned in decades of research about self-control. A few of his impulse control tips for kids *and* parents are included here.

Distraction. Even very small children can distract themselves from the object of their desire by looking around the room for something else to focus on. Dr. Mischel recommended singing a song, playing with their toes, picking their noses. Being able to willfully distract yourself from the literal or figurative marshmallow builds self-control.

"Cool" thinking. Dr. Mischel defined "hot" thinking as impulsive limbic system brain by-products. "Cool" thinking comes from the prefrontal cortex, the executive functioning part of the brain that isn't fully developed until kids are twenty-five. However, even first and second graders can tell the difference between "hot" and "cold" thoughts and try to regulate their mental temperature. Even waiting for a few minutes can make a difference. In a forty-year follow-up study in 2011, the "I'll wait" group's brain imaging of their prefrontal cortex showed more activity than the "can't wait" group.

Framing. If a child can transform the desired object into something other than what it is in their imagination, they can lessen their desire for it. For example, if the child mentally puts a frame around the treat, as if it were a picture and not actual food, they could wait longer to eat it.

"Our daughter's childhood was one long delay-of-gratification experiment. If Gracie said, 'Can I have a cookie with my milk?' our answer would be, 'Yes, in two minutes.' Everything was okay 'in two minutes,'" says Dr. Reinecke.

Make "yes, in a few minutes" a household mantra. Delaying gratification for a four-year-old can turn into a lifetime of strength and impulse control.

Scaffolding Strength for Kids

- **Structure.** Provide a safe physical and emotional space for children to be autonomous, try new things, take risks, and fall down. Learn to step away, and let the child do a puzzle or get dressed on his own before you step in to help. Institute a policy of delaying a child's instant gratification by a few minutes to teach self-control.

- **Support.** When the child falls down, be there to help her get back up, with praise for effort and by setting up the healthy expectation that anything worth doing takes some time and practice to get right.

- **Encouragement.** To bolster impulse control that predicts future academic productivity and social skills, cheer your child on from three giant steps back, without shouting instructions and demands.

You Can't Actually Die from Embarrassment

At my son Joshua's middle school, they held a big Thanksgiving Day assembly for students and teachers to read poems, play guitar, or do ballet routines. It was an opportunity for anyone in the community to put themselves in the spotlight. Imagine my surprise when Josh, a quiet kid, a boy of few words, told us that he'd decided to perform at the assembly with his friend Adam. I remember swallowing hard, trying to be encouraging. But Joshua didn't have a performer personality.

"That's great! What do you have in mind?" I asked.

"We're going to do a rap dance inspired by Michael Jordan to 'Jump' by Kris Kross."

He might as well have said, *I'm going to perform open heart surgery onstage! It's gonna be awesome!*

I knew Josh loved Michael Jordan. He had posters of the basketball star all over his room. Since he was two he'd been fascinated by break-dancers in the park and tried to spin on his shoulder blades on the floor of our kitchen. But that didn't mean he could pull off a rap dance onstage in front of the whole school.

I was terrified on his behalf. I thought, *He's going to die up there!* I've been a therapist for thirty-plus years, and so many patients of mine have told me about their childhood trauma of performance in public—and they were still processing the horror decades later.

I couldn't help myself from saying, "Well, I'm not so sure that's a good idea."

My wife, Linda, shot me a look and said to Josh, "That sounds great!"

Josh nodded. "It's going to be terrific! I've already started working with the dance instructor at school. She's helping me choreograph it."

Oh, God. He was really going to do this. It was just so out of character, so bold. And so dangerous. It could be social suicide.

Three days before the assembly, Josh informed Linda and me that his friend Adam had backed out.

I was absolutely flooded with relief. "Oh, well. It just wasn't meant to be," I said.

"No, I'm going to do it by myself."

Linda said, "Good for you."

"Everything in life has a cost and a benefit . . ." I started.

"Dad, don't worry. It's going to be great."

I was a wreck the whole day. I couldn't rearrange my schedule to be there, and I'll admit to feeling a little glad about that. Linda was an art teacher at the school. She watched the assembly from the back of the auditorium and called me right after.

I asked, "How was it?"

"It was amazing," she said. "The crowd went wild. He killed it up there."

A real-life *Napoleon Dynamite* twist! Relief, joy, and then the guilt. Why hadn't I had faith that my son knew what he was doing?

Flash forward to Joshua's thirtieth birthday party. His childhood friend Elias stood up and gave a speech. "Everyone knows how much I hate talking in public, but I really love Josh and will do anything for him," he said. "Josh doesn't know, but the first time I laid eyes on him was in middle school when he did a rap dance at the Thanksgiving assembly. Even at that age, I knew he was taking a big risk. And then the lights went out and the spotlight hit him. He was wearing a baseball hat backward and a baggy Chicago Bulls jersey. Kris Kross came on and Joshua started dancing and jumping and spinning on the floor. Within a minute, everyone was on their feet, screaming, 'Go Josh! Go Josh!' On Monday after the holiday, I saw him in the hallway with his head down, holding too many books. He was right back to being anonymous and marching to his own drum. I talked to my parents about his performance for years, saying if Josh could do that, then I could find the courage to put myself out there, too."

To this day, I'm relieved for Josh that his dance was a hit. But I also know that it didn't change his personality. In the movie *Parenthood,* Steve Martin stars as the ever-supportive dad who played catch every day with his uncoordinated son. Then, at the big game, the klutzy kid made a stunning, spectacular catch. Steve Martin did the happy dance, and his wife, played by Mary

Steenburgen, pointed out that nothing had really changed, that he was still a quirky kid and that catch didn't solve all his problems. The father's throwing the ball at his son a thousand times increased the chance that it would go into the glove. But he was still a klutz.

Josh's performance didn't change who my son was. But because he'd gone through with it, he inspired his friend Elias and probably others. And his world of possibilities opened. Later in life, he was a professional DJ for a while. I trace back a real change in his outlook to that Michael Jordan tribute. He risked embarrassment, and just by doing that, he gained powerful mental and emotional muscle.

If your child has the guts and grit to take a huge risk, please *don't* do what I did. Encourage him to go for it because you never know how it's going to play out. Yes, it might be fodder for his therapy sessions twenty years from now. Or it might be a turning point in his life or inspire others to be brave, too.

To scaffold a kid to risk embarrassment, you set the tone. When we're helping children learn healthy emotional habits, the first step is to consider how we handle similar situations in our own lives. So, as a doctor, I'm prescribing that, on family karaoke night, that you *demonstrate bravery* by grabbing the microphone and singing "I Will Always Love You."

If something goes wrong, *don't dwell* on it, as in, "I can't believe I did that!" Try to laugh it off and transmit or state the message, "*That* happened. Oh, well. Moving on . . ." Model resilience by brushing off mistakes.

Model emotional control and *remain calm* while in the throes of an embarrassing situation. While you are performing "I Will Always Love You," and people start throwing tomatoes at the stage, duck, but don't stop singing!

As for how to encourage risk-taking in your kids, *never belittle* them if they wind up embarrassing themselves. Even if the teasing is gentle and "in good fun," kids internalize shame and won't be in a hurry to risk embarrassment again.

Don't discount his feelings as overly sensitive. It's only natural for you to want to downplay your child's embarrassing experiences by saying things like "It's not as bad as you think." But discounting any of your child's big, really upsetting emotions invalidates them. He will think you don't understand or care that he's suffering. But don't go overboard with rehashing in this case. Validate the feelings and move on. Heaping too much attention on an embarrassing situation can make it worse, not better.

Reframe a negative experience into a positive one. So, if your kid blows her piano recital, say something that distances her from the bad scene and sprinkles in praise, as in, "I get why you're upset. You had a rocky start, but I was very proud of how you handled it. Only a brave person can start badly, regroup, and pull out a strong finish!"

Last, *teach a healthy perspective.* At some point in every person's life, he will fart in front of others. In childhood, letting one rip will be met with giggles. A lot of giggles. A child might believe that he will, forever after, be remembered as the Cheese Cutter. To your child, it feels like everyone is thinking about it as much as he is, when in reality, most kids will have moved on by the next day. You can help your kid gain a healthy perspective by telling him stories of your own mortifying gusts and get him laughing at you. Reinforce that you survived it and can joke about it now. Don't try to outdo his own experience; it's not a mortification competition. But let him know you relate. And then, drop the subject. If you give it short shrift, he'll realize that it's not as big a deal as he thought. This awareness will come to his rescue, should (when) something similar happen(s) again.

Like rejection and failure, embarrassment is part of life. It's tempting to try to shield your kids from all difficult experiences, but it's far more productive to scaffold him into learning a healthy way to deal with it.

Now, some of our patients fear embarrassment to such a degree that they become avoidant. Avoidant behavior might be a realistic response to bullying. If that turns out to be the case, parents and teachers need to step in and stop the bullying. Be on the lookout for disproportionate hesitation or avoidance, which delays development.

Is It Avoidance?

NORMAL	PROBLEM	DISORDER
Your child raises her hand in class, and gives an answer, even if she's not sure she's right. Her embarrassment seems proportionate to the situation. She gets over it quickly and tries again soon. She isn't thrilled to return to the scene of the embarrassment, but she musters her courage and goes back to class.	Your child hesitates to raise her hand in class, but if she's called on, she can give an answer, even if it might be wrong. He seems overly fretful and upset after an embarrassment and needs excessive encouragement before he can try again. He makes excuses to avoid the scene, and the people, associated with his embarrassment, but he eventually goes back to school.	Your child never raises her hand in class, even if she knows the correct answer. She loses sleep, stops eating, and becomes disproportionately anxious in response to an embarrassing moment and refuses to try again. She adamantly refuses to go back to school or to see certain people. He pretends that he's sick to get out of activities or quits them outright. If you force him to face the scene of the embarrassment, he will become very upset. Your child might have social anxiety–related avoidant behavior if she panics at the thought of participating in low-risk activities and obsesses over people's judgment of her. She withdraws from social interactions.

Bouncing Back

Much of what we call strength is resilience, the ability to recover quickly from adversity. Alfred said it best to Bruce Wayne, aka Batman: "Why do we fall, sir? So we can learn to pick ourselves back up." To scaffold kids to have the fortitude to pick themselves back up, reinforce your own bounce ability.

Adversity happens to everyone. But good bouncers look at it

in a way that allows them to get over it and move on. In the 1980s, psychologists Lyn Abramson of the University of Wisconsin and Northwestern's Lauren Alloy developed a theory called "attribution style," about how you look at the cause of bad things that happen to you.

According to their research, people who attribute negative outcomes (for example, a failed test) to *global* negatives ("I suck at math!") will "show helplessness deficits in new situations that are either similar or dissimilar to the original situation in which they were helpless." In other words, if a child goes global negative, she will feel helpless in all academic challenges and might fall apart about any upcoming test.

Those who attributed negative outcomes to *specific* negatives ("I had a hard time with that one algebra test, but I got an A in history last week") "will show helplessness deficits in situations that are similar, but not dissimilar, to the original situation in which they were helpless," per the study. Or, if a child has specific explanations for why a particular test went wrong, she might be a bit shaky about her next math test but won't fall into the trap of feeling helpless in other subjects, too.

Along with *global vs. specific attribution,* the researchers defined two other dimensions that can either raise or lower self-esteem and determine people's ability to recover after a setback: *internal vs. external* and *stable vs. temporary.*

An internal attribution for a bad outcome would be to blame yourself, as in, "I failed the test because I'm an idiot." An external attribution would be finding cause for a failed test outside of yourself, as in, "This teacher and I do NOT gel."

A stable attribution for bad things is like giving yourself a black mark on your permanent record, as in, "I always mess up. It's what I do." A temporary attribution is that a negative outcome is just a fluke, as in, "Shit happens sometimes."

Adding it all up, people who make global, internal, and stable negative attributions when a bad thing happens tend to become depressed, feel helpless and hopeless with low self-esteem, and they give up in the face of future negative events. To scaffold a child to be more resilient, you can help your child make specific, external, and temporary attributions.

So the productive pep talk might sound like, "Okay, you got a D in algebra, and that's not ideal. Let's not sugarcoat it. But if you study a little bit harder with my or a tutor's help, I think you can do better next time. Keep in mind you're not stupid. You got an A in history." Drive home your child's belief that he is capable of success and able to bounce back, and he's more likely to do so, again and again.

What's Grit for You Isn't Necessarily Grit for Your Child

Yes, back to this. It comes up in nearly every chapter because parents need to be reminded over and over again that your child is not you. The secret sauce that gave you confidence as a kid is not necessarily going to do it for your child.

"Whenever I needed a lift growing up, my grandmother said, 'Put on some lipstick, you'll feel better.' It was old-fashioned and a bit sexist, but there was something to it. I'd put on makeup and a pretty dress, and I felt more confident," said Polly, a mom at the Child Mind Institute. "My mother and grandmother were just like me in this regard and I have many happy memories of going shopping with my mom, and the two of us bonding over clothes and her guiding me about how to use style to feel strong enough to face the world."

However, Polly's daughter Jo is not like her mother, or grand-mother, or great-grandmother. "When Jo came home from school upset about something that happened, or if she got in a fight with a friend, I broke out the old chestnut, 'Put on some lipstick . . .'" said Polly. "Jo was not into that, at all. I pushed it once when she was in fourth grade, insisted on doing her makeup and outfit for

Selfies and Self-Esteem

A sentence that will surprise no one: Taking daily selfies, using filters and Photoshop to perfect them, posting and agonizing over likes and comments are destructive to kids' confidence and self-esteem.

According to a 2018 Canadian study, researchers put 110 female undergrads into three groups: the first group was required to take selfies and upload them untouched. The second group took and posted retouched selfies. The third group, the control, didn't take or post any selfies.

The moods and body image thoughts of all three groups were assessed before and after posting selfies. The findings: Regardless of whether or not the undergrads retouched their selfies, they all experienced adverse psychological effects, more anxiety, less confidence, and decreased feelings of physical attractiveness, compared to the control group.

If you knew for sure that your child was doing something that would damage her self-esteem, and it was happening right in front of you, dozens of times per day, wouldn't you do something about it? The best approach to decrease selfie taking and posting is to discuss the findings of this study, and to suggest that the next time your daughter wanted to take out her phone and pose in duck face, to say to herself, "Yes, in two minutes." And then two minutes more, and so on. Self-scaffolding leads to self-esteem.

her, and she could barely tolerate it. She washed her face as soon as I finished. It sounds superficial to say that I didn't understand my daughter because she rejected the girlie stuff. That turned out to be part of a much larger truth."

Jo, not her real name, came to us because she had symptoms of depression. But what our therapist quickly assessed was that her symptoms related to confusion and fear about her gender identity. Polly could not fully understand her daughter's problems. But she didn't have to personally relate to them to scaffold her through it with warmth, dispassion, and patience.

It's only natural to want to give our kids some of the same experiences that were good for us or to give them a better iteration of something we've experienced. But not every kid is exactly like his parents. He might be *very* different. It might go far beyond his not loving your sleepaway camp, or not being able to play the same sports as you did. Parents might not even realize how they subtly or overtly push their kids into sports, extracurriculars, or identities that match their own. You might think, *My path worked for me, so I'll put my child on the same path.*

In some cases, parents choose a hard path for their kids, one that made them miserable as children, in order to "toughen them up." I saw a child who'd been forced to go hunting with his father, starting at ten, a rite of passage that every male member of the family had gone through for generations. The father himself confessed that he hated his first hunt as a young boy and had nightmares about it for weeks afterward. And yet, he insisted his own son repeat the experience, with similar results.

When parents talk about toughening up a child, I tell them, "Well, that was a rough experience for you. Why do you want your child to relive it? What's the justification for it?" Forcing a child to be miserable is a strategy for developing distrust in your relationship, not the best way to guide a child toward grittiness.

Some of our patients' grandparents who grew up in a different time are skeptical, even fearful, about therapy and the "psychology stuff" we use to train parents to scaffold their kids. "They think kids should only speak when spoken to and that sparing the rod spoils the child," says Dr. Rachel Busman. "If your parents openly challenge your scaffolding of their grandchildren, we recommend you say, 'You're right. Things were harder and different for your generation. But we know more about the brain than we did then. We know more about how people learn and grow strong. Experts have figured out that a child develops grit by learning to identify obstacles and using strategies to get around them, not by parents and grandparents throwing *more* obstacles in their path. Misery does not have to be part of it. You can develop grit through positive experiences, too, like sticking with commitments.'"

And if that doesn't work, all I can tell you is to remember your planks of patience and dispassion.

Tenacity, Anyone?

Tenacity is staying power. Not giving up. Stickiness. It counts for more in life than just about anything, including brilliance. You can be supersmart, but if you quit, you won't accomplish anything.

By honoring commitments, no matter what, kids learn tenacity. Sometimes, tenacity must be forced upon them by you. A classic scenario is when your child expresses interest in an activity, starts doing it, and then decides he doesn't like it or isn't any good at it. Permissive parents would say, "Oh, you don't like it? Well then, you can just stop taking that activity."

But just letting a kid quit doesn't teach him stickiness. Your child will learn so much more if you tell him, "You didn't like karate as much as you hoped, but you made a commitment and you have to honor that. At the end of the session, if you decide it's something you don't want to do again, then we'll investigate other activities to get involved in."

Your child might not be too happy about having to show up for karate every week, especially since his best friend's parents had no problem letting him quit and now he doesn't know anyone there. But whatever strength he musters to get through eight weeks of karate will be far more beneficial to him than snapping your fingers and making the obstacle magically disappear. I have a friend who saw this situation as a simple matter of dollars and sense. "I paid for the classes so you're going, even if you hate every second of it!" she said when her kids complained about ballet or swim lessons. The message might be indelicate, but your kid needs to understand that his choice affects more people than just him. His personal preference is not the only factor in his showing up. If he joined a team, he can't abandon his teammates and the coach. Or if she got a lesser part in the play, she has to see it through or cause problems for the rest of the cast.

There is a difference between sticking with something and being stuck in it. "My son is in third grade. He's not super into team sports, but it's hard to just dabble in soccer," says Dr. Busman. "Now everyone is on the travel team and they all talk about being on this or that level. We feel like we've gotten this far and have to continue." But when the time comes for her son to give up soccer, he'll walk away knowing that he gave it a good, honest go and is ready to do the same elsewhere.

Parents often say they don't care if their kids fail as long as they're doing their best. But you have to consider the child's perspective. Doing his best and failing anyway can be upsetting, defeating. Mastery *is* self-esteem building. Excelling at something does make your kid feel more confident. If he's great at art, then load him up with drawing classes. There is nothing wrong with a child being exceptional and focusing on what he's good at and loves, and pushing out of his Comfort Zone within this one area of discipline. One warning, though. If your child feels pressure to excel—"My little Picasso!"—that can cause distress, which is more harmful than helpful.

Scaffolding can feel like a balancing act. You're supposed to encourage your kids to stick with their commitments even if they hate it, to pursue what they love and are good at, to be flexible and open to trying new things, but not to pressure them either way. It's a lot. The only way to really mess up is by doing too much for them and equating misery with grit.

Dr. Reinecke and his wife scaffolded their daughter, Gracie,

Scaffolding Strength for Teens

- **Structure.** Teach kids attribution style, so they can learn how to frame the way they think about their role if bad things happen. Make it a hard rule that teens are expected to honor their commitments and try to find ways to benefit from them. Create a style of using positive experiences to teach grit, like scaffolding a child to overcome an obstacle.

- **Support.** Give them opportunities to be great and build self-esteem. Give them opportunities to start slow and build tenaciousness. No matter how well they do, validate their feelings and keep giving them lessons on perspective. Not everything is such a big deal, no matter what social media or their friends say.

- **Encouragement.** Cheer them on when they take risks, even when you're terrified they'll make fools of themselves. Teens are easily swayed by their peers and the likes and comments on social media. Encourage them to look inward for validation, since external validation via posting selfies, even really good ones, negatively impacts self-esteem and body image. And role model risk-taking and bounciness in your own actions.

to do bold things, to take on challenges, and to be determined throughout her childhood, and now she's a strong, tenacious adult. "She really did become brave," he says. "When I give lectures on the subject of raising brave children, I usually tell two stories. One, when Gracie was nine or ten, she was climbing on a jungle gym at the park. It had two towers with a rope bridge between them. She climbed to the top of one of the towers and went to cross the rope bridge. There was a boy standing in the middle of it, the self-appointed master of the tower. Gracie moved along the rope bridge anyway. When the boy squared off to block her, she dropped into a karate pose, like Mulan, as if she were getting ready to kick his ass. I ran over to this jungle gym, and I said to the boy, 'You really need to let her go because she's about to unleash on you. This is not going to end well.'"

The boy said, "Yes, sir" and moved.

Dr. Reinecke says, "I wasn't encouraging my daughter to attack a random kid. She was practicing what she'd learned about being a brave girl, and I reinforced it. Our scaffolding and encouragement doesn't mean all her fears went away. She has normal anxieties about wanting people to like her and doing well in school. But she's not a fearful person the way she used to be and would have been if we hadn't changed course. Three years earlier, she never would have walked across the playground, climbed to the highest tower, and confronted the kid who was blocking her from what she wanted. But after years of bravery training, she did."

The other story he tells about Gracie's courage: "My daughter and I toured a black water swamp in South Carolina," he says. "It was 95 degrees. Mosquitoes were everywhere. Ferns were hanging from the trees. The swamp water was so black that if you put your foot in up to your ankle, you couldn't see your toes. I asked our guide, 'Are there alligators in here?' He said, 'Oh, yeah. Alligators. Water moccasins.' This was a scary place. My once-anxious daughter had the best time that day. She fearlessly canoed through the swamp, alligators and snakes be damned. I have a photo of her in that canoe, beaming. I bring it with me to my lectures, asking the crowd, 'Does this look like an anxious kid to you?'"

Nope. Not anxious. Just bold and healthy.

Nail Down Those Planks!

Strength is built, like muscle. Your version of "doing reps" is pumping scaffolding planks.

Patience

• If you expect children to delay gratification to develop big self-control muscles, you'll have to role model waiting as well.

• Since it's crucial to let kids try on their own, you'll have to be extra patient while watching them struggle, knowing you could jump in and solve the problem right away.

Warmth

• Since building their strength means allowing your child to take risks and be bold, use warmth to comfort them after a fall by validating their feelings.

Awareness

• Be conscious of pushing your own past on your child. What worked for you might not work for your child.

Dispassion

• Don't overreact to their embarrassment or failure or it'll inflate in importance in their heads.

Monitoring

• Vigilantly follow their progress as they become more autonomous. They might be able to do one thing on their own, and not another task of similar difficulty. Challenge builds strength and tenacity. But frustration and anxiety can lead to avoidance, which weakens resolve.

9

Set Realistic Limitations

The parental scaffolding around the child's building should never impede growth or block it from taking whatever shape it's going to take. However, the building needs to be safe. It has to meet standards. Like the head contractor at a construction site, the parents, from their scaffold, need to maintain quality control of the child's development and to make sure that its construction is "up to code." Parents have to point out what's not right and enforce changes in that area.

When my youngest son, Sam, was in eighth grade, my wife and I learned that he'd pregamed a party at our apartment, and got drunk or stoned or both, with some of his friends. A father from school called me and said, "I heard from another parent that your son and a couple of his friends were totally wasted on Saturday night."

It kills me even now that other parents were talking about my son's bad behavior. I'm the child psychiatrist! The other parents looked to me for advice and guidance, and here was my own son breaking clearly defined rules.

Initially, I reacted like any parent, and said, "You must be mistaken. My son would never do that."

The father said, "You have no idea how hard it is for me to make this call. I tried twice before and hung up." Not only because it was embarrassing for both of us for him to share this news, but my son was supposed to join his family on their upcoming ski vacation in just a couple of days. He knew that our plans might have to change now. How could I let my son go on the trip, given what I'd just heard?

What really bugged me was that I was there when Sam and his friends hung out at our place that night. Everything seemed as usual. I needed more information before I made any decisions. The father gave me the names of the other parents who could confirm the story. But before I started a full-scale investigation, I needed to hear what happened from Sam's own lips.

I wish I could say that I remained calm, but the truth is, I was enraged. He was my third son, and we talked about everything. Our lines of communication were wide open. Sam knew how Linda and I felt about marijuana use, and how it would affect his brain. We had a deal: He would not smoke pot until he graduated from high school. Apparently, he'd broken our deal, maybe not for the first time. I felt foolish, hoodwinked.

I called Linda and told her what our friend had told me. She refused to believe it, too. I was supposed to be on my way to an important event celebrating a colleague, but Linda said, "Forget the party. You have to come home. I'm not dealing with this alone."

I agreed with her and left a message on my son's phone to meet me at home ASAP, without his ever-present posse of friends. He probably knew he was in trouble. By the time I got to our apartment, Sam hadn't arrived yet. After one more urgent request that he "come home RIGHT NOW!," he showed up. My wife and I were in our bedroom talking about how to handle this when he knocked on our door. We told him to go into the living room and wait for us there.

I wanted him to sweat for a few minutes, and I needed a moment to calm myself before we talked. By the time my wife and I joined him, he was visibly upset.

I said, "We know everything."

He said, "What are you talking about?"

"What happened Saturday night?"

"We went to a party."

"Before you left, what did you do?" I asked. He seemed to be deciding if he should lie or not. "You're in deep trouble right now," I said. "I'm giving you a chance to get out. What really happened?"

He said, "We drank vodka."

"What about weed?" I asked.

Sam shook his head. "None of that."

"Where did you get the vodka?"

"One of my friends brought it," he said.

Linda asked, "How much did you drink?"

"Three shots."

It came out that his version of "a shot" was a full juice glass! My wife and I must have looked stunned. Our son started to cry from guilt, remorse, embarrassment, and shame.

I was devastated by his admission and to see him so upset. "You have lost my trust," I said. "I don't know what the consequences will be, but we're done for tonight."

We went to our own corners to think about it. I was as upset as my son about what I would have to do.

I remember growing up, hearing parents say about punishing their kids, "This is going to hurt me more than it hurts you." It's certainly not fun to set limitations on your child because he or she did something to betray your trust. But no one ever said scaffolding was easy. To live within a family, a community, and a society, there are rules of conduct. One of our jobs as parents is to teach, model, and reinforce those rules.

And if the rules are broken, there will be consequences.

"Don't Let's Start"

Let's all agree on this: Sometimes, kids can be impossible. In every home, in every family, there will be times when they behave horribly. One of the most common questions our therapists get from parents is, "Are they doing it on purpose to piss me off? Because it's working!"

Please don't take children's meltdowns personally. Monster moments are the by-product of their mushy prefrontal cortex. The reasonable part of their brains is still under construction. Kids aren't little executives who use logic. They are impulsive, emotional beings who run on wants and needs. This might not comfort you when your child is racing up and down the aisles at Trader Joe's, throwing a muffin at her sister's head, or screaming "I hate you!" before slamming his bedroom door.

Depending on the situation, you might have to respond to unruly children and rebellious teens with negative consequences, which I will lay out for you in just a few pages. Scaffolding limitations isn't *only* a matter of responding appropriately to a single transgression. It's creating a home environment and monitoring your own behavior so that your kids step out of line rarely.

So much of kids' punishment-worthy behavior—and your having to play the bad guy—can be prevented via effective communication, on your part and theirs.

Be absolutely clear. What, exactly, do you expect from them? Be as specific and clear as possible so there's no confusion. It's not about issuing orders. You're not a drill sergeant. But you are the authority figure, and your children look to you for direction. For example: "It's time for bed. Change into your PJs. Choose a book. Get in bed. I'll be there in five minutes." To an older kid: "You can go to the party, but please be home by midnight. If there is any reason you can't be home by then, you must call or text to let us know by 11:45." S-P-E-L-L I-T O-U-T.

Praise the good. To encourage and maintain prosocial, proactive behavior—in effect, playing nice—flood kids with positive reinforcement for specific actions. This strategy works for teachers who have to keep two dozen or more kids under control, so it will work for you. The trick is to be specific about the behavior you are praising, such as, "Great job sharing your toys," or "Great job helping me clean the dishes." Focus your positive attention on three skills at a time, prioritizing the most disruptive or dysfunctional behavior first for the biggest potential gains. As for the smaller annoyances, hold off on dealing with them until the big ones smooth over.

Express feelings with words. A lot of kids throw a tantrum because they want to be sent into a time-out. They have a sense that they need a little cooldown time, but don't know how to say that. If we teach them "functional communication training," aka to use their words, or for very young kids, to use cards that represent words, they'll be able to express the need for a break, and the whole scenario of them misbehaving won't happen.

Active ignoring. You could also call this strategy "choose your battles." If you sense your teenager, in particular, is trying to ping you to get a reaction, ignore it. One mother reported that her twelve-year-old daughter had started cursing at home. A lot. The extra salty words. She asked her daughter's therapist what the consequences should be, and he surprised her by saying, "Nothing. Ignore it." If the mom yelled or punished the daughter for swearing, she'd know exactly how to get under her mom's skin. The mother bit her lip and said nothing the next time her daughter cursed, and eventually, the cursing tapered off. Active ignoring worked beautifully . . . until one day, when the daughter used a particularly inflammatory word and the mother completely lost her cool. From that moment on, the daughter broke out the four-letter bomb whenever she wanted attention, and the mother had to double down on her active ignoring.

"I'm Telling You for the First Time"

Kids need to learn that their actions, good or bad, result in re-actions, good or bad, from you, teachers, and other supportive people *before* they go into the real world, or they are in for quite a shock when they start their first job and they have to report to a boss who will not take their crap for one second. Teaching them about consequences might not be fun for you or your kids, but it gives them a huge advantage in their professional and social lives as adults.

Sometimes, kids only need to come in contact with a con-sequence once or twice to absorb that crucial lesson. Just one time-out is enough to convince them that they never want to experience it again.

With some patients, Child Mind Institute psychologist Dr. Stephanie Lee teaches consequences by proxy. "I'll take a favor-ite toy like a teddy bear, and say to a kid, 'Mr. Bear is playing nicely and following directions and listening to his parents, so he can keep playing. When Mr. Bear doesn't follow directions, he has to sit in the chair.' Then we take Mr. Bear to the time-out room, put him in the chair, and tell the child that the bear can come back out in a few minutes." After Mr. Bear's time-out, she tested patients' self-control in the treatment room. Dr. Lee de-scribed bringing in a TV, promising the child that he could watch his favorite show, and then telling him the TV broke. Or letting the child's siblings play on their iPads while she asked the patient to do math homework. "The kids *still* didn't misbehave because they learned vicariously that it wasn't worth it."

Not every child is as sympathetic to the plight of Mr. Bear, however. "We have some kids that need to go to the chair repeat-edly," says Dr. Lee. "It varies depending on the kid, on his learn-ing history, and on the parents. Young kids—under four—don't need as much repetition of consequences because they don't have a long history of other types of patterns of behavior yet. Older kids who've been using other behaviors for a while need more consistent and reliable practice around consequences."

Teach them about consequences *before* they figure out how to get around them. It's easier to learn than unlearn. And it's easier to teach good behavior than retrain bad behavior.

"Get Yourself Together!"

While teaching kids about consequences, you have to train them simultaneously in coping skills to steer themselves away from consequential behavior. Such skills include the following.

Distraction. If a child can learn to turn away from the thing that's upsetting him and focus on something else, he won't necessarily have a meltdown. Describe it to him as "changing the channel in your mind."

Reframing. Self-control can be found by looking at a situation in a different way. If a child is upset because he has to do math homework while his siblings are playing *Minecraft* on their iPads, he can teach himself to cast it in a new light, perhaps, "Lucky me! I get to finish my work now, so I can play games later."

Scaffolding Limitations for Children

- **Structure.** Make sure kids know the house rules and codes of conduct about what's acceptable and unacceptable, and then set those standards in cement. Use time-outs consistently and repeatedly, from an early age.

- **Support.** Teach a child to support herself with coping skills that keep her emotions under control, like mindfulness, expression, and distraction.

- **Encouragement.** Encourage good behavior with praise and rewards. Discourage behavior by ignoring it or sending the child for a time-out.

Deep breathing. Mindfulness interventions like deep belly breathing and progressive muscle relaxation have been found to be similarly calming in children as well as adults. Simply saying to the child, "Stop and take a breath" and then doing it together has the potential to de-escalate any situation.

Expressiveness. Children misbehave because they want something they can't have. The simple act of expressing their frustration—"I'm upset that I can't have what I want!"—lessens its impact and allows the child to regain emotional control.

"I'm Telling You for the *Last* Time!"

When my toddler grandson doesn't get what he wants, he starts yelling and stamping his feet. Sometimes, he gets down on all fours and hits his head on the floor. I find this very interesting because his uncle, my youngest son, used to do the same thing. I asked Sam's pediatrician about it at the time, and he said, "When it really hurts, he'll stop."

Toddlers boil. Fortunately, they're small. Parents have physical control.

It's not entirely wrong to say that teenagers are no different from toddlers, except teenagers can drive a car. They boil when they're denied something, but they freeze, too. And you don't have physical control anymore.

With an adolescent, your finest scaffolding techniques might be rejected.

As kids move from childhood into adolescence, you will notice a change in how they test their boundaries and an uptick in provocative word choice, rule breaking, and back talk. To you, missing curfew might register as a teen being intentionally provoking, but what they're actually doing is expanding into any and all available space. The teenage brain is wired to seek out what's new, what's different. A novel experience for them might be testing the patience of the humans around them. It's their

The Escalation Trap

To steer your child toward seeing you as an ally, a partner, and make her more likely to take in the information you give her, scaffold with kindness and compassion, even when she is infuriating. If you react to her bad behavior with anger, she will see you as an adversary, and all your interactions will feel like going to war.

Gerald R. Patterson, an Oregon-based psychologist and pioneer in Parent Management Training, identified a pattern of escalation called the "coercive cycle." The child-parent argument gets progressively louder, meaner, and more insulting, until one of you "wins," but really, everyone loses his cool, dignity, and temper.

For example, a child sits on the floor of the hardware store, screaming "I hate you!" The parent yells at her to get up, or be quiet, and before too long, they are both red-faced and upset, resentment flowing like hot lava between them — not the intended outcome.

By fighting fire with fire, you give your child negative reinforcement and role model being out of control. Don't fall into the coercive cycle trap. Next time you feel the urge to lash out, remember that you are only making the situation worse for both of you.

Your prime parenting directive should always be building a strong, trusting relationship with your kids. To that aim, you mustn't take the bait when your child seems to be purposefully trying to goad you. Discipline strategy does not work when you're angry. It works when you're calm. Learn to meditate or, even better, give yourself a time-out. Say "I need a break," and role model emotional awareness by locking yourself in the bathroom for ten minutes.

developmental job to figure out how they fit into society (including the small society of the family), and to question everything. Authority figures are natural targets. Every argument they pick or rule they break is a test of what they can get away with, what happens when they challenge you, and whether you still love them if they say something awful.

Incidentally, teens will try to manipulate you in other ways, too. Accusing. Crying. But even then, they might not be doing it on purpose. If they grow up learning that crying gets them what they want 15 percent of the time, they will play those odds 100 percent of the time. *Charlie and the Chocolate Factory*'s Veruca Salt yelled, "I want it NOW!" and she got it. Why would she change her behavior if her father always did her bidding?

Despite a teenager's biological imperative to challenge your rules, you can scaffold compliance with this fixed-action pattern that's been designed to shape your child's or teen's behavior:

1. Direct with a calm voice.

2. Issue a warning for noncompliance with the same tone.

3. Give a short-term, small-dose punishment *consistently*.

4. Enforce the punishment without waffling.

5. Repeat as necessary.

If you stick with this pattern, your kid will learn to do what she needs to do to avoid consequences.

Warning: Before her behavior improves, you might have to withstand what we call an "extinction burst." It will get worse before it gets better. In therapy, we see this phenomenon often in family environments where everyone screams at each other. They are habituated to anger "working." But if you buck that entrenched dynamic, you can drag your family out of its (loud, hostile) rut.

The key is not caving in during one of those extinction bursts. Say you take away a teen's phone for noncompliance, and she rails at you, "You don't care if I have friends! We're group texting about weekend plans, and I need to be on it!" and so on. Role model empathy by listening and compromise by saying, "You can earn back phone privileges if you're well behaved over the course of the night."

If you give in because you feel bad for her or are worn down by her whining, you are committing the parental sin of inconsistency, and you will lose all credibility. Instead, communicate calmly that the consequence is short term but fixed. It's the only way kids will understand that you mean business.

Scaffolding Compliance in the Real World

When calling a kid to the dinner table, make your request with a neutral tone, "Please come to the table." Give her a second chance by repeating the directive, word for word. If she still doesn't listen, in the same neutral tone, say, "If you don't come to the table in the next three minutes, you will lose your iPhone for tomorrow." If that doesn't work, next level it by saying, "You didn't come to the table. Your phone will need to be checked in to its dock now and you can't touch it again for twenty-four hours. Now come to dinner." You can bet she'll show up that time.

Say your teenager did not put her dishes in the sink despite repeated requests.

Your instinct might be to react with anger and frustration. But if you let loose and say, "I had a long hard day and all I ask is that you do one thing. *Is that so freakin' hard?*" your speech will probably inspire "reactance"—a psychological term that means, basically, "You can't tell me what to do!"

Instead, repeat in a neutral tone, "Please put your dishes in the sink" until she does it.

After she complies, role model gratitude by saying, "Thanks. I really appreciate it when you help out around the house."

Being the Not-So-Bad Guy

At the Child Mind Institute, we don't like to use the word *punishment*. Punishment sounds punitive, like it's supposed to hurt.

Parenting should never be about inflicting pain and suffering on your child. And yet, Gen X and Millennial parents, thanks to *their* Boomer and Silent Gen parents, grew up believing that if punishments didn't inflict shame, guilt, loneliness, hunger, then kids wouldn't "learn their lesson." Too bad the lesson was, "My parents are cruel."

Unless a child cries or begs for mercy, you might doubt that a punishment is effective or impactful at all. If the kid shrugs it off or reacts to punishment with good cheer, you might think, *It's not enough. Should I scale up? Ground her for another weekend?*

Short answer: No. Consequences don't have to hurt to work.

A child doesn't have to demonstrate pain to reassure you that you're doing a good job as a disciplinarian. Remember, the scaffolding objective is to shape their behavior, not to make them suffer. If you issue a consequence, like grounding them for a weekend, you have made your point. Upping the ante just to get a reaction is overkill.

When delivering consequences, "Almost act like a robot or a cyborg," says Dr. Lee. "If you become emotional, you're doing what we call 'borrowing worry.' For example, when parents see their child not doing her homework, they start to borrow worry, thinking, *She's not going to pass the class, she won't get into a good college, she's going to be dependent on me for the rest of her life.* Parents borrowing worry adds to the intensity of their response in that moment, even though it's not called for." What's really going on when a teen slacks off is just developmentally appropriate, typical testing behavior. Parents don't help the situation if they're bogged down by their own negative thought process.

"Borrowing worry is a trap we set for ourselves," says Dr. Lee. "We want to stay focused on what is in front of us and, with dispassion, think about the best way to address a child's or teen's consequential behavior." We urge parents to stay calm and neutral. If that's not possible for you in that moment, take a break until you can regain self-control.

Attention Seekers

A child's breaking the rules can be a call for attention, a behavior that can follow them long into adulthood. I'm sure you can think of a few over-forty-year-olds off the top of your head who are hotly engaged in this strategy right now.

Kids want attention to be big, bold, and immediate. They don't care as much whether it's positive or negative. Young kids and teenagers have figured out that the quickest route to getting big, bold, and immediate attention is to behave badly.

Instead of concentrating on what your attention-seeking kid is saying, look at how you respond to it.

Are you in close proximity to your kid or far away?

Did the conversation last a while, or was it really short?

What tone did you use?

What volume?

Use the plank of awareness about how you may have reinforced negative behavior by rewarding it with your attention, even if it's negative. In the attention-seeking game, louder, closer, bigger, and more intense wins. So up the intensity of your praise when he does the right thing and lower the volume when he's doing the wrong thing. So, if you yell at your kid at level ten intensity, then you had better make sure to praise him at level eleven or twelve intensity. The attention he receives for negative behavior shouldn't be louder and more intense than the attention he receives for positive behavior.

Grounding for Life?

The fifteen-year-old daughter of a friend of mine, I'll call her Melanie, waited until her parents were asleep, found the car keys, and went for a joy ride that lasted for all of three blocks before she ran into a fire hydrant. The parents got a call from the police at midnight. They ran to the scene of the crash to find their daughter crying in the back of a police cruiser, the front bumper of their car crumpled, and the hydrant spouting water.

"It was like a car insurance commercial," said Melanie's exasperated mom. "Except our daughter wasn't on our policy." All told, between the fines and repair costs, the daughter's "escapade in the Escalade" cost her parents thousands.

They were *furious*! "She could have killed herself or someone else!" the mom said. "We've canceled her driver's ed. Forget about getting her license or a car. She'll never get behind the wheel again!"

Although what Melanie did was wrong and put people and property at risk, her parents issuing the driving equivalent of "grounded for life" was an ineffective strategy.

"We don't want to take something away for so long that the kid forgets about it or that the reinforcer loses its potency," says Dr. Lee. The reckless driver might be upset about her lifelong driving ban for a while but if she knows it's never going to happen, she'll adapt by relying on friends for rides and taking Uber. Eventually, she won't care about not getting her license. A reinforcer only works if the child cares about it.

"When I was a young kid, my brothers had nunchucks and we would always hit each other with them," says Dr. Lee. "One day, my parents had enough. They put the nunchucks on the top of the fridge where we couldn't reach them and said we could never play with them again. They're still there, a decade later. Taking them away wasn't a very good parenting technique, though. My brothers and I thought, *Okay, nunchucks are gone forever. We'll find something else to hit each other with*. If my parents had said, 'The nunchucks are going on top of the fridge for three days. If you play nice, you can have them back,' we would have complied. But instead, we just forgot about them."

The potency of the consequence shouldn't have to do with duration. If children feel like there's no way for them to ever earn back the object or privilege with good behavior, then they don't bother trying to adapt. Grounding for life, or putting nunchucks on the fridge forever, teaches kids not to bother trying to be better.

Don't Try This at Home

Hit your child.

Say you want to reinforce and model nonviolent behavior to a child who nunchucks his sister. Do you take away the weapon for a short duration, or do you whack the kid with the nunchuck yourself?

I have never advocated inflicting pain on a child for any reason. No part of scaffold parenting includes physically or emotionally harming a child. Spanking does both. The latest research from the American Academy of Pediatrics draws the same conclusion. Another recent study found that children who were exposed to corporal punishment have smaller brains and lower IQs than the control group. Dr. David Anderson, a Child Mind Institute psychologist, told the *Washington Post* in December 2018, "The negative effects of spanking outweigh any momentary payoff that might be apparent when a behavior stops. You can find alternate punishments that are less psychologically injurious and can still reduce the behaviors in question, such as the removal of privileges. If you want to teach a child how to navigate situations with better interpersonal skills or with more respect, the only way to do that is to work with the child in those situations to teach, promote, and reinforce the skills you'd like them to practice."

Monitor for Underlying Causes

Gordon was increasingly frustrated that his eleven-year-old son Jasper was always late for the school bus. "No matter how early he got up or how much I yelled at him to hurry up, he would miss the bus and then I had to drive him to school," said Gordon. "It wasn't just the bus, though. He was late for dinner and activities all the time. I increased his chores to be more helpful around the house, since his lateness was so unhelpful for everyone else. He did the chores, no problem, no pushback. But it didn't matter. The next morning, we'd go through the same pattern all over again."

I asked Gordon to do some at-home investigating. Instead of yelling at Jasper to "hurry up!" from the bottom of the stairs, he needed to monitor his son getting ready for school to better understand the holdup.

"What I saw nearly broke my heart," said Gordon. "Jasper wasn't goofing off in his room. He was pacing between the door and his bed, over and over again. When I asked him what he was doing, he said, 'I lost count. Now I have to start over.' Then he started pacing again, counting his steps. They had to be an even number, and he had to make an even number of laps, before he could safely leave his room."

Jasper wasn't willfully missing the bus. He had obsessive-compulsive disorder (OCD), a brain-based disorder of having unwanted, stressful thoughts and fears that can only be alleviated with compulsive rituals. Jasper told his clinician that he was consumed by the idea that if he left the house in the morning without pacing his room thirty times, with six steps per lap, that the bus would crash, or his parents would get in an accident on their drive to work. He never explained what he was doing out of confusion and embarrassment. "I was doing it for Mom and Dad, to protect them from getting hurt," he said. "I felt like I had to do it, but if I told Dad, he'd drag me out of my room before I could finish, and then something bad would happen."

We worked with Jasper and his parents to treat his OCD with a combination of medication and cognitive behavioral therapy, and after a few months, he was able to stop pacing and make the bus. If Gordon hadn't changed his own routine, and checked on the cause of his son's lateness, he'd still be trying to apply consequences for bad behavior, and Jasper would still be suffering in silent shame.

When consequences don't make an impact on behavior, we as clinicians take a closer look at what's really going on. There might be a bigger issue than you realized.

Is It OCD?

NORMAL	PROBLEM	DISORDER
Your child has realistic fears that, after a discussion with you, are mollified.	Your child has exaggerated anxieties about germs, illness, accidents, bad things happening. He expresses his fears to you several times a week.	Your child has exaggerated and unrealistic fears and thoughts about germs and contamination, or his things being in disarray.
She repeats certain behaviors or tasks, like rebuilding the same block structure over and over, but she eventually masters it and moves on to a new game.	He likes things to be "just so" in his room and gets very upset if he thinks someone has rearranged his things.	He is compelled to perform rituals like handwashing, counting, touching things, hoarding, and cleaning that give him a temporary "just right" feeling.
She asks questions, follow-up questions, and once she's satisfied with the answers, moves on to a new topic or activity.	He shows signs of being superstitious about walking on a certain side of the street or only doing things in the right order but can change routine if he has to get something done or with parental supervision, without experiencing distress.	He has "magical thinking," that if he does something, like scratch his arm, he can prevent bad things from happening.
She isn't afraid of germs and has to be reminded to wash her hands after using the bathroom and before meals.		He seeks reassurance from adults about any anxiety.
		He asks questions repeatedly.
		He can't function normally because his rituals distract him in the classroom and hinder friendships.

Let the Punishment Fit the Crime

All attention is reinforcing. To reinforce opposite (good) behavior, take away the thing kids want the most (attention) when they demonstrate bad behavior. Time-outs are appropriate, effective, and endorsed by the American Academy of Pediatrics and the American Academy of Child and Adolescent Psychiatry, even for children with ADHD and ODD. Some parents (and experts) aren't too sure about separating a child from the group, that isolation, even for a minute or two, might cause anxiety or depression. According to a longitudinal study of fourteen hundred families and children from ages three to twelve, there is no downside to using time-outs to reinforce positive behavior.

Some tips: Label the behavior before sending him to the time-out chair, as in, "If you hit your friend, you get a time-out"; choose a consistent place devoid of toys, TVs, phones, and computers; keep it to one minute per age (a five-year-old gets five minutes); ignore him for the duration; when it's over, praise him for good behavior, as in, "You're playing nice, great job!"

Making a tween or teen sit in a chair to reinforce and shape behavior isn't realistic or age-appropriate. Back in my day, you could send an adolescent to his room to force him to quietly contemplate his actions. But nowadays, a teen will say, "Cool. I was going there anyway."

For teens, use the time-out technique with his favorite objects. Their iPad, cell phone, or car gets into time-out until the teen can earn it back via target behavior and demonstrating adaptive skills. If a teen misses curfew, to earn her phone back, she must come home on time every day for three or four days in a row to prove that she's capable of being reliable. If she misses curfew again, repeat the consequence with consistency and predictability. It might seem like you're stuck on repeat, that every four days, she breaks curfew and you take away the phone. But don't give up. Eventually, the teen will realize that it's just easier for her to comply.

When I was growing up, parents would punish their kids by declaring, "No dessert for a week!" Cake takes a time-out. Parents would send their children to bed without dinner.

It's inappropriate and flat-out wrong to deprive a child of food as a form of punishment. Look, we're not in *Oliver!*. No child should learn to associate parental disapproval with hunger. It can set up food issues for life, sometimes serious eating disorders. I've found this form of punishment is hard for parents to give up if their parents did it to them. As a scaffolding parent, you're taking a kinder path, one that includes praise and dessert. You will not fail your kids by letting them eat cake (in moderation), even when they've done something wrong.

Rita discovered that her daughter Erin was stealing money from her. If Rita's phone was left on the counter unlocked, Erin quickly sent herself $20 via Venmo. Since Rita hardly ever used that app, she was none the wiser . . . until she got an email with that month's transaction history and realized what was going on.

If possible, to determine the appropriate consequence, start with a discussion about the "crime," in this case, a theft. I recommended that Erin's parents sit down with her and ask, not interrogate, some questions:

"Why did you feel the need to steal?"

"What were you spending the money on?"

"How did you feel about it?"

"Do you understand that stealing is wrong?"

Rita reported, "At first, she denied it. But I showed her my account history of five $20 transactions from my account to hers. Who else would do that but her? The Venmo fairies? After showing her the evidence, she shut down completely and just stared at the wall. Do we have to punish her now for stealing *and* lying?"

First order of business was to put Erin's phone, the means of her transgression, into a time-out. Her parents deleted her Venmo account.

Since Erin was not willing to discuss it, I advised her parents to give her a chance to think about what she'd done and delay meting out consequences for lying. The delay also gave Rita and her partner a chance to agree on what to do instead of impulsively under- or overconsequencing. Since Erin tried to get something for nothing, the target adaptive skill was to teach her that, to get what you want, you have to work for it. "I handed her a pair of rubber gloves, a bucket, and a mop and sent her to clean out the basement," said Rita. "I felt a bit like the evil stepmother in *Cinderella*. But, then again, Cinderella didn't steal." As for the lying, it seemed like overkill to punish her for trying to protect herself, even if it was wrong.

Obviously, there are levels of bad behavior. No one would equate leaving the milk on the counter with throwing a house party when you are out of town. You need to respond appropriately, or, as the case may be, not react at all. Save your most severe consequences for major offenses.

If a child lies about someone else, have her retract it and tell the truth to any people the lie might have harmed. A lie told online should result in a short-dose ban on social media.

If a child cheats, first figure out why the cheating happened. Was it because the child didn't understand the material and felt like cheating was the only way he'd pass? Then he needs a tutor *and* a consequence.

If a child breaks curfew, drinks, does drugs, limit freedoms by cutting off contact with friends for one weekend. If she does it again, make it two weekends.

If a kid studies hard for a test but fails, what should the consequence be? Limit fun time and replace TV, games, and friends with hours of study?

No. You scaffold by rewarding good behavior and correcting bad behavior. Reward the effort of studying hard. All success comes from effort. Associating effort with success will lead to better performance eventually. The outcome—a bad grade—doesn't really matter. To scaffold a child who works hard and fails, arrange for extra help with the teacher, hire a tutor, or have some educational testing.

Enforcement Strategy

When enforcing consequences, scaffolding parents always play the good cop, the nice one who offers a beverage and speaks softly.

You might be tempted to play the bad cop if your child doesn't go along with your consequences, but that will only make things worse.

"We took away our son's phone because he was on it all night instead of studying for a test," said a father in our practice. "We said he could have it back if he studies hard for the next one, and he tearfully agreed. We put his phone in the kitchen drawer. I would have bet my life he was on board with the plan. The next night, he was studying for a test, as he promised he'd do. Just out of curiosity, I opened the kitchen drawer to make sure his phone was still there. It was. But when I picked it up, it was warm. I asked my son to unlock it, checked the usage history, and saw he'd been on and off his phone all day."

If a teen secretly uses a phone or computer when it's supposed to be powered down, you can increase the duration of the ban in incremental doses. You can also use an app to track a kid's phone usage and movements. Add additional time to your teen's grounding or take away additional privileges if she's not where

Scaffolding Consequences for Teens

- **Structure**. Establish house rules and a fixed pattern of how you react to their behavior. Consequences should never come as a surprise; they should know what to expect for breaking the rules the first, second, or third time.

- **Support**. Support their learning adaptive skills by making the punishment fit the crime. Separate breaking the rules from normal, developmental testing-out behavior that empowers growth.

- **Encouragement**. Encourage compliance by playing the good cop, keeping a neutral, robotic tone, avoiding the coercive cycle of "whoever yells the loudest/longest wins," and sticking to your rules, despite their best efforts to budge you.

she's supposed to be. When you confront her, remember to maintain the cyborg neutral expression and tone. Enforcement is not emotional or personal. It's just what you have to do to uphold the established household rules.

When my wife and I confronted our son Sam about sneaking vodka into our house and drinking it with a group of his friends before they left for a party, it took everything I had to tolerate my own discomfort in that situation. My instinct was to scream, "Grounded for life!" But that would have role modeled impulsivity, the same behavior that got him into this mess in the first place.

After the three of us agreed to think about it and decide on consequences the next day, my wife and I made a brief appearance at a party my friend was throwing, but we weren't feeling too festive. We knew that, soon, we would have to make some difficult decisions and have some awkward conversations with the parents of the other two boys who'd been drinking under our roof.

Incidentally, one of those mothers said to me, "They did it again?" She hadn't shown me the same consideration of telling me what she knew about previous incidents, and I was irritated by her attitude. "What's the big deal, Harold?" she added. "They're just kids being kids." Exactly. That's why they need adults!

It was a tough call, but Linda and I allowed Sam to go on his planned ski trip, which was paid for and would disappoint our friend's family as much as it hurt our son if he didn't go. But when he returned, for the next month, he was not allowed to hang out with his crew after school or on weekends. For a social kid who loved being the mayor of his friend group, it was a harsh consequence. But he was not locked up in his room. Linda, Sam, and I went out to dinner and the movies on the weekends. Granted, a fourteen-year-old might not think chilling with his parents on a Saturday night is fun. But that was sort of the whole point. A punishment doesn't have to be agonizing. But it has to feel like a sacrifice to have an impact.

And it did. Sam didn't bring alcohol into our house again (I think). If he had, and we found out about it, we would have handled it the same way. In fact, Sam was such a stickler about not smoking marijuana until he graduated from high school, his friends got on board with his abstinence as well, by not bothering to pass him the joint when they smoked as a group.

The upshot is, we taught, and he learned, a valuable lesson—and it wasn't not to drink vodka. It was that if he didn't respect the rules, he'd pay a price. The price wasn't horrible; paying it didn't hurt him unduly. But his actions caused reactions, and they always would.

Nail Down Those Planks!

Being a disciplinarian doesn't have to be soul crushing for you as long as you tread lightly yet firmly on the planks.

Patience

• It'll test your patience when a kid breaks the same rule again and again, despite your sticking to the fixed pattern. But keep going. If you remain calm, you'll wear him down.

Warmth

• Remember to be the good cop, the one who asks, "Can I get you a Coke? Are you comfortable? Good. I know this is tough, but let's talk about what happened last night." The objective is to teach her to follow the rules, and you'll get her on your side if you're kind and compassionate.

Awareness

• Always check your tone, volume, and posture when meting out consequences.

• Be conscious of whether your punishment style is a holdover from your own childhood, and make kinder, more compassionate changes that are aligned with scaffolding techniques.

Dispassion

• Try to come off as robotic when you set and enforce consequences.

Monitoring

• Don't assume the child will comply. Make sure he does by monitoring his phone usage, physical location, and chores.

10

Support Unconditionally

The architecture of your child's building might not be to your taste. You prefer a proud Federal or no-nonsense Colonial. But your child is growing into a luxury condo.

Your personal preferences do not matter. What does matter is that the child's building is stable and strong, and that your scaffold is there to provide structure and to catch pieces that fall off. If you try to change his condo into a whimsical Victorian (you just love turrets and dormers!) or fool yourself into believing that it'll one day miraculously transform into your dream house, your scaffold won't fit the construction or provide the necessary support. Accept his building architecture for what it is, even if it seems strange to you. When it's all done, he'll live in it. You won't.

When Barbara, mother to then nine-year-old Leah, came to the Child Mind Institute for the first time, she'd done so at the suggestion of Leah's fourth-grade teachers. "They had a meeting about my daughter, and then called me in to tell me what they all decided. It felt like an ambush," said Barbara. "The ringleader was the math teacher, who spoke for the group. I'd never liked this man. He seemed hostile to Leah from the start. He told me that the school had brought in learning and behavioral specialists to observe my daughter in the classroom *without telling me*! I was furious. Was that even legal? What gave them the right to have people spy on my daughter?"

For the record, it would have been better policy to inform Barbara that her child was being observed, but many schools have specialists who are brought in or on staff. It's considered due diligence, not spying. The objective is early prevention for students who might have a learning or behavioral problem. The earlier parents and educators intervene, the greater the likelihood of the child learning skills to overcome a disability. However, I also understand how the idea of someone watching your child, looking for problems, can feel intrusive and Big Brother-y. Barbara's first instinct was to protect and defend her daughter.

"What did the specialist say?" I asked.

"They think Leah's anxious, has an attention disorder, and OCD," she replied, outraged. "It's ridiculous!"

"Why do they think she has OCD?"

Barbara waved it off. "She has this annoying habit where she pulls on her eyelashes. It's just a tick. Nothing for anyone to worry about."

"Does she pull them out?"

Barbara shook her head, but said, "Yes. But they grow back."

It sounded like Leah might have trichotillomania, aka "hair pulling disorder," which is classified as a type of obsessive-compulsive disorder, affects approximately 1 percent of the U.S. population, and often co-occurs with anxiety. The sufferer has a compulsive urge to pull out his or her hair on the head or anywhere on the body. The disorder can be treated with cognitive behavioral therapy, medication, or a combination of both, but it is very tenacious and needs intervention. It's unrealistic to think that Leah would just stop on her own one day.

But Barbara seemed resistant to her daughter's having any mental health problems, let alone being open to treatment. I convinced her to bring in Leah for an assessment, and we'd discuss our findings. When the girl arrived, I noticed immediately that she had almost no eyelashes on both lids, and that her eyebrows were patchy. She was quiet and quite anxious. During her two-hour assessment, her mind wandered, and we had to gently bring her back to the task at hand.

I agreed with the specialists from Leah's school—ADHD, anxiety disorder, and OCD—and shared my diagnosis with Barbara. I explained that despite Leah's problems, she could have a normal, happy life—and full eyelashes—if we began treatment as soon as possible.

Barbara looked at me like I had lost my mind, and said, "You can't diagnose my daughter with all that."

"I can't?"

"What if she wants to be president one day?"

"I think we're getting ahead of ourselves," I said.

Barbara took Leah and left the Institute. I had no idea if we'd see them again.

Two things were going on here. The first part is about parental expectations. The second is about the stigma of mental health disorders. Both of Barbara's blocks would have to be overcome before she could support her daughter unconditionally.

The Gap Between Expectations and Reality

Most of us don't believe our kids will really grow up to be president, but we do have dreams for them. It's hard to accept your child's deficits, as well as his assets, if they don't line up with what you'd envisioned. You might feel disappointed your kids don't hug you and say "I love you" after every argument like a sitcom family. It might be that you wanted a sports star and got a klutz. You assumed your child would be an easy-A student, but he has dyslexia. She isn't the social butterfly you were. Maybe you just expected your child to be more obedient. In whatever way, your expectations might clash with reality.

Many parents put on blinders about their child's natural

limitations. Barbara's outrage at all the trained professionals who were just trying to help her daughter is one example. I'm also thinking of a father I know who pushed his son into engineering grad school even though the boy struggled in science classes throughout his education. After a semester, he failed out. The father's refusal to align expectation and reality set the kid up for failure, made him feel bad about himself, and caused tension and stress in the relationship that hasn't gone away.

One of the most important pieces of advice we give to parents, one that is hard for many to understand, is, "You don't decide who your child is." Your child is his or her own person, and he has his own path and his own journey to follow. That may not be what you hoped, but for you to decide what his journey should be shows a lack of empathy.

Scaffolding means providing support and encouragement to your child no matter what her reality happens to be. Perhaps in your day, parents were authoritarians, benign dictators, and their word was law. If Dad said you were going to grow up to be a doctor, then you applied to medical school, even if you swooned at the sight of blood. But the research shows that when children are involved in deciding their own future, they make better decisions with better outcomes. Parents who give their kids the freedom to make and regret bad decisions are actually helping them learn to make smarter ones. To stop being authoritarian and allow your child to be her own person, stand down and let her make up her own mind.

For kids, childhood should be a time to believe anything is possible. A little girl who loves to sing should be allowed to dream of Carnegie Hall, even if she can't hit a high C. Kids will reckon with adjusting their dreams when they grow up and enter the real world. With parental support, children will have an easier transition from the fantasy of "I want to be a movie star!" toward a reality that is happy and satisfying.

"Once, I gave a talk to a group of two hundred parents in a wealthy area in Illinois," says Dr. Mark Reinecke, clinical director

Try This at Home

Let your kid call the shots.

Encourage a child's executive functioning by letting her make age-appropriate decisions. Make it clear that you still have veto power. As always, model decisiveness and reinforce your child's decision-making competence with praise.

- **Toddlers.** Introduce the concept of decision-making by presenting limited choices. Eating their veggies is not up for discussion but let them decide if their carrots should be cut into sticks or circles. They have to dress appropriately for the weather, but a toddler can choose between two pairs of pants.

- **Kids.** Expand the number of choices from one of two, to one of three to five. Teach them that once they make a decision—cookie, piece of candy, or fruit—they have to stick with it. Next time, they can make a different choice, but they'll have to wait for the opportunity. Build in a pause—"Think carefully"—before they can make a snap decision.

- **Tweens.** Up the stakes by giving them bigger choices, like activities and privileges. Again, If they choose karate over ballet, they have to stick with it for the entire cycle. Allow them to make some bad decisions and scaffold them through the evaluation and learning process so they'll make wiser ones in the future.

- **Teens.** Drive home the link between consequences and decision-making and that their choices impact other people. When they drive drunk, for example, they're making a decision for every other person on the road. When they decide to blow curfew, it affects their tired, worried parents back at home. If you teach teens to be considerate, trust that they will make the right decisions most of the time.

of the Child Mind Institute in the San Francisco Bay Area. "And I said, 'We want to teach our children that you can be happy and successful in life without going to an Ivy League college.' Half the people in the room stood up and started applauding, and half of them were horrified. The horrified half said things like, 'I went to Harvard and my son will, too.' I asked, 'Why?' Why does a child have to follow in the parent's footsteps? They don't and shouldn't. Every child should find her own way, and find her own areas of strength and competence, and things that excite her and that engage her. But it's going to be different from what the parents expect."

When you cling to expectations, it can damage the parent-child relationship and do severe harm to your child's ability to cope and function independently. "I was working with a young man who was having difficulty in college," says Dr. Reinecke. "He had to take a leave of absence and come home. His parents' shame about his not succeeding in college was so great, they would not allow him to go outside the house on his own during the day because they were afraid the neighbors would see him and realize he'd left college. They made him put on a hat and sunglasses when he was in the car and they were pulling into the driveway."

The reason we send kids to college is so that they will get an education and learn to live independently. The irony here is that the parents were so full of shame, they isolated the son and made it impossible for him to be an independent person. At nineteen, he couldn't take a walk to a sandwich shop to buy himself lunch. "I asked him, 'Do you want to be home?' and he said, 'No!'" says Dr. Reinecke.

The tension between parents and the college dropout was based on all their exceedingly high expectations—including the son's. "He told me that he felt like he had to win the Nobel Prize in literature, that if he didn't, he'd consider himself a failure," says Dr. Reinecke. "I told him, 'You're a teenager! Most people win that in their sixties.'" Next-level perfectionism was what sent him off the rails at college. Whether it came from his parents or from inside himself almost didn't matter. The problem existed, and it had to be dealt with. "We talked about his having reasonable expectations, and to remind himself of the things he had accomplished. He was very bad at giving himself credit for doing just all right," said Dr. Reinecke. "If he couldn't learn to do that, he'd be locked away in his parents' house for a long, long time."

Eventually, the young man enrolled in another college and started over, and he did well there. The college was farther away from home, which was a good idea in this case. The key to his success was putting aside shame about failing to meet unrealistic expectations, and to just live with both feet on the ground.

Why do parents expect or want their kids to walk the same path they did? Because they were happy and fulfilled every moment of their entire lives and wish the same for their children? I have yet to meet someone who could make that claim. People have a psychological leaning toward taking comfort in the familiar, even if the familiar isn't comfortable. It gives parents a cozy feeling of continuity for their kids to go to the same schools and camps, to have the same interests and play the same sports. When their child succeeds, it validates their past experiences. When I hear parents say things like "That's my boy!" or "She's a chip off the old block!" after their kid scores a goal or wins a prize, I inwardly cringe. They might as well be bragging, "I have great genes!"

The flip side of that is when a child stumbles on his parents' path. The child who doesn't succeed in the arena you chose for him is also "your boy" and "a chip off the old block." Your children deserve the same love, even if they aren't just like you. Prove your unconditional support by allowing them to diverge from your path and find their own.

Accentuate the Positives

Of course you want your children to be their best selves and to be happy in the long term. It's extremely helpful to examine what that really means. One way to see your children's future long-term happiness is for them to grow into adults who can function in the world, live independently, seek out their own happiness, and know what they're good at.

To scaffold a child to seek out his own happiness, teach him to recognize his positive attributes on a consistent basis. "Actually write them down, highlight them, think about them in a consistent way," says Child Mind Institute psychologist Dr. Stephanie Lee. "Recently, I said to a mom, 'You have told me that your son is really funny. You talked about his humor. Over the next week, I want you to write down three jokes that he told you and bring those back to me so that we can focus on that good stuff. It's not just parents reminding kids what they do well, it's helping parents see more of the positives in their kids, too," she says.

One pitfall is when you convince yourself of positives that don't really exist.

I'm friends with a couple in Silicon Valley. Tim, the father, fifty, looks twenty-five. He's athletic and is always outdoors. His wife is the same way. They are what I call "California fit." We all went hiking together and I could barely keep up.

His nine-year-old son, Ethan, is a bit awkward, an indoors-type kid who is sharp as a tack. As an only child, he banters with his mom and dad like a pseudo adult.

The weekend I stayed with them, I was surprised to hear about Ethan's sports-heavy schedule packed with lacrosse and baseball practices.

I said, "I didn't realize he's so jocky."

Tim said, "Well, we're trying to find his sport."

I looked at Ethan and he shrugged. I could tell that he was just playing along, putting on the uniform, being "game." And that was fine, for now. At a certain point, sports get very competitive. The kids get really into it and can be savagely cruel to their less-competent teammates. Parents scream from the sidelines like crazy people and aren't always so nice to the kids who drop the ball. Did Tim want to put his son through all that? These were smart, thoughtful people, but Tim had a blind spot. His son was never going to be the athlete he wanted him to be.

Scaffolding is about recognizing all your child's assets *and* deficits. And then, once you have a clear view of the way things really are, you can work toward reshaping deficits into assets. For example, anxiety that is harnessed can be reshaped into productivity. I joke with parents that if I didn't have anxiety, I wouldn't have completed a research fellowship.

Stubbornness can be reshaped into persistence. The child who digs in her heels might grow up to use that persistence in a career where it's an essential ingredient to success, like law or science research.

Macy, twelve, came to the Institute because of her social anxiety. Her mother, Susan, was afraid that her daughter would never make friends because she sat by herself and drew sketches in her notebook. We asked Macy to bring her notebook to therapy. She'd created cartoon panel drawings of human-size cats in a classroom setting, like a graphic novel. They were quite impressive from an artistic standpoint. But what really interested our clinician was how she portrayed people as animals, assigning character traits to them and making it all very funny. Her social anxiety might have made it hard for her to talk to her classmates, but it hadn't stopped her from observing them and learning about social interactions. Our clinician pointed out to Susan that Macy had a talent for drawing and observing human nature, a gift she could use in any number of future careers—including psychology. Macy could also develop her powers of observation as a coping skill in her relationships once she learned how to overcome her social anxiety. Suddenly, the once-fearful mother was proud of her daughter's deficit. The shift in Susan's attitude caused an immediate, impactful change in their relationship. All it took was a little reframing.

Reinforce Yourself

You have your own work to do in order to scaffold your kids. It's only natural for you to push your children to do things you either did successfully or to right your wrongs, or to want to share your interests with your kids. But it's essential that you recognize your own biases, actively question their validity, and work to change your behavior in real time.

Gary was a teenage boy who had zero interest in watching professional sports on TV. His father, Ed, had been a lifelong New York Giants and Mets fan and had many loving memories of going to ball games and Super Bowl parties with his father. Ed had a very hard time accepting that Gary just wasn't into something that was so important and special to him. So whenever there was a big game on TV, Ed insisted Gary sit and watch it. When he was younger, Gary would do what his father demanded, but he couldn't fake excitement when the Giants and Mets won, and he could never satisfy Ed's need for him to learn the players' names and understand the subtleties of sports strategy. It was frustrating for both of them to disappoint the other. As a teen, Gary predictably rebelled, and either refused to watch or would pointedly stare at his phone throughout the game. Ed's attitude was, "What's wrong with him?" until our clinician suggested that the problem was in his own expectations. She suggested that instead of getting stressed out that Gary didn't want to watch games with him, he could just watch on his own or with friends who cared as much as he did.

Reinforce corrections in your own behaviors with rewards. If you give yourself something good, you're more likely to continue making the positive change. Ed the sports-loving father who let his son Gary off the hook could say to himself, *I didn't stress out my son or create tension between us today. Great job, me! I'm going to reward myself with a cold beer!* Keep those cold ones coming to reinforce the change in yourself. (Beer as a parenting tool? You read it here first.)

It's like if you were trying to get in shape, and you made a deal with yourself that if you exercised three times this week, you'd splurge on a new jacket or a nice dessert. This might sound familiar, because I've talked about using external reinforcers earlier in this book with your kids. The strategies you use to change your child's behavior are the same ones you can use to change your own.

If multiple caregivers are involved, reinforcing behavior is that much easier. You can work together as partners to help each other. Ed's wife, Leslie, for example, could reassure Gary that it was okay to do his own thing on Sunday afternoon, and reinforce Ed's letting go of expectations with praise and by having a beer with him. When everyone is working together on a common goal—in this case, a harmonious, accepting relationship between father and son—it's within reach. Once you begin this practice, and you notice your partner backing off on something that he or she traditionally nagged or criticized your kid about, praise him or her for it. Say, "I noticed that you didn't make a big deal out of it, thanks" or "Great job letting that go." The more we praise ourselves, our kids, our partners—the whole village of extended family and friends—the more we're all going to be loving, supportive, and encouraging with each other.

Go There

When you give up on expectations and explore your child's interests, you'll find out that, very often, you have more common ground than you thought. So you might not be artsy and your kid might not be into sports. But maybe the common ground is music. You both love classic rock or show tunes. Once you crack that, you've found something to bond over that is meaningful to you both.

"You have to be accepting and willing to do some things that you might not enjoy as you try to find that common ground," says Dr. Stephanie Lee. "You also have to be willing to have conversations with your kids and be open to hearing things you might not want to hear. Supporting them unconditionally is accepting what they like, what they think, and how they feel, even if it makes you bristle. Teach kids how to explore by participating and trying new things to find common ground and bonding opportunities. A little parental openness and willingness to participate goes a long way."

Dr. Lee mentioned a family she's working with, and her efforts to convince a judgmental father to open up. "Conor is fifteen and he's into skateboarding and gaming. His older sister, Lyla, is into basketball. Their father, Paul, relates to Lyla's interest in sports and goes to all her games and is very involved in looking at colleges with her. As a result, Conor feels left out," she says. "I made a big point about Paul going to watch Conor *just once* at the skateboarding park and coached him about how to behave there, like no eye rolls or judgmental comments." Paul did show up, didn't say anything snarky, and left after twenty minutes when the urge to roll his eyes got too strong. But even that small gesture meant so much to Conor. "It's been months since then, and Conor continues to bring it up in therapy, telling his dad how great it was to look up and see him there. Their relationship is not completely recovered or great by any means, but Paul's showing up was a starting point."

The reason Paul was so negative about skateboarding and gaming was because he doubted that Conor's hobbies would turn into a career. "I said, 'And you think your daughter is going into the WNBA?'" says Dr. Lee. "The father and I could discuss and debate whether professional sports or gaming was a more viable career path. I'd say the odds are about the same. But what I was trying to explain to him was that discouraging what was important to his son was damaging their relationship and preventing them from connecting."

If you can "go there" with your child when he's a kid, you'll establish a closeness that'll last into his adulthood. "It's not the kid's job to come to you. It's your job to go to them. Find out what they like and join them where they want to be," says Dr. Lee.

Scaffolding Acceptance with Children

- **Structure.** The ability to make confident decisions is a valuable life skill. Let your child call (some) shots from toddlerhood to teach him a sense of agency and show him that you accept his opinions and thoughts even if you don't always agree with them. You have veto power, but give some latitude.

- **Support.** Concentrate on validating kids' emotions, not forcing them to be more like you, and participating in their interests. Try to find common ground so that you can do things together.

- **Encouragement.** Help your child to be his best self by noticing and praising the positive attributes while keeping it real about his deficits, too. Model acceptance of your own assets and deficits, and call attention to them.

The Stigma Is Real

I'd said earlier in this chapter that there were two factors that can keep parents from supporting their kids unconditionally. The first had to do with expectations. The second? The stigma, fear, and shame parents feel about their child's or adolescent's mental health problems.

The stigma of mental illness has greatly diminished over time, but it's still present. Having a diagnosis is essential for treatment, but parents often worry about forever concepts, like "he'll never get better," "she'll be on meds for the rest of her life," and "she'll be saddled with this label forever." Many reject a diagnosis out of hand due to fears about overdiagnosis and overmedication. Those fears don't change the fact that some kids really do have problems and parents need to accept this.

"I work with a family right now where the mom just cannot say that her child has autism," says Dr. Lee. "He's almost seventeen. There is no question that he is autistic. She knows he has problems, but she can't use the word. I've told her that he was the same guy before and after his diagnosis. We need to have a diagnosis because it informs the care the child and parents are receiving. But a diagnosis doesn't define the child. He's not a bunch of checked boxes. If a parent gets stuck on the word *autism*, or any other diagnosis, we might say from the start, 'Let's not talk about that. Let's talk about what the child or teen is doing well, and what he's struggling with. Let's talk about the goals that you have for him, and whether those goals are realistic.' What we consistently find is that when parents concentrate on supporting their child to reach realistic goals, they are more accepting of the diagnosis."

The parents of nonclinical kids can do the same thing: From your scaffold, you have a clear, unobstructed view of your child's building. You can spot the strengths he can build upon, and his limitations that you can help him to reshape into strengths. Everyone has things he's really good at. Everyone has things he needs to work on. There is no shame in having a problem, whatever it might be. Instead of getting hung up on labels—anxious, depressed, compulsive—focus your energy on what's going to move the needle for your child.

For kids with mental health disorders, intervention will move them forward. Ignoring or denying problems sets them back. We say that every kid has limitations. Well, every adult does, too. Your limitation might be getting stuck on what's wrong with your child, preventing you from seeing all the great things about her.

Moving the Needle

When Joshua was two, I took him to some of his activities and was amazed by how articulate some of the girls his age were. They could speak in complete sentences, like, "Mommy, can I please have a peanut butter and jelly sandwich with the crusts cut off the bread?" At that point, Joshua was just pointing and grunting. I remember saying to Linda, "How come we had the slow kid? Thank God he's good-looking!" His language development was very average, but compared to those extraordinary girls, he seemed tragic. It was shocking to me that he wasn't a genius.

By nursery school, my opinion shifted. It wasn't that he wasn't smart. He was just a reticent, pensive kid with a keen attention to detail. His preschool teachers used to call him professor because, if they did any routine out of order, he'd say, "No, that's not the way you do it. You broke the sequence." Other than that, he didn't talk much at all.

One of Joshua's uncles was socially reticent. At a birthday party for my nephew, I watched my brother-in-law and Josh walking hand in hand, and noticed their strong resemblance, their slightly awkward gait and prominent ears. I thought, *He's got the social anxiety gene.* The same way my colleague Mark Reinecke had his revelation and announced to his wife, "We're going to raise a brave child!," I made a vow the day of that birthday party, "I'm going to raise a socially competent child." Not that I intended to turn Josh into someone he wasn't. He would never be a chatterbox. But we could give him the tools he needed to engage more fully in the world. Learn to accept your child for who he is, recognize his assets and deficits objectively, and support him to move the needle in the right direction to correct problems with realistic expectations.

My wife and I started scaffolding Josh about how to interact with people, practicing a firm handshake and teaching him to look people in the eye until you can see the color of their irises. We went over endless "you" questions. People like to talk about themselves and if he got them going, he didn't have to speak too much himself.

When Josh was in second grade, the mother of one of our son's classmates was the head of a nonprofit organization that raised money to maintain Central Park. Through this mom, our family was invited to a charity event at the park near the boathouse on the lake. Henry Stern, the New York City commissioner of parks and recreation, was at the party, and he came up to introduce himself to me. I proceeded to introduce Henry to Joshua. Joshua gave him a handshake (firm not fishy; check).

I said, "Josh, Mr. Stern is the commissioner of parks."

Joshua knew he was supposed to ask "you" questions, and said, "What do you do?"

"I make sure the lake is filled with water and the horses are fed and the grass is green."

They were chatting! My wife and I were optimistic! Josh was doing so well.

"That is a very interesting job," he said. "How do you get a job like that?"

Henry, a very quirky guy, said, "When you go to school tomorrow, look around and figure out which one of your classmates is going to become the mayor one day, and stay friendly with him."

Linda and I laughed. The joke went over Joshua's head but that was okay. When Henry said goodbye, he and Josh shook hands again. Joshua leaned in and put his face so close to Henry's, he could have been doing an ophthalmological examination.

After Henry walked away, Josh said, "His eyes are brown."

Linda whispered into my ear, "He needs a little more rehearsal."

That might be true, but we'd turned a kid who rarely talked into one who could chat with confidence at an adult party with a VIP guest. I chalked that up as a scaffolding victory.

Acceptance Is a Thankless Job

Major acceptance challenge for parents: You will do a lot of difficult adapting to scaffold a kid you don't necessarily relate to. Don't expect much appreciation for it. I hear this often from parents, that they pay for everything, take the kids everywhere, get them to school, activities, and therapy, and in return, they have to bite their tongues and be endlessly supportive even when their kids act jerky or make boneheaded decisions they know are wrong.

When your child has mental health disorders, parenting can feel even more like "all give, no get." But kids don't ask to be born. They don't ask to be anxious or have a learning disability. They certainly didn't ask to be depressed, and yet 3.2 million teenagers will have at least one depressive episode in the next year.

"My daughter just got in bed one day and didn't want to get out," said the mother of a fourteen-year-old girl with depression. "I kept trying to get her to do things I know she likes, like come shopping with me or go out to lunch. But whenever I asked her to do something, she burrowed into her bed. It was really frustrating for me. I yelled at her a few times, trying to get through to her. That didn't work, either. She wouldn't be normal, no matter what I said or did." The mom's trying to get her daughter to "be normal" certainly didn't help her feel better or strengthen their relationship.

Is It Sadness or Depression?

NORMAL	PROBLEM	DISORDER
Your child experiences sadness related to a specific experience or event. She can say, "I'm sad because . . ." and give a clear reason for her feelings.	Your child experiences sadness unrelated to a specific experience or event. She can't say exactly why she feels down, just that she does.	Your child has been sad or irritable most of the day, most days in a week, for at least two weeks.
Crying and venting her feelings provides relief.	When "moody," she has low energy and motivation but bounces back when she feels better.	She has lost interest in things that she used to really enjoy.
Your child's sadness passes or diminishes after a few minutes, hours, or a day.	Crying and talking it out don't provide much relief.	She has changed eating or sleeping habits.
	Her feelings pass within two days.	She has little energy, motivation, or concentration to do much of anything.
		She feels worthless, hopeless, or guilty about things that aren't her fault.
		She has a drop in grades.
		She has thoughts of suicide. If so, contact a mental health professional and go to the ER immediately.

If your child's building is crumbling, you shouldn't yell from the scaffold, "Hey! Stop crumbling!" In this case, the mom kept telling her daughter, "You're not worthless! Stop saying that!" Loving concern can come off as criticism. Instead, approach a depressed teen with compassion and empathy. Ask about how she feels and listen without judgment. Validate her feelings by saying, "I hear you and understand that what you're going through is really hard."

It might not make sense to validate what you think of as irrational feelings, but what you're doing is communicating your acceptance, no matter what. That will mean more to her, and benefit her more, than any "fix."

Depressed or otherwise, very few kids will be able to grasp and appreciate your unconditional support. So appreciate yourself whenever your child has a breakthrough or experiences success. Those victories are the result of your teachings and the gifts that you've given her. You can pat yourself on the back when a depressed child trusts you enough to express herself without shame and guilt. Or when your anxious teen who freaked out over every test winds up harnessing her anxiety into straight As. Or when your son, the boy who hated sports and loved comic books, whom you took to ComicCon in a Spider-Man costume despite feeling embarrassed as hell, gets a job at Marvel. Then, you can gloat inwardly about having done the small and big things to prepare him for life.

Barbara wasn't ready to accept her daughter Leah's complex of problems—ones identified by her school's specialists—when we first met her. Even after we'd evaluated her daughter, Barbara clung to the belief that Leah was faking her symptoms for attention. And then, there was what became known as "the subway incident."

"We were on the train platform, going uptown to visit Leah's grandmother like we'd done many times before," said Barbara. "Leah got very upset and started to pull on my arm. She said she had to get out of there. I told her to just relax, the train would be

Scaffolding Acceptance with Teens

- **Structure.** Develop executive functioning by linking good and bad decision-making with consequences that reach beyond just the teen himself.

- **Support.** Show up for your teen, participating in his interests, even if you think they're weird and stupid. Always be on the lookout for areas of common ground and bonding opportunities. Look for ways to move the needle for your child with realistic expectations.

- **Encouragement.** Motivate your own accepting behavior with rewards. Encourage your teen to explore prosocial, proactive, healthy ways to be happy.

here any minute. She said she felt like her chest was pressing on her, and that she needed air. I kept telling her to chill out, but she just got more and more upset, until she was in a full panic attack on the platform. The expression on her face was terrifying. She struggled to breathe, started to sweat, and clung to me like it was a matter of life and death. I'd never seen a panic attack before. But this was real. There was no way she was faking it. No one would choose to go through that."

Barbara was able to get Leah aboveground, and they took a taxi straight home. "It was the saddest ride of my life," she said. "I realized that I'd been really mean to my daughter. I had no patience for her problems or with the teachers who warned me about her issues. I thought they were attacking me, but they were trying to help."

Leah has been getting therapy and medication for a year now, and Barbara has been doing Parent Management Training with us. "I still slip into 'get over it' mode with Leah when she gets anxious over some tiny thing," Barbara told me. "With her eyelash pulling, I say, 'Just stop doing it,' which usually makes her cry and then I feel awful. She's not going to change completely overnight, and neither am I. But we're both working on it."

Suddenly open to all strategies, Barbara invested in an electronic bracelet* that buzzed whenever Leah made the motion of lifting her hand to pull out her eyelashes. When she felt the buzz, she knew to lower her hand and do something else, like take some deep breaths or go for a short walk. "It worked really well and now Leah has eyelashes again. She feels much more confident about facing the world. I think I'm more relieved than she is about it," said Barbara.

It was a long, bumpy road between Barbara's ignoring Leah's problems to accepting them and empathizing with her. But as soon as she made that shift, Leah's symptoms, and their relationship, improved rapidly.

Nail Down Those Planks!

Just accept your child for who she is, scaffold with love and attention, and you can expect good things for your relationship and her future.

Patience
• Be patient with yourself! It's not easy to put aside all your expectations and fears and to let go of taking comfort in the familiar.

Warmth
• Be kind to yourself! When you accept your child taking her own path, you will grieve about her not choosing yours. It's okay to feel sad about it.

---

* For more information, go to habitaware.com.

Awareness

• Always ask, "What are the goals?" and "What will move the needle for my child?" Keep focusing on what you can do to solve problems, instead of thinking about what's wrong.

Dispassion

• When your child makes decisions and explores avenues toward his own happiness, you might have some comments and questions to make. Use your cyborg nonemotional, nonjudgmental voice.

Monitoring

• When you show up for your child at his activities or therapist's office, watch and listen, and be open to greater understanding of who he is. Monitor how your own thoughts and judgments can get in the way.

11

Repair and Minimize Cracks

As the building goes up, the construction team is always looking for cracks. Not all of them are significant. Some are just cosmetic and take very little to cement over. But some force the crew to stop everything else and work exclusively on repairs. Along with scanning for cracks in the building itself, you need to check the scaffold, too. If the scaffold breaks, it can't provide structure and support to the building. Keeping the scaffold in a state of good repair is just as important to the construction as scanning for cracks in the building itself.

Tanya, forty-four, is the mother of four, including her eldest son, John. John had been an athlete in middle school, and when he transitioned to high school with older kids, he was bumped down the roster to second string. "He was really upset," she told me. "I scaffolded him by encouraging him to stick with it anyway, that he could work out a bit more to show the coaches he had heart. I said, 'It's not you, it's just your size, and that will change in time. Nothing to worry about.' He seemed happier and more pragmatic about it and stepped up his workouts. I thought to myself, 'You're a scaffolding genius.'"

Six months went by, and Tanya noticed that John seemed to

be working out all the time. It didn't worry her, though. "He was with friends, and he looked good," she said. "His grades didn't suffer. And his father got involved and they started lifting weights in the garage together. It seemed only positive."

Until it wasn't. John started to be very picky about what he ate. No carbs, ever, and two huge protein shakes per day that he made himself. He was so rigid about his eating and workout schedule that the family had to plan their outings around it. "It wasn't until eight months went by that I realized we had a problem," said Tanya. "I took something into the garage for storage and saw John in there, lifting weights all alone, staring at himself in the mirror he'd installed. I hadn't seen him with his shirt off in a while, and his body had totally changed. His muscles were bigger, and exaggerated, like every fiber was clearly defined under his skin. No fat on his body at all. The sight frightened me. He used to have a normal athletic body. But this was too much for a sixteen-year-old. When he heard me gasp, he self-consciously pulled his shirt back on."

Tanya and her husband overlooked their son's problem because they were so busy with their three other kids (one of whom has an anxiety disorder) and because they thought, as many people do, that boys don't get eating disorders. In fact, though boys are less likely to suffer from an eating disorder than girls, about 25 percent to 33 percent of people affected by eating disorders are male, and those numbers are rapidly increasing. Tanya knew to keep an eye on her girls for signs of their pushing away food or making postmeal trips to the bathroom, but not her sons. She had never heard of muscle dysmorphia or "bigorexia," the disorder of boys and men (for the most part) becoming obsessed with getting more defined muscles. Like people with anorexia, they develop compulsive eating and exercising routines, but with reverse objectives. They are trying to get larger, not smaller.

"I beat myself up really good for not noticing sooner," Tanya said. "I wasn't monitoring him like I should have been. Scaffolding fail."

I assured her that she shouldn't blame herself. Granted, she'd missed some warning signs, but she'd been watchful of others, like a sudden drop in grades or social isolation, which hadn't happened.

Despite your best efforts, sometimes things will get by you. You won't notice that your daughter's BFF seems to have dropped out of her life. Or that your son is failing history (until the report card arrives). The crack in your scaffold might be your backsliding into nagging and yelling or becoming lax about sticking with your consequences policies.

When you get a sinking feeling, "Oh, no, I let a lot slip by me," don't waste time and energy on guilt. A friend of mine—not a psychologist, just someone who had a manipulative mother—calls it "a worthless emotion." It's true. Guilt does nothing good for anyone. What does you the most good is breaking out your own coping skills toolbox, and getting to work on repairing your scaffold.

Facing Problems Head-On

The scaffolding crack of back-burnering is putting a problem to the side with the intention of addressing it later, if at all. You have a lot on your plate and can't do everything at once. But there are some issues that can't be back-burnered, like connecting your child with a professional, such as a tutor or a doctor. Do not hesitate to make that call. On average, a parent waits two years from the first sign of symptoms to seek help about a learning or mood disorder, which is far too long. Once a child is in treatment and doing better, you can beat yourself up for delaying. But in most cases, remind yourself that you didn't know the signs to look for. When you got the information, you responded to it.

If there is any doubt in your mind, please go to childmind .org and use the symptom checker—an interactive question-and-answer tool to help inform you about potential diagnoses—and/or to get an evaluation. The sooner a child with learning disabilities, spectrum disorders, OCD, ADHD, anxiety, depression, gets treatment, the better his or her prognosis.

For more information about how to recognize signs of children's
mental health disorders and to check your child's symptoms,
go to childmind.org/symptomchecker.

Ignoring these disorders doesn't make them go away. But parents often lack a sense of urgency about getting treatment (even those who don't fear a label or reject all disorders out of hand). Forty percent of kids with diagnosable ADHD don't get treatment. For kids with depression, it's 60 percent. For anxiety, 80 percent. I don't mean to be alarmist, but of the 6,000-plus teen suicides each year, 90 percent had a mental health disorder. Between 2007 and 2015, the number of children and teens taken to an emergency room for suicidal ideation or attempts doubled, reaching a high of 1.2 million in 2015. This means that every minute in the United States, there are two suicidal teens going to the ER.

Using anxiety as an example, while you are delaying treatment, your child will predictably avoid any situation that exacerbates his anxiety. Avoidance feels good; it takes away the worry temporarily but does nothing to address the underlying condition. If a child is stuck in that pattern of avoidance for years, he'll miss key developmental milestones. He might stop making friends or lose the ones he has. He won't raise his hand in class. He'll quit after-school activities that once raised his self-esteem but now embarrass him. Don't wait to talk to someone until your child has completely isolated himself and is defined by his disorder. In addition to those demoralizing behavioral symptoms, these disorders also work at a neurobiological level to change the way the brain works. Those changes increase the risk for depression later. In other words, anxiety disorders not only limit your child's activities but are literally bad for his brain.

"You Can't Make Me"

Parents don't have an exclusive on back-burnering. Teens in particular are often resistant to getting treatment. Seeing a therapist means they'll have to sit in a room with a stranger and reveal their deepest, darkest secrets, feelings, and vulnerabilities. Besides that, teens are worried about labels, embarrassed about having a problem, or afraid of being thought of as "crazy" by their peers. Due to pre-existing bias—things they've heard from friends, the media, or past experiences—they might think therapy or medication won't help.

You already know it's hard to get a teen to do something small that he doesn't want to do, like take out the garbage. Saying, "I'd like you to see a therapist"—another way to take out the "garbage"—is a big ask of a reluctant adolescent who is testing out her autonomy, as she should.

Try using the scaffolding strategy of reframing to gently nudge a troubled teen into accepting help.

The therapist is just a doctor. If your child had a stomachache, you'd get the symptoms checked out. Same thing here. Say to your child, "You seem very unhappy. As your parents, it's our job to figure out what's wrong so you can be as productive and happy as possible. You have symptoms that are causing you pain and we want you to see someone to make that pain go away. We can't fix it, and you can't fix it. So let's get help from someone who can."

Therapy isn't about problems. It's about priorities. Instead of describing therapy as a time the teen should talk about what's wrong with him, say it's an opportunity to talk about what he wants for himself, his priorities, not yours. What is he looking for at this stage? What does he want to improve on, academically and socially? If he's focused on what's in it for him, based on what he cares about, he'll be more open to working together with a professional.

I understand the impulse for inaction. If you have a cold, you don't run to the doctor. You wait for it to get better on its own. With kids' mental illness, you won't necessarily recognize symptoms. Our nation's health-care system is complicated and overwhelming. It can be a challenge to find a doctor on your insurance plan and take time off from work to get your kid to a therapist. Parents also blame themselves for their child's illness for a host of reasons (divorce, their own anxiety or depression, financial stress, etc.) and feel so bad about it they choose to ignore it. Mental illness is no one's fault, but the reality is, if you delay intervention, you can make things worse. Scaffold your child by making that one appointment and take it from there.

To this day, my middle son, Adam, insists that my wife and I back-burnered his dyslexia.

The first inkling came when he was four. After spending a day with him on vacation in Florida, my mother-in-law said to us as we were leaving, "I love listening to Adam speak, but I don't understand what he's saying."

I said, "Well, his articulation is not very mature."

"No, I don't think that's the problem," she said. "His stories are out of order and hard to follow. He went to a party, something about a clown and a pool? It's all mixed up and I can't figure it out. And I don't think he remembers my name. He calls me 'Mel's wife.'"

On the plane back home, I said to Linda, "Your mother is never really super positive or negative. The fact that she gave us this critique at all means we have to pay attention to it."

My wife called the nursery school and asked if they noticed the same thing. The head of the school said, "I'm not sure everyone understands what he's saying, but it doesn't stop him. He's a boy, don't worry about it."

But it did worry me. I found a speech and language therapist to evaluate him. After hours of testing, she brought him to the waiting room and said to us, "He is very bright! He is going to score exceptionally well on the ERB (the entrance exam for the independent schools)."

"What about the fact that he can't remember his grandmother's name?" asked Linda.

Word retrieval is a symptom of dyslexia, but she assured us he was okay. I pushed it at his nursery school, and they connected us with another speech and language therapist. Adam got significantly better and, as the first expert predicted, he got in the 99th percentile on the ERB.

He moved on to kindergarten, then first grade and second grade. We thought we were on top of it with language therapy twice a week and a reading tutor. And then, when Adam was in third grade, he punched another boy in the nose and we got called in. I knew he was not an aggressive kid and that there had to be an explanation. We sat down and talked with Adam at home. The boy he hit had called him "stupid" and others joined in. Throughout elementary school, Adam said he had been two steps ahead in math and three steps behind in reading. That week, in math, they had started doing word problems—such as, "If Jane had two dollars and she wanted to buy apples at fifty cents apiece . . ."—and he was stumped. With tears streaming down his face, he said, "I'm in the Sparrows reading group and the smart kids are in the Hawks reading group and hawks eat sparrows."

I thought, *No, you're not stupid. The teacher who came up with those names is stupid.*

We had him tested again by a wonderful neuropsychologist, Dr. Rita Haggerty, who said, "His comprehension is great. If you read to him, he can answer the questions. But he doesn't know how to decode the language. He has memorized thousands of words. But his computer is full. When he sees Sally, Susan. and Sarah, he knows it's a girl's name, but he's just guessing. If you show him a nonsense word, he has no way of decoding it."

This was bad news. We had been working with many specialists and Adam was steadfast in all his efforts, and now we were told there had been little progress. We had a problem that needed to be on the front burner.

We found an intensive (four hours a day, for one month) reading program with one-on-one specialized tutoring called Lindamood-Bell, then located in Belmont, Massachusetts, that could teach our son how to decode and, in turn, read. Linda and Adam went to Belmont during the week and came home for weekends. My parents helped watch Josh and Sam while I was at work. After the four weeks, back in New York, Adam did an hour of daily homework with a tutor to practice the skills he'd learned. He was highly motivated and cooperative, especially when he realized that tutoring was working.

We also used an external reinforcer with Adam to make sure he got as much as possible from the program. I said to him, "If

Is It a Learning Disability?

The range of "normal" learning speed and skill varies greatly. Some kids will always be faster than others, better at spelling, comprehension, and vocabulary. But a child who can't decode, spell, or take notes by eight most likely has dyslexia. I want to make sure you understand that dyslexia and intelligence are unrelated. As Dr. Sally Shaywitz and Dr. Jonathan Shaywitz describe in their book *Overcoming Dyslexia: A New and Complete Science-Based Program for Reading Problems at Any Level,* dyslexics are often above average in intelligence, articulate, curious, imaginative, and creative. The disorder is brain based, not intelligence based. It is a problem to be managed, not a life sentence. If your child has dyslexia, he or she:

- Has trouble learning simple rhymes

- Is speech delayed

- Struggles to follow directions

- Has difficulty with short words: repeats or leaves out *and, the, but*

- Has trouble differentiating left from right

- Has significant difficulty learning to read, sounding out new words, and counting syllables you're cooperative, you get a dollar a day. If you're not coopera-tive, you only get fifty cents."

He said, "What's cooperative mean?"

I said, "If you give her attitude, you only get fifty cents."

"Oh," he said. "I gave her attitude today."

By the end of the summer, he was decoding on the fourth-grade level. We thought we took care of it. But he needed more intervention during the school year. He went to his regular school for four hours a day, and then he worked with a Lindamood-Bell

- Continues to reverse letters and numbers when reading after age eight
- Struggles with taking notes and copying down words from the board
- Has difficulty associating sounds with letters, and sequencing and ordering sounds
- Has trouble spelling even familiar words
- Lacks fluency in reading, continuing to read slowly when other kids are speeding ahead
- Avoids reading out loud
- Shows signs of fatigue from reading
- Has trouble understanding logos and signs
- Has difficulty learning the rules to games
- Struggles to remember multistep directions
- Has trouble reading clocks and telling time
- Has a particularly hard time learning a new language
- Has emotional outbursts as a result of frustration

tutor for another four hours in the afternoons. It was a significant expense, but our son had to learn to read.

Our family rearranged our lives for Adam to get this treatment. Looking back, I'm proud of how we handled it. We didn't find the right solution between the ages of four and eight. But he was still very young when we finally found an evidence-based program that worked.

He thinks we should have intensified sooner. But Adam is a very intense guy.

According to Dr. Shaywitz, codirector of the Yale Center for Dyslexia and Creativity, up to one in five children have dyslexia, making it the most common learning disorder. It affects 20 percent of the population and accounts for 80 to 90 percent of all learning disabilities. For the Child Mind Institute's #MyYoungerSelf, a campaign to eradicate the stigma of mental health and learning disorders, I've met and interviewed many famous people who have the disorder. Once, I had a long discussion with the actor Orlando Bloom about it. When Adam met Orlando, he said, "Is it true you told my father dyslexia is a gift? Because if it's a gift, can you tell me where I can return it?" Adam still does read slowly, and writing requires a concerted effort. I'm sure his dyslexia affected his middle and high school experience. Which is why he does not want to hear me, Orlando Bloom, or anyone talk about turning deficits into assets.

But he did learn to read. The tenacity and effort to do so helped him get into Brown University and later Columbia Business School. He's very successful in his field. Not bad for a kid who couldn't read until eight. (You've got to let me brag about him just a little; it's a scaffold parent's prerogative.)

On the other side of the coin, you see kids who get to eleventh grade without learning to read. They slip through the cracks of the system. Maybe their friends help them get by. Their parents aren't paying close enough attention or are fixated on performance, thinking, *If he's not failing, he's okay*. But when they go off to college, it's a disaster.

What I want to stress is that parents need to reinforce their own effort over performance principle. You have to make the effort to know your kid is a bungalow, not a skyscraper. Make the effort to listen to him and pick up on the cues like Adam's grandmother did. Make an effort to find him specialists who can teach him to read. Your hard work for him will be rewarded in his success.

Fixating on What Matters

Brian's ten-year-old son Michael has ADHD. His condition interfered with his learning, but not to such an extent that Michael needed special accommodations—extra time for tests, for example—to do his schoolwork. Brian, however, instructed Michael to flub a learning assessment so the boy would qualify for accommodations that gave him an edge academically.

There's no other way to say this: That's so wrong! Telling a ten-year-old who's eager and wants to please to intentionally screw up is a complete misstep. To scaffold, praise and reward effort, not performance. The child who studies for hours to get a C deserves more praise than a smart kid who slacks off and gets an A. Brian's suggestion was far worse than fixating on performance. He coached his son to game the system.

Always tell your kids to do their best. Never communicate to them that they shouldn't be trying their hardest. No matter what the circumstances, parents need to send the consistent message that kids should strive to do well, even if doing badly might in some way help them.

I tried to do so gently, but I had to admonish Brian for coaching Michael not to try as hard as he could, to be dishonest. "Would you tell Michael to go out on the ice at his next hockey game and throw the game?" I asked. That seemed to get through to him. He believed doing poorly on the test would help his son in the future, but if you think really long term, teaching him to cheat would have far greater consequences. Kids don't fully know the risks of tricking others. They might believe that they can be slicker than they actually are and get into serious trouble.

It's developmentally appropriate for a ten-year-old to learn that people sometimes say things that others don't recognize as being true or false—white lies—and that capacity allows you to be nice to people at times when you don't want to be. But teaching a child early on that trickery is okay is *not* okay.

Even kids who have real struggles should always be trying to the best of their ability. Social interactions are complicated enough, so why add unnecessary layers to them? Honesty really is the best policy. There's no substitute for good regular conversation with your kids about social situations and the benefits of being truthful and working hard.

Try to Stay Flexible

You might feel like you have to stick by your original action or "final decision," even if you realize that it's wrong or flawed. Let that one go. It's not written in stone that you are required to stick with *any* decision. Do-overs are allowed. Not everything is up for negotiation, but many decisions and choices can and should be reevaluated.

What's more, depending on your child's age, she should be involved in the decision-making process. If you can sit down and say, "I was wrong that time. I realize I made a bad call. So let's talk about what to do now," you are role modeling compromise, thoughtfulness, flexibility, and humility. By admitting you're wrong, you are communicating to her what is really important, aka not being "right" all the time. Have these talks early on—from age five to seven—to scaffold your child for a lifetime of adapting readily to change.

Let's say one parent said yes to something and the other says no. Mom and Dad didn't communicate ahead of time and now you're in a bind. It's actually a great opportunity to show your kids that you're human. We all misstep sometimes, just like your kids do, so apologize if an apology is warranted, make amends, and move on.

My colleague, Dr. Rachel Busman, had to apologize to her son about being away from home so much during conference season a few years back. "I was gone for three or four days in September and had two more conferences in October," she said. "The night before the second trip, I was saying good night to my son and said, 'I'm leaving for San Diego tomorrow.' He got upset and said, 'Mommy, you went to Chicago and now you're going to San Diego. It's too much.' It was heartbreaking, but I couldn't not go to the conference. I said, 'You know what, Jackson? You're right. It is too much. It's too much for you, and for me.'"

She felt awful about leaving. "I went into my bedroom and cried, thinking, *I'm a jerk*. I vowed to myself, and told Jackson in the morning, that as soon as I finished what I'd committed to, my going away so often was over," she said. "This example stays with me because it's about admitting my mistake, saying 'I hear you and I'm sorry,' and also about balancing work and being a mother. I could have said, 'Isn't it fun when you and Daddy get to stay home alone?' Or, 'You know that when I go away I always bring you back something,' but that would have been my making myself feel better. Comments like that are a smoke screen. They invalidate the child's feelings. Better to acknowledge his feelings, and my own, apologize, and try to do something in the future to change."

And then there are those moments when the scaffolding slips and you lose your temper. Cyndi, mother of seven-year-old Jamal, told me, "Oh, I really messed up. I really lost it this time." I braced myself for the worst, and then she shared a story about her handling a tough situation well. Yes, she got angry. Jamal asked her the same question thirty-five times in a row when she was on a work call, which would be frustrating for anyone. "I yelled at him to shut up," she said. "He cried and I felt awful. I gave him a hug and said, 'Okay, I got mad. I'm sorry I raised my voice, but you can't do that when I'm trying to talk to someone. It's too hard!'"

I reassured her that she'd done a good job and that she is, after all, a human being with feelings. Her loss of temper was a learning opportunity for them both. Jamal learned not to bug her for attention when she's on the phone. Cyndi learned that what she thought was terrible parenting was actually pretty good.

Most of us go into our interactions with the best of intentions. It's in the delivery that we lose it. And that's okay, as long as you can admit your mistake and say, "I'm sorry."

Limit TV Time and Tone

Most parents have read and absorbed the proverbial memo about limiting screen time for their kids. But too many don't stick with the scaffolding strategy of watching their kids' programming *with* them. Even if you do, and closely monitor what your child is exposed to at home, you still need to watch out for what they see at friends' houses and other places.

"My daughter had a complicated first-grade experience because of some media other kids were exposed to," says Matthew Cruger, a pediatric neuropsychologist at the Child Mind Institute. "The social interactions in that show could be characterized as snarky and sarcastic and conflict-ridden. The dialogue that kids see on TV tends not to be as wholesome as most social interactions could be. In our family, we don't talk that way. But my daughter's friends were taking cues from the show and saying things like, 'If you hang out with that other girl, I'm going to kill you.' The tone was confusing and upsetting to her."

When you hear your child using a certain tone or saying words or phrases you don't approve of, there needs to be a discussion about where the new messaging came from, and whether you like the sound of it or not. "In this particular show," says Dr. Cruger, "the ultimate message was for people to be nice to each other. But the tone the characters used to communicate with each other was too obnoxious. The core message got lost and came off like a sarcastic punch line. So the kids weren't modeling niceness. They picked up the sarcastic style of communicating."

Many schools are working toward developing an early curriculum that's focused on the social, emotional success of the kids in the classroom, as opposed to strictly focusing on academics. But even if that curriculum is one day effective, you should be the value setter for the social emotional curriculum that you teach your kids, rather than discharging those responsibilities to school or television.

This is not to blame you! You are no doubt taxed by your kids' demands to watch TV, and all your other responsibilities. It's a lot to ask that you take *every* opportunity to interface with your kids around their values and lessons. It's far more expedient at times to just give in and say, "Fine, go watch TV."

If you're going to be a value setter, though, you really do have to sit down, watch TV together, and react to the snarkiness as it happens with comments, like, "That remark doesn't reflect how the character really feels. She doesn't really want to kill her friend."

Scaffolding Maintenance with Kids

- **Structure**. Scan regularly for cracks about upholding house rules and values.

- **Support**. Enlist help with your scaffolding from a partner, friend, or family member. Ask, "Am I nagging, yelling, impatient, inflexible as a parent lately?" Just as you should expect your child to accept corrective feedback, do the same when you receive it.

- **Encouragement**. Salute your own efforts to scaffold your kids, even if you let a few things go. It's impossible to be a perfect parent, so cut yourself some slack for making mistakes.

I know it's a time suck. But there's really no substitute for taking the time to interface with your kids and talk to them about the nuances of social interactions.

Don't Forget Your Basic Training

Remember all the way back in Chapter Four, I talked about Parent Management Training, bonding rituals, and nonjudgmental quality family time? It's hard to keep that going when kids get older and want to spend more time with their friends.

Do Not Do This at Home

Smoke weed.

I don't want to be a buzzkill or anything, but if you smoke marijuana at home, your kids will be exposed to it, too, even if you do so in another room in the house. In a Colorado study, kids as young as six tested positive for marijuana if their parents were frequent users. Just because it's legal for adults (in some states) doesn't mean it's safe for young, developing brains. And if children and adolescents know you use pot, you are modeling tacit approval of it to them.

I'm just sharing the science. If you or your child has an anxiety disorder, it will get worse with chronic marijuana use. Being high can trigger a panic attack. For kids with ADHD, being high feels like a warm blanket, but when they're sober, they're left in the cold. Pot is detrimental to any learning disability.

When my sons were young, I talked to them about the developing brain and explained that if they start smoking as a teen, it could develop into a habit and it would affect short-term memory, which they needed to learn.

I asked each of them to abstain until they graduated from high school and got a different outcome with each child. Josh made it

Middle-school kids' outlook is shifting from family life to their extracurricular social lives. That's also the time when you start testing the waters with allowing them to have social media accounts, ideally with your monitoring and supervision. What happens is kids spend less time at home, anyway, and when they are around, they're on their phones or in their bedrooms on their computers with the door closed.

Tweens and teens definitely need more alone time than elementary-school kids. But you can still expect and require them to spend a reasonable amount of time in common areas of the house, even if they're engaged on their computers. Have kids

until the summer between junior and senior year, and immediately told us about it, saying he tried it four times. Adam pretended not to smoke and later told me, "It's hard to tell you something that you don't want to hear." He smoked for the first time his senior year after he got accepted to college early decision, but he was so anxious about it, he had a terrible time and didn't smoke again until college. Sam kept his word and used his friends to help. He announced to his crew that he made a deal with his dad not to smoke pot until he graduated, and even though most of his friends did smoke, they helped him keep his pledge by not passing him the joint. He made them part of the social pressure. And he definitely did smoke after graduation.

I feel pretty good about their not smoking until relatively late compared to their friends. An under-twenty-five-year-old's brain is not developed enough to make executive decisions and be appreciative of the consequences of their actions. It might not be realistic to expect a kid to stay away from pot until he's old enough to rent a car. But every year you can delay their exposure is a bonus for their brains and lessens the chance pot (or cigarettes, for that matter) will open the door for experimentation with other drugs.

do their homework in an open space where they're with other members of the family until eighth grade. If it ends up turning into a huge argument or debate, you can take the opportunity to teach them about negotiating, rather than just insisting they do it your way.

That said, a teen's alone time needs to be balanced with family interactions, no matter how skilled a negotiator your teen happens to be. I have spent decades doing therapy with families, and for all the knowledge we have about child and adolescent psychology and parenting strategies, we can't underestimate the impact of family meals together. Life doesn't always afford that, so don't be overly critical of yourself if you can't hit the gold number of three dinners together per week. But that old standard and tradition is worth aspiring to. If you can only manage one family bonding ritual time per week, it's better than none.

Skip the Nagging

Anecdotally, nagging behavior has a very high recidivism rate. You will have to remind yourself, as we remind parents every day, that nagging is not an effective motivator. When you stop doing it, you can see the good outcomes in your kids' behavior. But then, if your child slacks off a bit, you might zoom right back in to nagging. If you feel like you can't trust your kids to, say, do their homework, it requires superhuman self-control to hold off on checking up on them, and throwing in, "Time to do your work." If your child says, "Time for you to leave me alone," the interaction will go straight downhill from there.

Kids are highly motivated not to fight with you, especially about homework. To shift away from nagging (again), which messages a lack of confidence in your child's work ethic and abilities, focus on trust and respect. Start by asking him to list his assignments for the night and then say, "I'm sure you have a plan for getting it all done. If you don't think so, I can help you organize."

If he says he can do it on his own, you can poke your head in now and then to ask if he would like something to drink, but otherwise, back off.

If your kid doesn't get the job done, offer assistance in organizing a work schedule for him to do the assignments independently, but do not yell or nag. Praise and reinforce his efforts, and reward follow-through. It doesn't have to be a monetary reward. It could be letting him pick what restaurant the family goes to on Friday night, which is the win-win of bonding ritual and positive reinforcement in one fell swoop.

Scaffolding Maintenance with Teens

- **Structure.** No matter how busy you and your teen are, always make time to spend time together doing things you both enjoy. Family meals, that old standby, is a great time to bond and check in.

- **Support.** Listen to the sound of your own voice. As soon as you hear yourself nagging or yelling, know that your teen has completely tuned you out.

- **Encouragement.** Inspire your teen to be his best self by being your best self. Model and reinforce the behaviors you want to see in kids by living them.

Tanya, mother of John, sixteen, who became so obsessed with building muscles that he developed an eating and exercise disorder, already had one child under our care, so her search for someone to help John was simple: She called the Child Mind Institute. But her experience is not the norm; parents often encounter problems in finding good help and going through the process of matching their child with the right doctor. A rule of thumb: Frequently, it will take speaking to two or three clinicians before you make a commitment to one.

During John's first session, his therapist learned that he was under a lot of pressure to bulk up from his coach and the other players on the football team. He wasn't the only kid who'd crossed the line into obsession. Tanya's scaffolding support for her son exposed a danger to other kids in their community, and the right people were notified and admonished. This serves as a reminder that when you scaffold your own child, the impact can ripple out into other families for the benefit of all. It really does take a village.

John is doing well. "He's eating normally, but he still loves his workouts," said Tanya. "We negotiated with John that he limit his nonsports workouts to thirty minutes a day. And I check in with him every evening about how he's doing as unobtrusively as I can. He rolls his eyes like I'm annoying, but I can tell that he's glad I'm there and that I care. In the end, that's really what scaffolding is. We're all doing our best to be and to raise good people."

Be there and care.

Tanya summed up scaffolding beautifully in just a few words.

Nail Down Those Planks!

There is no better way to scaffold your kids than by standing strong on your planks.

Patience

- No matter how "crazy" your kids make you, take a deep breath and remind yourself that parenting might seem endless and really hard, but it goes by in a flash. What once drove you crazy might be something you miss when they've gone off and started their adult lives. If you can bring that perspective into scaffolding, you might be able to summon that two-second pause to find your patience before you react in another way.

Warmth

• No parent will look back on the scaffolding years and say, "I really wish I had been colder and crueler to my child when she was young and vulnerable." You are her first source of warmth and love. Maintain that same feeling in your heart, even when she pushes back against it.

Monitoring

• You can't know you've slipped unless you make a habit of checking in with yourself. So every month, when you do something routine like pay the mortgage or the rent, ask, "How's my scaffold holding up?" And then make the necessary repairs.

When the Scaffold Comes Down

A scaffold is not actually holding up the building. It provides a structure, supports, and guides, but it's not weight bearing. So if a contractor takes down a scaffold prematurely, the unfinished building might be able to stand on its own, but it's not necessarily safe to be occupied. That won't stop squatters from moving in, though. If a storm comes in or any external pressure is applied to the building and a wall falls, people might be hurt. The next thing you know, the Occupational Safety and Health Administration will get involved and the contractors who took down the scaffold too soon are going to get sued.

Now, no one is going to call OSHA if you dismantle your parental scaffold prematurely, but it's still reckless. You want to make sure that your child's building can stand on its own and be occupied safely. So the big question is . . .

Are They Ready?

When a teenager or a child says, "I can do it on my own. I don't need you," it might be technically true. She can tie her own shoes or drive to the mall to buy her own prom dress. But her building construction is not necessarily done. She's not able to move out, get a job, do her taxes, and live independently.

Case in point, your kid drives to the mall to buy a prom outfit, but on the way, the car runs out of gas. She's stranded on the highway, and she freaks out. Or say he makes it to the mall, and his wallet gets stolen. If the scaffolding was ready to come down, your kid would have been able to cope the way an adult would. Finding a police officer. Reporting the crime. Self-soothing in a strategically effective way.

We scaffold kids *toward* "I can do it" self-efficacy, a positive feeling of competence and independence. We scaffold them *away* from the opposite view, "I can't do it," a negative feeling of incompetence and dependency. You want to instill in them a sense of optimism that nice things will happen in the future, but also the sense that "Whatever happens, I can handle it."

That perception of competence comes from learning through mistakes, their doing things on their own and overcoming difficulties—all the adaptive skills that you've modeled, reinforced, and guided your children to develop. When you encourage your kids by saying, "I know it's hard, but I think you can handle it—you're going to be fine," you reinforce the perception of competence. You're not saying, "You're the best in the world!" or "You're the worst!" You are encouraging them based on their own past experiences and successes.

When your child has the sense that he can deal with stressors, one part of the scaffolding can come down.

A sign of true maturity: When his wallet gets stolen at the mall, your child calls you second, after he calls the cops. He finds his own doctor, apartment, and job recruiter when he moves to a new city. If your child always calls you first to say, "I need to find a plumber," he isn't self-supporting, aka self-scaffolding, quite yet.

Another sign of readiness is what Carol Dweck, professor of psychology at Stanford University, called "the growth mindset," aka "I can learn it." If he tried to, say, hire his own plumber and got ripped off, the growth mindset would be his saying, "Okay, it didn't work out that time, but I can figure it out next time. The fact that I got ripped off just means I didn't do enough research." The growth mindset doesn't perceive failure as that big a deal. It's a problem in need of a solution that you will eventually figure out.

When your child is confronted with a problem he can't manage, if he responds with "I'm not smart enough" or "I'm not good enough," he's toast. And you have more scaffolding to do to encourage, support, and guide him toward a growth mindset, coping strategies, and self-efficacy.

If he can roll with challenges and has a sense that he can learn to figure things out—and does—another part of the scaffold is ready to come down.

You might prefer a more mathematic measure of a child's readiness. In therapy, we evaluate progress systematically. After each session with a patient, the doctor answers, "Is the child much worse, worse, slightly worse, slightly better, better, or much better compared to last time?" "Better" or "much better" three sessions in a row means it's time to go from weekly to biweekly or monthly sessions. Use a similar rubric for whether your scaffolding is ready to come down. Ask, "Is my child self-advocating?" Self-advocacy skills are the ones you've been scaffolding all along: making wise decisions, solving problems, goal setting and reaching, self-awareness, emotional intelligence, standing up for herself, getting things done on her own or seeking out appropriate help on her own.

If the answer is any level of yes 85 percent of the time, then the scaffolding in that area is ready to come down.

We worked with Eric for several years to help him manage his anxiety disorder. When the time came for him to apply to colleges, his disorder might have been his undoing. But, with his parents' guidance and support, Eric arduously prepared for the part of the process that was most stressful for him: the admissions interview.

Before each interview, he practiced answers to likely questions, which eased his symptoms tremendously. When the admissions officer asked Eric his opinion about a random topic, one he didn't have an answer for, his heart would start to race, and his hands got sweaty. It could have been a disaster, but his parents had scaffolded him so well, he was able to scaffold himself. He knew immediately to start using countermeasures, like taking deep belly breaths and to repeat the question to give himself time to calm down and think of something to say. When Eric got into his first choice, we couldn't have been prouder of his perseverance and resilience. If his parents hadn't given him support, structure, and encouragement during his childhood, he probably wouldn't have mastered those interviews and may not have been accepted where he really wanted to go. His parents didn't fear his diagnosis, ignore it, or see it as a negative. They allowed him to try and fail, gave him corrective feedback and labeled praise, taught him to name his emotions, learn from mistakes, and bounce back from them.

When your child masters such life skills, and does them without instruction on your part, the scaffold can come down.

When your child is self-motivated and feels a sense of accomplishment and validation from within, the scaffold can come down.

When your child can advocate for his or her own needs . . .

When your child can express emotions and use them to understand himself better . . .

When she isn't afraid to come forward and ask her teacher, boss, friends, partners for what she needs . . .

There is the possibility that you may misread the situation and prematurely dismantle the scaffolding, even if your child seems to be self-advocating well. The good news is that you can always put it back up. A friend of mine scaffolded his daughter Jennie well and sent her off to college with high hopes that she'd be successful. There was no reason to fear that she would struggle. But within a week of dropping her off, Jennie started calling home every night with new problems to report. She wasn't making friends, forgot to sign up for a science lab, was under so much stress, wasn't eating.

Jennie's bumpy transition to college didn't mean that her parents failed to provide her with enough support and encouragement growing up. It just meant that her scaffolding needed to be reassembled and kept up a bit longer to make the necessary repairs.

That's one of the beauties of the scaffold. It can go down, and it can go back up as needed, around the whole building, or just one part.

I advised Jennie's mom to resist the urge to swoop in to save the day, but to continue scaffolding strategies that she'd done throughout her daughter's childhood: to be emotionally available and present; praise positive prosocial, proactive behaviors; support her by helping her find a doctor or a tutor if needed; and validate her feelings and encourage her to use her coping skills. When Jennie eventually adjusted to college, her accomplishment was her own, and she felt great about herself.

And then her parents complained that she didn't call home *enough*.

They missed her, but that is the bittersweet gratification of scaffolding success. We all want our children to be confident, competent. With the ten strategies I've discussed in this book, you will provide them with everything they need to become all that they, and you, desire for them.

Are *You* Ready?

Your natural urge is to protect your child. But you can't protect him or her from every adversity in life. What you can do is help kids to learn to cope independently. Otherwise, you'll be reinforcing dependence, the perception that they can't handle life on their own. That sends the wrong message. When your kids are ready for the scaffold to come down, you need to be ready, too.

You might be reluctant to dismantle it out of wariness, as in, "What if my child needs me and I'm not there?"

But remind yourself that you are, in fact, there. You are standing and enjoying the view from outside the building. You're just not surrounding it anymore.

As parents, we live our lives caring for and guiding our children. And when they start to get independent in high school, more so in college, then get jobs and move away, it leaves a big hole in our lives. We'd built something, and then all of a sudden, it's gone. We have to look for something to fill that space.

But when parents say, "I'm going to take care of you *forever*," it's not a love story. It's a horror story! You have to give your kids light and space to grow.

"On my desk, I have a photo of our daughter taking her first steps," says Dr. Reinecke. "Gracie was about fourteen months old. We were in a rose garden in Evanston, Illinois. She was holding on to the low brick wall surrounding the garden while she toddled along, while my wife and I were looking at something else. And all of a sudden, Gracie turned away from the wall and started taking steps toward us. My wife whipped out her camera and got the picture. Gracie was three steps away from the wall, her hands are up in the air, and she was beaming. The look of excitement on her face as she let go of the support is a reminder to me every day of what we're trying to achieve. She took her first steps to walk toward us and learned the skill that would ultimately take her away from us."

From the first brick of your child's building, from the first plank of your scaffold, you are rising and growing together, in constant connection and communication. The scaffold is an essential part of the building's construction. Tools and materials come up via the scaffold. The scaffold guides and supports, provides a safety net for catching pieces as they fall. And then, eventually, the day comes when the building is complete, and the scaffolding is superfluous.

Remember and then remind yourself once again: The scaffold was never meant to be permanent. Its purpose is to lend structure and support, and it necessarily becomes less and less important over time, until it's not needed at all. Getting rid of it might make you nervous, but if your child is ready, it has to come down. Otherwise, it just blocks the view.

Dismantling the scaffold will be your moment of glory. You can stand back and admire the fine, strong building you raised with pride and joy. And then you can set off to build something new that's completely your own.

Notes

2: Secure Yourself First

27 *In a recent German study*: Reinecke, L., Hartmann, T., and Eden, A. "The Guilty Couch Potato: The Role of Ego Depletion in Reducing Recovery Through Media Use." *Journal of Communication*, 2014.

28 *"We were a bit surprised"*: Mikolajczak, Moïra, Gross, James J., and Roskam, Isabelle. "Parental Burnout: What Is It, and Why Does It Matter?" *Clinical Psychological Science*, August 2019.

28 *Parental Burnout Inventory*: Roskam, Isabelle, Raes, Marie-Emilie, and Mikolajczak, Moïra. "Exhausted Parents: Development and Preliminary Validation of the Parental Burnout Inventory." *Frontiers of Psychology*, February 2017.

30 *Follow-up study*: Mikolajczak, Moïra, and Roskam, Isabelle. "A Theoretical and Clinical Framework for Parental Burnout: The Balance Between Risk and Resources." *Frontiers in Psychology*, June 2018.

3: Draw a New Blueprint

45 *A recent Canadian study*: Dickson, D. J., Laursen, B., Valdes, O., et al. "Derisive Parenting Fosters Dysregulated Anger in Adolescent Children and Subsequent Difficulties with Peers." *Journal of Youth and Adolescence*, 2019.

45 *Damage a child's self-concept*: Storch, Eric A., et al. "The

Measure and Impact of Childhood Teasing in a Sample of Young Adults." *Journal of Anxiety Disorders,* 2004.

53 *A fascinating experiment:* Rosenthal, R., and Jacobson, L. *Pygmalion in the Classroom.* Holt, Rinehart and Winston, 1968.

56 *Overdiagnosis:* Merten, Eva Charlotte, et al. "Overdiagnosis of Mental Disorders in Children and Adolescents (in the Developing World)." *Child and Adolescent Psychiatry and Mental Health,* 2017.

56 *Overmedication:* Sultan, Ryan S., et al. "National Patterns of Commonly Prescribed Psychotropic Medications to Young People." *Journal of Child and Adolescent Psychopharmacology,* 2018.

57 *One in five depressed subjects:* Madsen, T., Buttenschøn, H. N., Uher, R., et al. "Trajectories of Suicidal Ideation During 12 Weeks of Escitalopram or Nortriptyline Antidepressant Treatment Among 811 Patients with Major Depressive Disorder." *The Journal of Clinical Psychiatry,* 2019.

57 *Suicide rates increased:* Cuffe, Steven P. "Suicide and SSRI Medications in Children and Adolescents: An Update." *American Academy of Child and Adolescent Psychology,* 2007.

4: Lay a Solid Foundation

61 *Childhood obesity:* Hales, C. M., Carroll, M. D., Fryar, C. D., and Ogden, C. L. "Prevalence of Obesity Among Adults and Youth: United States, 2015–2016." *NCHS Data Brief,* 2017.

61 *Obesity and depression:* Sutaria, S., Devakumar, D., Yasuda, S. S., et al. "Is Obesity Associated with Depression in Children? Systematic Review and Meta-Analysis." *Archives of Disease in Childhood,* 2019.

64 *These techniques work for teachers:* Perle, J. G. "Teacher-Provided Positive Attending to Improve Student Behavior." *TEACHING Exceptional Children,* 2016.

75 *Affects roughly 3 percent of children:* American Psychiatric Association. *Diagnostic and Statistical Manual of Mental Disorders.* American Psychiatric Publishing, 2013.

77 *Behavior disorders like ODD:* Brestan, E. V., and Eyberg, S. M. "Effective Psychosocial Treatments of Conduct-Disordered Children and Adolescents: 29 Years, 82 Studies, and 5,272 Kids." *Journal of Clinical Child Psychology,* 1998.

77 *or ADHD:* Evans, Steven W., Owens, Julie Sarno, Wymbs, Brian T., and Ray, A. Raisa. "Evidence-Based Psychosocial Treatments for Children and Adolescents with Attention Deficit/Hyperactivity Disorder." *Journal of Clinical Child & Adolescent Psychology,* 2017.

78 *But according to a 2011 study:* Kross, E., Berman, M. G., Mischel, W., Smith, E. E., and Wager, T. D. "Social Rejection Shares Somatosensory Representations with Physical Pain." *Proceedings of the National Academy of Sciences of the United States of America,* 2011.

5: Hold Steady

86 *Express herself openly:* Eisenberg, Nancy, et al. "Parental Reactions to Children's Negative Emotions: Longitudinal Relations to Quality of Children's Social Functioning." *Child Development,* April 1999.

88 *One in two million:* Holland, Kristin M., et al. "Characteristics of School-Associated Youth Homicides—United States, 1994–2018." CDC, January 2019.

90 *Parents hiding their emotions:* Karnilowicz, Helena Rose, Waters, Sara F., and Mendes, Wendy Berry. "Not in Front of the Kids: Effects of Parental Suppression on Socialization Behaviors During Cooperative Parent–Child Interactions." *Emotion,* 2018.

91 *". . . Transmitting those emotions":* Washington State University. "Emotional Suppression Has Negative Outcomes on Children: New Research Shows It's Better to Express Negative Emotions in a Healthy Way Than to Tamp Them Down." *ScienceDaily,* 2018.

94 *The parentification risks:* Jankowskia, Peter J., et al. "Parentification and Mental Health Symptoms: Mediator Effects of Perceived Unfairness and Differentiation of Self." *Journal of Family*

Therapy, 2011; Jurkovic, Gregory J. *Lost Childhoods: The Plight of the Parentified Child.* Routledge, 1997.

95 *"The loneliest"*: Cigna's U.S. Loneliness Index, 2018: https://www.multivu.com/players/English/8294451-cigna-us-loneliness-survey/.

95 *Poor mental health:* American Psychological Association, Stress in America Survey, 2018. Gen Z research: https://www.apa.org/news/press/releases/stress/2018/stress-gen-z.pdf.

96 *Hooked up couples:* Gottman, John, and Silver, Nat. *The Seven Principles for Making Marriage Work: A Practical Guide from the Country's Foremost Relationships Expert.* Random House, 2015.

97 *The Worry Hill:* Pinto Wagner, A. *Up and Down the Worry Hill: A Children's Book about Obsessive-Compulsive Disorder and Its Treatment.* Lighthouse Press, 2000.

6: Stay on Their Level

104 *For a 2007 UCLA study:* Lieberman, M. D., et al. "Putting Feelings into Words: Affect Labeling Disrupts Amygdala Activity in Response to Affective Stimuli." *Psychological Science,* May 2007.

111 *Eight hours per day:* Rideout, V. "Generation M2: Media in the Lives of 8- to 18-Year-Olds." Kaiser Family Foundation, 2010.

111 *That is too much:* Council on Communications and Media. "Children, Adolescents, and the Media." *Pediatrics,* November 2013.

111 *The impact of social media:* Child Mind Institute. *Children's Mental Health Report: Social Media, Gaming and Mental Health,* 2019.

116 *It's usually diagnosed:* Wong, P. "Selective Mutism." *Psychiatry,* March 2010.

121 *According to a meta-analysis:* Coles, N. A., et al. "A Meta-Analysis of the Facial Feedback Literature: Effects of Facial Feedback on Emotional Experience Are Small and Variable." *Psychology Bulletin,* June 2019.

7: Empower Growth

131 *Support of an adult:* Vygotsky, L. S. *Mind in Society: The Development of Higher Psychological Processes.* Harvard University Press, 1978.

135 *College admissions scandal:* Medina, J., Benner, K., and Taylor, K. "Wealthy Parents Charged in U.S. College Entry Fraud." *The New York Times,* March 2019.

137 *Anxiety and depression:* Gonzalez, A., Rozenman, M., Langley, A. K., et al. "Social Interpretation Bias in Children and Adolescents with Anxiety Disorders: Psychometric Examination of the Self-report of Ambiguous Social Situations for Youth (SASSY) Scale." *Child Youth Care Forum,* 2017.

145 *Acceptance rate:* https://www.princeton.edu/news/2018/12/12/princeton-offers-early-action-admission-743-students-class-2023.

146 *They did a study:* Kahneman, D., and Deaton, A. "High Income Improves Evaluation of Life but Not Emotional Well-Being." *PNAS,* 2010.

8: Build Strength

153 *Kids from diverse backgrounds:* Perry, N. B., et al. "Childhood Self-Regulation as a Mechanism Through Which Early Overcontrolling Parenting Is Associated with Adjustment in Preadolescence." *Developmental Psychology,* 2018.

153 *"The kids reacted":* "Helicopter Parenting May Negatively Affect Children's Emotional Well-Being, Behavior." APA.org, 2018.

155 *"One treat now":* Mischel, W., and Ebbesen, E. B. "Attention in Delay of Gratification." *Journal of Personality and Social Psychology,* 1970.

156 *1989 follow-up study:* Mischel, W., Shoda, Y., and Rodriguez, M. I. "Delay of Gratification in Children." *Science,* 1989.

156 *2013 follow-up:* Mischel, W., et al. "Preschoolers' Delay of Gratification Predicts Their Body Mass 30 Years Later." *The Journal of Pediatrics,* 2013.

156 **Title of a book:** Mischel, W. *The Marshmallow Test: Mastering Self-Control.* Little Brown, 2014.

156 **Forty-year follow-up:** Mischel, W., et al. "Behavior and Neural Correlates of Delay of Gratification 40 Years Later." *PNAS,* 2011.

163 **"They were helpless":** Alloy, L. B., Abramson, L., et al. "Attribution Style and the Generality of Learned Helplessness." *Journal of Personality and Social Psychology,* 1984.

165 **2018 Canadian study:** Mills, J. S., et al. "'Selfie' Harm: Effects on Mood and Body Image in Young Women." *Body Image,* 2018.

9: Set Realistic Limitations

177 **This strategy works for teachers:** Perle, J. G. "Teacher-Provided Positive Attending to Improve Student Behavior." *TEACHING Exceptional Children,* 2016.

180 **Calming in children:** Zoogman, S., et al. "Mindfulness Interventions with Youth: A Meta-Analysis." *Mindfulness,* 2014.

187 **The latest research:** Abbasi, J. "American Academy of Pediatrics Says No More Spanking or Harsh Verbal Discipline." *JAMA,* 2019.

187 **Another recent study:** Tomoda, A., Suzuki, H., Rabi, K., Sheu, Y. S., Polcari, A., and Teicher, M. H. "Reduced Prefrontal Cortical Gray Matter Volume in Young Adults Exposed to Harsh Corporal Punishment." *NeuroImage,* 2009.

189 **Time-outs are appropriate:** "How to Give a Time-Out," American Academy of Pediatrics via healthychildren.org

189 **Children with ADHD and ODD:** "Oppositional Defiance Disorder." American Academy of Child and Adolescent Psychiatry, 2019.

189 **According to a longitudinal study:** Knight, R., et al. "Longitudinal Relationship Between Time-Out and Child Emotional and Behavioral Functioning." *Journal of Development & Behavioral Pediatrics,* 2019.

10: Support Unconditionally

198 *1 percent of the U.S. population:* Huynh, M., Gavino, A. C., and Magid, M. "Trichotillomania." *Seminars in Cutaneous Medicine and Surgery,* 2013.

200 **Learn to make smarter ones:** O'Connor, E., et al., "Do Children Who Experience Regret Make Better Decisions? A Developmental Study of the Behavioral Consequences of Regret." *Child Development,* 2014.

213 **Depressive episode:** Depression stats per the National Institute of Mental Health, 2017. https://www.nimh.nih.gov/health/statistics/major-depression.shtml.

11: Repair and Minimize Cracks

220 **Rapidly increasing:** Lavender, J. M., et al. "Men, Muscles, and Eating Disorders: An Overview of Traditional and Muscularity-Oriented Disordered Eating." *Current Psychiatry Reports,* 2017.

222 **Suicidal teens:** Burstein, Brett, et al. "Suicide Attempts and Ideation Among Children and Adolescents in US Emergency Departments." *JAMA Pediatrics,* 2019.

226 **and Dr. Jonathan Shaywitz describe:** Shaywitz, Sally. *Overcoming Dyslexia: A New and Complete Science-Based Program for Reading Problems at Any Level.* Vintage, 2008.

228 **It affects 20 percent:** http://dyslexia.yale.edu/dyslexia/dyslexia-faq/.

234 **Marijuana at home:** Wilson, K., et al. "Marijuana and Tobacco Co-exposure in Hospitalized Children." *Pediatrics,* 2018.

Acknowledgments

There are so many people to thank for their work on *The Scaffold Effect* and the Child Mind Institute.

First, I want to thank my agent, Michael Carlisle. He has been after me for years to write this book. If he hadn't kept at it, the wheels would not have been put in motion. Thanks to Eliza Rothstein for seeing it through with such close attention and care.

Marnie Cochran has been the perfect editor. Her comments and expertise have elevated the book to the highest level. I couldn't have asked for a smarter publishing partner.

Huge gratitude to Valerie Frankel, a very talented writer, who worked closely with me to get all my stories and strategies onto the page and help me grow a one-page outline into a fantastic book. And thanks to Dana Points for introducing me to Val.

The mission of the Child Mind Institute is the transformation of the lives of kids struggling with mental health and learning disorders by providing the highest standard of care. The litmus test for me in bringing people into our institute is whether I'd trust them with my own children. Every one of our clinicians passes the test. They are what makes CMI so special. All of them have contributed to the formation of the core concept in *The Scaffold Effect,* but I want to thank especially the doctors who added their voices and stories to these pages: Drs. David Anderson, Jerry Bubrick, Rachel Busman, Matthew M. Cruger, Jill Emanuele, Jamie M. Howard, Stephanie Lee, Paul Mitrani, and Mark Reinecke.

Our researchers share their data before they publish, altruistically, nobly, and pragmatically, making sure that we're accelerating the pace of discovery. Thanks to Michael Milham, vice president of research, and his incredible team.

A special thanks to our Scientific Research Council, made up of researchers and scientists from national leading academic medical centers, for all their wisdom and support.

Thanks to Mimi Corcoran, our executive director, and our leadership team, including Amie Clancy, Brett Dakin, Julia Burns, for making sure the trains run on time and helping me turn my vision into reality.

Blythe Gillespie was indispensable in bringing order to an unruly project (and to my unruly life).

Our communications department educates the public about scaffold parenting principles on childmind.org and are just as essential to our mission as our researchers and clinicians. Much thanks and appreciation to editorial director Caroline Miller and our press officer Haleigh Breest for their dedication and hard work.

Very special thanks goes to Harry Kimball, director of communications special projects, for always making me sound so smart and working on some of the research for the book.

I'd like to thank the Child Mind Institute's board of directors for its endless support and belief in my vision and dream of creating the institute against the odds and the prevailing belief that this was not possible as an independent national nonprofit. With special thanks to: Brooke Garber Neidich, cofounder and co-chair; Ram Sundaram, co-chair; Debra G. Perelman, cofounder and vice chair. Our board members are generous with their time, creativity, intelligence, and financial support: Arthur G. Altschul, Jr.; Devon Briger; Lisa Domenico Brooke; Phyllis Green and Randolph Cōwen; Mark Dowley; Elizabeth and Michael Fascitelli; Margaret Grieve; Jonathan Harris; Joseph Healey; Ellen and Howard Katz; Preethi Krishna; Christine and Richard Mack; Anne Welsh McNulty; Julie Minskoff; Daniel Neidich;

Zibby Owens; Josh Resnick; Linnea Roberts; Jane Rosenthal; Jordan Schaps; Linda Schaps; David Shapiro; and Emma Stone.

Thanks to extraordinary donors Helen and Chuck Schwab, Linnea and George Roberts, and Devon and Pete Briger, and supporters and friends in the San Francisco Bay Area, led by our West Coast Advisory Council, including Megan and Harris Barton, Cori Bates, Ashlie Beringer, Suzanne Crandall, Stacy Denman, Abby Durban, Eve and Ross Jaffe, Liz Laffont, Andrea McTamaney, Karen and Ronnie Lott, Jen Sills, Christine Tanona, and Angelique Wilson. Thanks for helping to make the Child Mind Institute bicoastal.

Thanks to Bloomingdale's, our first corporate sponsor when no major national brand was adopting child mental health as their cause. I want to thank Anne Keating for being stubbornly supportive, former CEO Michael Gould for listening to her, and my friends Frank Berman and CEO Tony Spring for taking it to a new level of partnership.

Over the years we've had the great opportunity to work with actors, authors, musicians, journalists, entrepreneurs, politicians, and other notable and creative people in our public education campaigns and events, and they have done so much to bring our message to people everywhere. Thank you to Reese Witherspoon, Kevin Love, Jesse Eisenberg, Charles Schwab, Lindsey Stirling, Whoopi Goldberg, Lorraine Bracco, Naomi Judd, Brian Grazer, Trudie Styler, Orlando Bloom, Governor Gavin Newsom, Goldie Hawn, Glenn Close, Katie Couric, George Stephanopoulos, Ali Wentworth, Cynthia McFadden, Elizabeth Vargas, Secretary Hillary Rodham Clinton, Jimmy Buffett, Michelle Kydd Lee, Adam Silver, Bill Hader, Kim Kardashian, Jim Gaffigan, Mark Ruffalo, Al Roker, Deborah Roberts, Meredith Vieira, Patrick Kennedy, and Scott Stossel.

During my career I have been blessed with many remarkable and wise mentors who have shared their brilliance, support, and love. I thank them all and especially Drs. Rachel Klein and the late Don Klein, Robert Cancro, Gaye Carlson, Alan "Avi" Gistrak, Tom Insel, Bennett Leventhal, Cathy Lord, Kathleen Merikangis, Nora Volkow, and Ruth Westheimer.

Many thanks to all my wonderful friends, colleagues, and dedicated supporters, and specifically Virginia "Ginger" Anthony, Ann and Fred Axelrod, Emary Aronson, June Blum, Alex Briscoe, Kenneth Cole, Geoff and Sarah Gund, Jenji Kohan, Edi Kornell, Linda Rosenberg, Daniel Lurie, Wes Moore, Chris Noxon, Gail and Len Saltz, Lisa Schultz, Klara and Larry Silverstein, and Ron Steingard.

I get so much joy watching my son Adam and daughter-in-law, Zaneta, parent our grandson, Jackson, so naturally. And thanks to my sister, Edith Koplewicz, for always being able to make me laugh.

Life is so much easier when you have a best friend. I'm so fortunate that Brian Novick has been mine since medical school. Thanks, Brian, for all the support and for taking so much pleasure in other people's happiness.

Finally, you might have heard that behind every successful man is a strong woman. My wife, Linda, does not stand behind me or anyone. She's been standing next to me, and always asking me what's truly important and keeping me focused on our goals for our family and our lives. Thanks for everything we are, have been, and will be, Linda.

About the Author

Harold S. Koplewicz, MD, is one of the nation's leading child and adolescent psychiatrists. The founding president and director of the Child Mind Institute in New York City and San Mateo, California, he has been repeatedly named in *America's Top Doctors, Best Doctors in America,* and *New York* magazine's "Best Doctors in New York." He has appeared on *Today,* CBS News, CNN, *The Oprah Winfrey Show,* and *Anderson Cooper 360°,* and he is quoted regularly in *The New York Times, USA Today,* and *The Wall Street Journal.* He lives in New York City.